THE DOCTRINE OF PROPHECY

*AN INVESTIGATIVE REPORT USING THE
101 CLASSROOM EXPERIENCE*

APOSTLE SHERMAN D. FARMER

The Doctrine of Prophecy
Copyright © 2014 Sherman D. Farmer

All rights reserved. No part of this book may be reproduced, distributed or transmitted in any form by any means, graphics, electronics, or mechanical, including photocopy, recording, taping, or by any information storage or retrieval system, without permission in writing from the publisher except in the case of reprints in the context of reviews, quotes, or references.

Unless otherwise indicated, scripture quotations are taken from the Holy Bible, *King James Version*®, KJV®. Copyright © 1982 by Thomas Nelson, Inc. All rights reserved.

Unless otherwise indicated, scripture quotations are taken from the Holy Bible, *New International Version*®, NIV®. Copyright © 1973, 1978, 1984, 2011 by International Bible Society®. All rights reserved.

Unless otherwise indicated, scripture quotations are taken from the Holy Bible, *Amplified Version*®, AMP®. Copyright ©1954, 1958, 1962, 1964, 1965, 1987 by Zondervan®. All rights reserved.

Published by: Purposely Created Publishing Group™

Printed in the United States of America

ISBN: 0-692-32010-5
ISBN-13: 978-0-692-32010-5

Special discounts are available on bulk quantity purchases by book clubs, associations and special interest groups. For details, email: Sales@PurblishYourGift.com or call (866) 674-3340.

For more information, log onto
www.PublishYourGift.com

DEDICATION

I would like to dedicate this book to the countless brilliant minds who are awakening to their prophetic genius. Continue to prophetically emerge and dare to use the full power of your prophetic creativity. For in that fullness, your prophetic gifting determines the true destination of your unlimited potential and divine greatness in Him.

For whomever God forbears, no man can discredit or discount.
You are here for the grace and by the grace of the Almighty God.

But you are primarily here to prophesy within the grace of God!

TABLE OF CONTENTS

Dedication	iii
Acknowledgments	xi

PART I

BIBLICAL FOUNDATION	1
The First Introduction: A Biblical Foundation About Prophecy 101 – Part 1	2

Chapter 1: Biblical Survey of the Scriptural Prophets

Who Are the First and Final Prophets of Scripture?	5
A General Overview	6
✓ Who Are the First Biblical Prophets	7
✓ The Old Testament's Historical Progression of the Prophetic Voice	17
✓ Prophetess versus Prophet	21
✓ Who Are the Last Biblical Prophets	23
✓ The Convergence of a New Prophetic Generation, Covenant and Dispensation	24
✓ The Last Prophetic Voices of the New Testament Era.	27
Conclusion of Lesson 1	30

Chapter 2: The Genesis of Becoming a Prophet

What is a Prophet?	33
✓ His Foundation Begins with Naturalness	34
✓ His Spiritual Elevation is Based on Prophetic Relevance	41
✓ His Assignment is to Be a Messenger of God	47
✓ His Governmental Authority is Given by God	51
✓ His Identity is a Composite of Ancient and Ascension Gift	53
Conclusion of Lesson 2	58

Chapter 3: True Prophets –vs- False Prophets; Christian Prophetism -vs- Christian Socialism

When is a Prophet Most Needed?   61
    The Ministry of True Prophets Counterattacks the Manifestation of False Prophets   62
    The Termination Date for the Spirit of False Prophecy   67

Conclusion of Lesson 3 69
- ✓ Conflict Resolutions Christian Socialism versus Christian Prophetism   69
  - o The Identification of Common Problems   69
  - o The Identification of Universal Solutions   78

Chapter 4: The Definition of Prophetic Honors and Rewards

Where is a Prophet Most Prevalent?   87
- ✓ The Overview   88
- ✓ The Prevailing Conflict of Honoring a Prophet   91
- ✓ The Intoxication of Prophetic Persecution   99
- ✓ The Conclusion of the Conflict Concerning Prophetic Honor   101
- ✓ The Proper Honor Due to a Prophet   102
- ✓ The Primary Point to a Prophet's Prevalence is Honor   102
- ✓ The True Definition and Application of a Prophet's Reward   107

Conclusion of Lesson 4 111

Chapter 5: The Relevance of Today's Prophets

Why is a Prophet Still Necessary?   113
- ✓ Vision and Visionaries   114
- ✓ How Should a Contemporary Prophet Begin?   116
  - o Jesus Christ   117
  - o The Spirit of Prophecy is the Testimony of Jesus Christ: 118
  - o A Lifetime Commitment and Study of Both Testaments   122

Conclusion of Lesson 5 127

PART II

AN APOSTOLIC REVELATION ABOUT PROPHECY 101   129

The Second Introduction: Revelatory Prophetic Fundamentals 101 – Part 1   130

Chapter 6: Revelatory Prophetic Fundamentals 101 – Part 1

How Does the Prophetic Operate? – Part 1   131

The Conventional Prophetic Mediums   132
- ✓ Overview: The Supreme Medium is Always God   132
- ✓ The Three Conventional Prophetic Mediums   134
- ✓ The Prophetic Mediums of Similitudes   136
- ✓ The Prophetic Medium of Visions   139

Three Greater Revelations About Prophetic Visions   143
- ✓ The General Prophetic Visionary Experience   143
- ✓ The Simultaneous Prophetic Visionary Experience   144
- ✓ The Ripple-Effect Prophetic Visionary Experience   146

The Prophetic Medium of Dreams   148

The Interpretation of Dreams   150

Conclusion of Lesson 6 153

Chapter 7: Revelatory Prophetic Fundamentals 101 – Part 2

How Does the Prophetic Operate? – Part 2   155

Prophetic Dispensations, Methodologies, Dimensions, Graces, and Diversities   156

The Dispensation of Grace versus the Dispensation of Law   156

The Three New Testament Prophetic Messages of Grace   158
- ✓ The Message of Prophetic Edification   159
- ✓ The Message of Prophetic Exhortation   160
- ✓ The Message of Prophetic Encouragement (Comfort)   161

Conclusion of the Three Prophetically Graced Messages   163
- ✓ "Thus Saith the Lord" versus "Thus Saith the Spirit"   153
- ✓ Forth-telling versus Fore-telling   167
- ✓ Revelation versus Confirmation in Prophecy   171
- ✓ The Gift of Prophecy versus the Gift of Word of Knowledge   172

Conclusion of Lesson 7 173

Chapter 8: The R.O.A.M Mission – Part 1

How Does the Prophetic Operate? – Part 3 — 175

Prophetic Regions and Operations — 176
The Overview of Prophetic Regions — 179
- ✓ The Local Prophet — 181
- ✓ The National Prophet — 183
- ✓ The International Prophet — 184

Conclusion of the Three Prophetic Regions — 186
The Overview of Prophetic Operations — 188
- ✓ The Revelation of the Governmental Prophet — 190
- ✓ The Revelation of the Serving Prophet — 191
- ✓ The Revelation of the Charismatic Prophet — 192
- ✓ The Old Testaments' Confirmation of the New Testament's Revelation About the Three Prophetic Operations — 193

Conclusion of Lesson 8.. 195

Chapter 9: The R.O.A.M Mission – Part 2

How Does the Prophetic Operate? – Part 4 — 197

Prophetic Administrations and Mantles — 198
- ✓ The Three Administrations of a Prophet — 198
  - o The Overview of Prophetic Administrations — 198
  - o Pre-Exile Prophetic Administrations Paradigm — 199
  - o Exiled Prophetic Administrations Paradigm — 200
  - o The Combination of Exiled and Post-Exilic Prophetic Administrations Paradigm — 201
  - o The Tri-fold Exilic Prophetic Administration Paradigm — 202
  - o The Greatest Exile and Diaspora of the Bible — 203

Conclusion of the Three Prophetic Administrations — 204
- ✓ The Three Mantles of a Prophet — 206
  - o The Overview of Mantles – What is a Mantle? — 206
  - o The Biblical Revelation of the Three Mantles — 209
  - o The Realm of Divine Sight — 210
  - o The Realm of Divine Exploits — 213
- ✓ The Ream of Divine Hearing — 215

Conclusion of Lesson 9 217

Chapter 10: Prophetic Power 101 – Part 1

How Does the Prophetic Operate? – Part 5 — 219

The Overview and Observations of Prophetic Placement and Sensitivity — 220
- ✓ Distinguishing Between Denominational Prophets versus Christian Prophets — 220
- ✓ Distinguishing Between the Gift of Prophecy versus the Office of the Prophet — 221

Proper Discernment of Prophetic Sensitivity – A Lesson That Takes Time — 223
- ✓ The Primary Fundamental of Prophetic Sensitivity: Anthropomorphizing God — 223

Prophetic Sensitivity Lessons — 226
- ✓ Lesson #1: Carrying a Heavy Word During Uncertain Times — 226
- ✓ Lesson #2: Deciphering Self-Consciousness from God-Consciousness Moments — 227
- ✓ Lesson #3: Detoxing from the Prophetic Ruts of Complacency — 229
- ✓ Lesson #4: Decoding Prophetic Messages from Angelic Visitations — 231

Conclusion of Lesson 10 234

Chapter 11: Prophetic Power 101 – Part 2

How Does the Prophetic Operate? – Part 6 — 235

Proper Development of Your Prophetic Productivity — 236
- ✓ The Three Sources of Prophetic Power — 236
- ✓ The Spirit of God — 236
- ✓ The Consistency of Prayer — 238
- ✓ The Application of Incremental Fasting — 240
- ✓ Conclusion of Prophetic Productivity — 241

Proper Distinguishment of the Conduits of Prophetic Vocality — 241
- ✓ The Three Conventional Conduits for Prophetic Vocality — 242
- ✓ Overview: The Most Common Conduit is the Speaking Voice — 242
- ✓ Dark Speeches — 242
- ✓ Prophetic Parables — 243
- ✓ The Conduit of Music — 245
- ✓ The Conduit of Written Word — 247

Conclusion of Lesson 11 250

PART III

The Third Introduction: The Final Dissertation About Prophecy 101   252

Chapter 12: Final Scriptural Thought

The Third Introduction: The Final Lessons on Prophecy 101   255

An Old Testament Prayer Fulfilled   256

An Apostolic Charge   258

The Final Conclusions 260

    ✓ Prophesying is Greater than Speaking in Tongues   260

    ✓ The Prophetic is Interpretation of the Will and Purposes of God   260

About the Author 265

ACKNOWLEDGEMENTS

To my parents, Chief Deacon and Deaconess, Elton Sr. and Deborah Pittman; my siblings, Prophet Elton Pittman Jr., Deacon and Deaconess, Sharon and Lynue Chambers; my nieces, Shaylah, Nylah, Madison and Mackenzie; and last but not least, to my nephew, Jacob, I truly thank you for loving me and following me as your apostle, son, brother, and uncle. I am complete because you have never changed who you are to me! Your love-legacy alone is the very reason I am strong enough to complete God's task. Thank you for being my center and my heart.

To my apostolic team: Chief Pastor Jerome Sherman Jr., Executive Pastor Cheronda Walls, Pastor Justin Walls, Pastor Arnetta Whitaker, Pastor Anthony Hill, Prophetess Tarinna Terrell, Pastor Monta, and Pastor Staci Burrough, thank you for operating in the straightway principle. Your immediacy of employing the apostolic work is not only flowing with zeal and passion, but I truly received the agape love you have towards the fulfillment of our ministry. Thank you for your seeds of faithfulness for they will never be forgotten—surely not by me, and assuredly they will never be forgotten by God!

And lastly, to the members of New Gibeah Ministries for Christ and Redeeming Touch of Love Ministries, thank you for being the best churches on this side of heaven. I will forever and continuously thank God for each and every one of you as I stand with joy, as your leader, before our heavenly Father.

Your seeds of faithfulness and commitment has tremendously helped push the visions of NGMC, RTOLM, SAM, and now the New Kohath Prophetic Institute.

God has made me who am because He has made you to help me fulfill this work. Therefore, it's my honor to be your spiritual leader, and it's my desire to serve you until the Lord Jesus calls us home or up and out of this world following His soon return.

– Maranatha!

And Agape in Christ,

Chief Apostle

PART 1

Wisdom is the principal thing; therefore get wisdom: and with all thy getting get understanding (Proverbs 4:7).

THE FIRST INTRODUCTION

A Biblical Foundation About Prophecy 101

The Bible describes the word of God as a lamp unto our feet and a light unto our path (Psalm 119:105). Another scripture says that faith comes by hearing and hearing by the word of God (Romans 10:17). Did you know that you need the bible and your faith in order to become a better prophet? The answer is yes! Prophetically speaking, one's faith and divine direction cannot grow without a consistent study and prayer life. Additionally, there must be a certain yielding conduciveness to the lifestyle of God's prophet! This yielding is best discovered through using the word of God as a roadmap. But it also takes faith to reach the realm of what we call the spirit of prophecy.

And just like every invention comes with instructions, in the same manner, Christian prophets need a more pliable manual. To assist you with the dos and do nots of contemporary prophesying, I have created this manual like an introductory college course. I have placed the profiles and practices of Hebrew and Christian biblical prophets inside this manual as a methodology to expand prophetic thinking and vocabulary.

This is why it is time to awaken prophetic sobriety by revisiting the "rightly dividing" of God's word (2 Timothy 2:15). For the best means of prophetic sobriety come from linking sound biblical teaching with practical understanding. And this is what the word doctrine (or teaching) fully means and embodies. So we are called to learn the teachings of God diligently as we progress in our operating of the prophetic anointing. Thus, an intimacy with the doctrinal world will bring longevity and balance unto all who are called to prophesy.

Most importantly, the foundation of prophecy is that a prophet should only prophesy to the proportion of his faith (Romans 12:6), through God's *agape*-love (1 Corinthians 13), and by the unction of the Holy Spirit. It is, therefore, important for prophets to be strengthened simultaneously in their biblical knowledge and experiential prophetic practices. And using classic investigative tools (i.e. who, what, when, where, and why), along with biblical knowledge and my prophetic experience, I have comprised this section of the book to teach you general facts, and even a few advanced ones.

But this course is only designed for the humble prophetic student. And that type of student is one who seeks to hone his prophetic skills through the perpetual "classroom of prophecy." I trust you have purchased this book because you are that type of student, and you are truly interested in this particular series and lessons. Reading this book means you are consenting to the challenge of increasing your prophetic gifting, and if you are assigned to this type of classroom and challenge, then welcome. Welcome to the greater dimension of defining your prophetic shape and destiny.

Now that you have received proper welcome and orientation, let the new semester officially begin. The bell of Christ's university has rung. Class is now in session.

You may start taking notes, for quizzes and tests are sure to follow...

CHAPTER 1

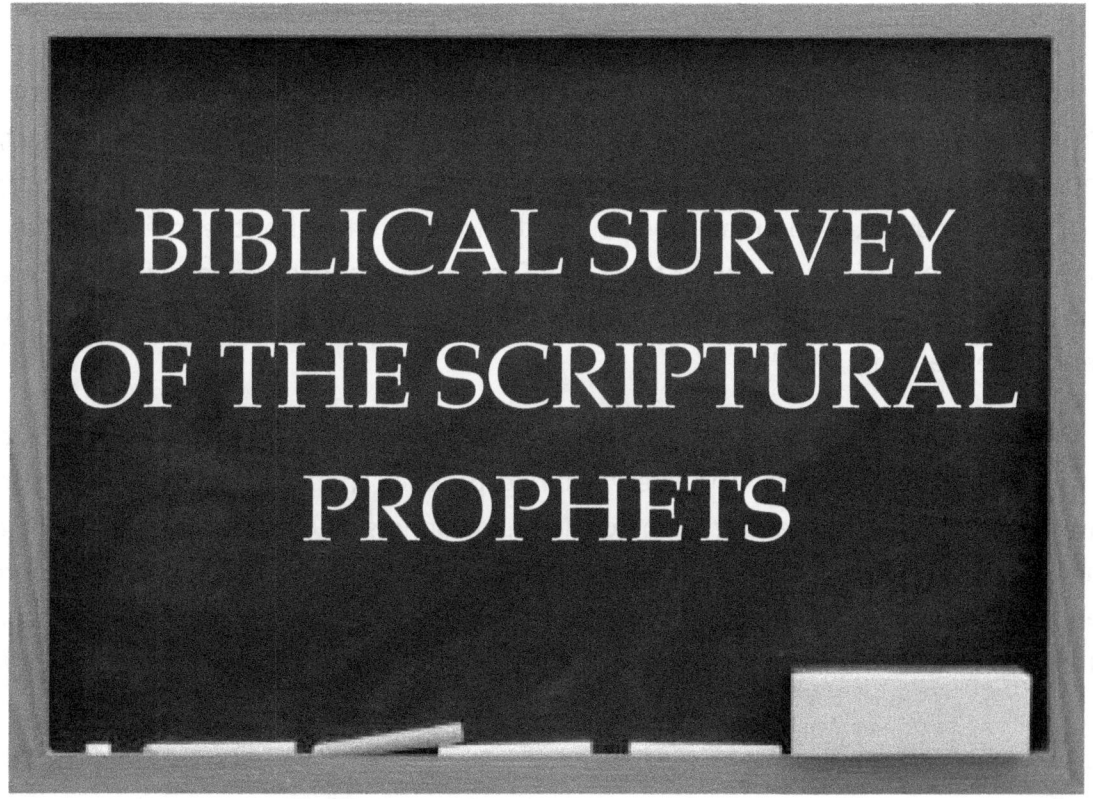

Who Are the First and Final Prophets of Scripture?

I have also spoken by the prophets, and I have multiplied visions, and used similitudes, by the ministry of the prophets (Hosea 12:10).

The Doctrine of Prophecy

A General Overview

The Bible declares that every word is established in the mouth of two or three witnesses (Matthew 18:16; 2 Corinthians 13:1). And a threefold cord is not easy to break (Ecclesiastes 4:12). Scripturally speaking, there are two Old Testament personalities, which are what I term "foundational prophetic voices" of scripture. These two voices bring into the world the beginning of, and solidification of, biblical prophetic ministry. With such solidification, their presence in the prophetic office is undeniable and irrefutable.

And it is your responsibility to learn and know these two main biblical prophets by heart. Yes, their names are synonymous with the foundational teaching on prophecy. In fact, their teachings are considered part of the canon of prophecy (or what is properly called the prophetic books of the Holy Bible). If you remember them, then you'll remember the initial foundation for what prophetic ministry is according to the Bible. The purpose of such memorization is to ensure that you are on the right track with your prophetic compass, which should lead you to more prophetic understanding.

For we must realize God has created a prophetic hall of fame when he selected the Hebrew and Christian prophets. And every aspiring prophet should know who these prophets are! Simply put, this lesson is about learning the first prophets' names and their testimonies just like one must learn the ABCs of speaking and writing. If you know their names and purposes, you can grow in your purpose as an emerging prophet, whereby one day you may join this incredible league of extraordinary vessels.

WHO WERE THE FIRST BIBLICAL PROPHETS?

The Foundational Prophetic Voices:

Enoch

The first prophetic voice actually receives full clarification not from the Old Testament, but from the New Testament accounts. This prophetic voice is none other than Enoch. Enoch's storyline is found in the book of Genesis (Genesis 5:18-24), but confirmation of his prophetic office is provided by the Apostle Jude:

And Jared lived a hundred sixty and two years, and he begat Enoch: And Jared lived after he begat Enoch eight hundred years, and begat sons and daughters: And all the days of Jared were nine hundred sixty and two years: and he died. And Enoch lived sixty and five years, and begat Methuselah: And Enoch walked with God after he begat Methuselah three hundred years, and begat sons and daughters: And all the days of Enoch were three hundred sixty and five years: And Enoch walked with God: and he was not; for God took him (Genesis 5:18-24).

The seventh son of Adam, Enoch also prophesied saying, Behold, the Lord cometh with ten thousand of his saints, to execute judgment upon all, and to convince all that are ungodly among them of all their ungodly deeds which they have ungodly committed, and of all their hard speeches which ungodly sinners have spoken against Him. These are murmurers, complainers, walking after their own lusts; and their mouth speaketh great swelling words, having men's persons in admiration because of advantage (Jude 14-16).

Enoch is the first foundational prophet of scripture, who was born in the Adamic generation (Genesis 5:1). The Apostle Jude classified his generation as seventh from Adam. This teaches an important lesson about biblical genealogy, which is very important within the constitution of the Bible. Biblical genealogies are comparable to what we call modern-day family trees. They are created to reveal Israel's history and heritages. God uses biblical genealogy to confirm each tribe of Israel's distinct purposes within the world. Some Israelite genealogies reveal farmers, shepherds, and yes, some even define those who are called to be prophets. This, then, is the purpose of enduring the litany of any genealogy.

One primary confirmation that biblical genealogy also provides is the first commandment God had given to Adam and Eve. God exhorted Adam and Eve "to be fruitful and to multiply" (Genesis 1:28). When you review the "begot" and the "begets," you will discover that

The Doctrine of Prophecy

Adam and Eve's descendants completed this objective every time a new child was born in the family of Adam. Thus Genealogies also appear in scripture to mention birth, lineage, marriage and death. But they are present to reveal man's obedience to the first commandments given to the generations of mankind.

But here it mentions something more. We also discover that biblical genealogy reveals and defines true prophecy. For biblical genealogy also reveals which family God created the genesis for the prophetic assignment within the congregation of Israel. In my first book, *The New Prophetic Generation*, we tackled this issue with intense observation. For genealogies are not something we should overlook or lightly glance at, especially if they reveal the nature of understanding and various spiritual purposes. Take, for example, Enoch's storyline and how some of it is written in genealogical form.

Enoch's storyline and genealogy purposefully signify his initial prophetic encounter with God. They also signify his miraculous final days before God transitions him from earth into heaven (Genesis 5:18-24). Even more, they also clarify the length of his prophetic ministry before he leaves the face of the earth for heaven. This was his generational assignment, and this was also his prophetic assignment.

Combining these two scriptural references with these factors, it is easy to understand how God called Enoch to be a prophet in the beginnings days of man. This is why he is seventh from Adam. Enoch's assignment was to become the first prophet among the first generation of mankind. Enoch was sent to help mankind begin its return to God, for mankind was taking the presence of God for granted. This mishap occurred because Adam brought transgression into the known world.

The text says that Enoch's father, Jared, begot Enoch when he was 162 years old. Jared lived another 800 years before dying at the age of 962. The Adamic generation definitely had a longer lifespan than any other generation of mankind. Enoch was approximately 65 years old when the prophetic calling manifested. The defining moment for his prophetic call likely commenced after the birth of his son, Methuselah. This is why genealogy and prophecy are interrelated. We will discover that they assist each other throughout all scripture.

The text in Genesis 5 says that at age 65, after Methuselah was born, Enoch walked with God. Enoch's ministry was possibly the longest among the prophets of scripture. The Bible says that Enoch was 365 years old when he transitioned from earth into the heavens. Therefore, Enoch ministered for God, after the birth of his son, for a possible interval of 300 years.

Can you imagine carrying out prophetic service and duty that long? For most prophets, even a few years in the prophetic ministry can be stressful. Even seeing and knowing God isn't always the happiest experience for a prophet. And carrying such weight requires the strictest forms of discipline. Nevertheless, Enoch was the master of prophetic ministry because of the length in which he ministered.

This further reveals Enoch's truest assignment: walking with God and being God's prophet. Beyond that, his greatest achievement was to produce the 8th generation of Adam: Methuselah. Further content of Enoch's ministry is unknown, but the Apostle Jude's pericope (which is an excerpt from the apocryphal book of Enoch) indirectly provides legitimate means to our study.

This explains the reasoning for Jude's usage of this inordinate material because the entire book of Enoch is not canonized for Holy Scripture. Maybe this reasoning is attributed to us learning that Enoch was not just a man who God took from the earth, but more importantly, that Enoch was God's first prophet of recorded scripture. Moreover, the allowance of this specific apocryphal excerpt brings an ethical principle about the fearlessness a prophet must have when speaking prophetically before a people. Enoch certainly exhibited such courage. Therefore, we must thank Jude for his additional submission of divine inspiration and information.

Jude asserted within a letter to the church of his age that God had given every man of God prophetic clarity of what would come within his distinct generation. Enoch is no exception to the rule! Thus, every prophet is placed in a specific generation. And it is that prophet's responsibility to speak on the behalf of God within his generation.

This dynamic of Jude's revelation is an apostolic technique that we must clearly mention. Jude's technique is a common system among certain apostles who have written works within the Bible. This apostolic system oftentimes involves pulling from either the Old Testament or non-Testament writings; this has now become acceptable among the apostolic college of all true apostles in every age. For, by using such means, apostles often provide greater clarity concerning the prophets of old. Another example is the Apostle Peter's comments about Hebrew Prophets of yesterday, which is now recorded in the first epistle of his scriptural writings:

Concerning this salvation, the prophets, who spoke of the grace that was to come to you, searched intently and with the greatest care, trying to find out the time and circumstances to which the Spirit of Christ in them was pointing when He predicted the sufferings of Christ and the glories that would follow. It was revealed to them that they were not serving themselves but you, when they spoke of the things that have now been told you by

those who have preached the gospel to you by the Holy Spirit sent from heaven. Even angels long to look into these things (1 Peter 1:10-12, NIV).

This system is the true definition of what we call "binding and loosing" (Matthew 16:19). Binding and loosing is not just used to explain demonology. This system is used to express deeper revelations through conveying the Old Testament's connection with Christ and his testimony. Thus, Enoch's message in Jude's letter was a prophetic warning about the church's allowances of Christ's testimony that was to be disrespected. In this manner, when converging apocryphal writings mixed with Old Testament messages, the outcome was usually one of order and acceptance by Christian scholars and theologians alike.

For the comparative pericope from Genesis and Jude now work together as one central message. Enoch's vision served to correct the wickedness he dealt with during his time. In like manner, Jude corrected the church's predicament of whether to compromise. False believers were blaspheming the testimony of Jesus Christ. And Jude's decision to use harsh words (within his rebuke) was similar to that of Enoch's testimony, in which he preached a fiery sermon unto those who took God for granted.

Jude's apostolic message was that the secret was out, and one day, very soon, God would send reinforcements through Jesus Christ (Revelation 19:11-16). Jude explained that very shortly all the confusion against the gospel of Jesus would be eradicated. The prophetic gift in Enoch further revealed how Christ and his saints' pre-millennial entrance and reign would become the means of dissolving every level of ungodliness within the known world.

Enoch also confirms Jesus' return to the world as a symbol of the end of "the spirit of this world" and the beginning of the new reformation. Simply put, when a new sheriff comes to town, the inappropriate practices of law enforcement will no longer be allowed to go unnoticed. Jesus will come and set a new order. Everyone rejecting this compliance will certainly see an immediate ramification of his or her disobedience.

First, Jesus and the return saints' presence will reprove habitual practices of ungodliness. Then their manifestation will have a mirror effect. As a means of exposure (like a mirror does with every man's image), their presence will reveal to the fullest extent how ungodliness is practiced within them. Whereby the source of ungodliness will be bound for 1,000 years (as Revelations foretells in Revelation 20:2-3). Of course, that source is Satan himself. Afterwards, the final judgment of the earth will be at the mercies of God (Revelation 20:11-15). In short, Jesus will take care of all wrongdoers. This will happen when he returns to the earth in the experience known as the Second Coming.

This teaches another important truth: God is always in the lives of his people. And every person must deliberately choose which place he wants to be in. Joshua said, "As for me and my house we will serve the Lord" (Joshua 24:15)! Therefore, the presence of God and those who are godly serve as lights to those willing to come out of this world's darkness. The verdict is clear: If a person decides to stay in sin, judgment will be severe. But if he chooses the light, which comes by God and His holy church, he will find mercy. Jude and Enoch's scriptures harmoniously work together to convince the lost to return to God. And such a return is accomplished by submitting to the Gospel of Jesus Christ.

This also implies that a heaviness of ungodliness blinds those who are practicing ungodliness. For the ungodly cannot see past their own wickedness. Notice what the text says about ungodly sinners (verse 15). What this reveals is that there are several groups of sinners that must be addressed. First it implies a group of sinners who are consistently ungodly (i.e., the unsaved soul). But there is another implication. That implication possibly reveals a second group who frequently practices ungodliness with hypocrisy (i.e. the so-called saved believer who has professed Christ and become part of the church, but only in name and not with sincerity).

Thus, Enoch's prophetic ministry serves the saved, the unsaved, and those destined to be saved. It is very important that every generation comes to obey God. This message is the prevailing message of each prophet in every generation. And Jude uses Enoch's voice and message of his time to speak such a message to the people within the church of his day and time. But we must also speak to the church ages that have come and are yet to come. When God is correcting, he leaves no room for error. The prophet's message is explicit for this very reason!

This is why Enoch labels those who murmur, complain, and seek their lusts as ungodly sinners. He explains how these men take full advantage of seducing others in order to continue wickedness. Enoch reveals that their ability to convince is a blatant means of deception. But the prophet promises that God will bring justice. The Apostle Jude uses the prophetic ministry of Enoch and his messages as a strategy to correct the current errors among his current audience (circa AD 70). And that message rings loudly, even today, some 2000 years later! So the question now arises: Are you for God? Or are you for the god of this world?

There is so much room left for speculation about this text, and the prophet who provides it. One thought comes to mind: Does Enoch's entire prophetic ministry speak with this same tone? Or is this an isolated prophetic word? As we know that there is nothing that will be done in the earth without a prophet of God seeing it first. When that prophet sees such a thing, his prophetic word comes and manifests as a means of ensuring that God's will is always said and done. It is powerful how timeless a prophetic word can become once it is initially uttered. Who knew that the first prophet of all prophets would have a word that is still relevant today?

But what we must also learn is that a prophetic word may last for many lifetimes. This is why a prophet must be careful about the words that he speaks. A prophet must make sure that God gives him specific utterances. For the gravity of such words will hold weight and continual purpose for generations to come. Jesus teaches that we are justified or condemned by the words we speak (Matthew 12:37). Therefore, Enoch was responsible for the words he spoke in his day and so was Jude.

We, too, must follow this same pursuit. For the Bible is surely right – the word of God is a two-edged sword (Hebrews 4:12). The apostle, prophet, and believer alike are responsible for what they hear and for what they speak unto a people. It is a prophet's job, then, to make sure that he is the first partaker of such words. Enoch apparently had very little struggle with this commandment. His obedience was possibly the reason why he was taken instead of terminated by means of a natural death.

In this we must see why Enoch is the first within the hall of fame of scriptural prophets. His life and his mission are now memorialized because Enoch was not partial in his prophetic assignment. This reveals how the word of God is a precious process within the life of God's prophet. And the words from God are not always easy to come by. Nor are they easy to digest or disseminate. Despite Enoch's discomfort, his example teaches that one must stand and do as God commands when one is called of God. And with a stance like this, and the divine audacity within Enoch's ministry, there is no wonder why God would take him at the end of his prophetic work. For we also know Enoch pleased God, and every prophet must be a pleaser of God and never of men (Galatians 1:10).

So God makes Enoch's transition the first unusual transition among humanity. Instead of dying, the Bible says he is taken. The word "taken" is another word for "transition." And the process of transition connects us with the testimony of Jesus Christ. For there are two other known transitions similar within scripture. Enoch is the first, and the prophet Elijah is the second (2 Kings 2:11). Again every word is always established three times within three distinct mouths or lives of true witnesses. Thus, we have our biblical three: Enoch and Elijah are the first two, and Jesus Christ is the third person God uses to bring relevance to this confirmation (Acts 1:9-11).

The confirmation of this phenomena is similar to the experience the church will call the rapture (1 Corinthians 15:51-54; 1 Thessalonians 4:15-17). The rapture is the process of when the church will be taken out of the world, just as Enoch, Elijah, and Jesus miraculously ascended into the heavens.

For, just as Enoch, Elijah, and Jesus were taken, we, too, will be taken. God establishes Enoch as our spiritual trendsetter. This event is predetermined, and only God knows the date of its occurrence. Until then, we must preach and look for his imminent return. But while we preach, we must prophesy with the knowledge that Enoch is our first prophetic minister. So we conclude Enoch began the prophetic work within the world and God's kingdom. And Enoch is the first name that one must memorize when thinking about prophetic ministry. When thinking of his name, we must not just think of the ominous words that were spoken; we must also find hope in what Enoch's ministry has done. In the case of the church and the cause of Christ, Enoch's perfect position within the generation of Adam speaks to the perfect place we will one day have in the generation of Jesus Christ.

Abraham

Abraham is mainly known as the father of the Jewish Nation. His complete storyline is found in the book of Genesis (Chapters 12-25). This storyline begins when God randomly creates an encounter with Abraham, instructing him to leave his extensive family. Abraham, his wife, Sarah, and his nephew, Lot, left a town called Haran. The crux of the story centers on Abraham's father, Terah. It is Terah who decides to take his immediate family from Mesopotamia (which is called Ur or Chaldees in Genesis 11:31. See also Acts 7:2). And Terah left his land with the intentions of going to another land called Canaan, but his death prevented such fulfillment.

Yet the result of Terah's derailment of life is actually the will of God. God was not responsible for Terah's decision to move his family. But God was positioning his will for Abraham, who was one of Terah's sons, to complete such an action. This storyline reminds us of King David and Solomon. God gives David the blueprints to build the temple, but it is Solomon, David's son, who completes this action (1 Kings 8:17-20).

In like manner, God visits Abraham. Instead of Terah leading the generation, it would become Abraham's responsibility. The reason being is that God predetermined Abraham to become his family's generational leader. Generationally speaking, within the generations of the Jewish people, God usually works in cycles of four, seven, and ten. We recently learned how Enoch was 7th in the generation of Adam. And from the New Prophetic Generation book, you will also learn how the 4th generation of Israel was the primary generation for whom God sent major movements of deliverance within cycles of every 400 years (Genesis 15:16a).

The Doctrine of Prophecy

Within the generation of Shem (Noah's son), Abraham is not 4th or 7th in his generation. He is actually the 10th male born within his generation. Again, generations, genealogies, and genetics do matter. The prophet of God has to come from somewhere. Realistically, a prophet starts his journey from a specific family, and that family is based upon each generation. For Abraham's storyline shows the importance of connection and relationship as it relates to what it means to be truly prophetic. This also demonstrates how a prophet is not only prophetic by name and family. A prophet is also prophetic because of the world he is called to live in and experience:

And Terah lived seventy years, and begat Abram, Nahor, and Haran. Now these are the generations of Terah: Terah begat Abram, Nahor, and Haran; and Haran begat Lot. And Haran died before his father Terah in the land of his nativity, in Ur of Chaldees. And Abram and Nahor took them wives: the name of Abram's wife was Sarai; and the name of Nahor's wife, Milcah, the daughter of Haran, the father of Milcah, and the father of Iscah. But Sarai was barren: she had no child. And Terah took Abraham his son, and Lot the son of Haran his son's son, and Sarai his daughter in law, his son Abram's wife; and they went forth with them from Ur of the Chaldees, to go into the land of Cannan; and they came unto Haran, and dwelt there. And the days of Terah were two hundred and five years: and Terah died in Haran (Genesis 11:26-32).

Before we proceed further in this storyline, we must clarify the difference in prophetic administrations between Enoch and Abraham. Enoch had a more publicized ministry of prophetism. But Abraham's mantle was more private than public. We further add that there are no additional scriptures explaining Abraham's formal call to prophetic ministry. Neither are there any written prophetic utterances ascribed to Abraham anywhere in the Bible. But God's honoring of Abraham as a prophet appears more like an evangelical witness rather than the typical demonstrative works of a publicized prophet.

Nevertheless, like Enoch, Abraham had some prophetic qualities that only God can explain. And it is God who clearly defined Abraham's prophetic purpose. We know that the voice of God reached Abraham on a particular day. Jeremiah said it in this manner: "The word of the Lord came to me" (Jeremiah 1:2, 4, 11, 13). This explains the true position of prophetic posture when receiving a word from the Lord. A prophet cannot be a prophet until the Lord comes and releases the prophetic anointing by way of a specific word that will change that prophet's life.

And this is not a word that the prophet seeks, but rather one he will sense when it is coming. Consequently, this provides us an interesting parenthetical note, which is that a prophet who doesn't have contact with God is a questionable prophetic voice. God has to have a direct line of communication with a prophetic vessel in order for that vessel to be truly deemed prophetic. If the word of God never comes, then how can one confirm his or her prophetic office? Truth be told, there is no other way but this way. So not only does a prophet need a direct line, but he or she also needs confirmation of a prophetic purpose that is clarified in some random choice or individual who can attest to God's calling of that prophet.

In the case of Abraham, God did not send the word directly to him. He sent the word indirectly unto another. In fact, when God spoke about this prophetic title concerning Abraham, there existed only one major witness. Ironically, this witness was a pagan man. This teaches an even greater truism. Gentile nations have experienced the prophetic anointing for a very long time. Just as Jesus would release the apostles to minister to Gentile nations because of the Jewish Diaspora, this Old Testament foreshadowing provides glimpses into the New Testament mission. So God speaking to the pagan man through Abraham's life can be likened unto Jesus Christ speaking to the world.

Though Abraham is not a publicized prophet, his prophetic ministry is still formally relevant. For the following official prophetic recognition was first given to the pagan king, Abimelech. This revelation of the prophetic mantle of Abraham came as a private warning to the pagan king. Like Enoch, the prevailing relevance of God's first prophets seemed to stem from the necessity of warning someone about the dangers of inappropriate activity:

"Now therefore restore the man his wife; for he is a prophet, and he shall pray for thee, and thou shalt live: and if thou restore her not, know thou that thou shalt surely die, thou, and all that are thine" (Genesis 20:7).

This is the first time the word "prophet" is actually used in the Old Testament. Here it is used to convey what God considered Abraham as he revealed the destiny of Abraham unto the foreign king. God wanted Abimelech to become a witness not only of God, but also of God's servant. This revelation of Abraham's true calling is the first witness among the non-Jews (Gentiles) that God was the only true and living God. Again, I must stress that God is not prejudiced. He will speak to any and every man. This is why the Bible says that God desires for no man to perish (2 Peter 3:9). So even though the prophet is called to prophesy unto his own people, if need be, God will make an exception. And the goal of that exception is to always bring any man closer to Him!

We see countless examples of Jesus explaining that His mission is to the lost house of Israel (Matthew 15:24). But every now and again, the Gospels record that Jesus would make an exception to the rule. John's gospel even records the existence of other sheep outside of the congregation of Israel. This parable alludes to those of the Gentile nations that will one day accept Jesus as the Christ:

And other sheep I have, which are not of this fold: them also I must bring, and they shall hear my voice; and there shall be one fold, and one shepherd (John 10:16, KJV).

Returning to the story, by nature, Abraham was extremely fearful and lacked bravery. This is why he convinced Sarah to lie about being his wife. (Similarly, Moses had an identity crisis as well – Exodus 3:11; Exodus 4:1; Exodus 4:10.) The lesson here is that even current prophets have to work hard at not allowing their identity to fall into crisis. So Abraham and Sarah lied out of fear of death, and the lie involved calling Sarah his sister instead of his wife.

Thus, when Abimelech viewed Sarah, he immediately wanted her for marriage. But when Abimelech prepared to marry Sarah, God spoke to him the night before in a dream. Not only was this a direct warning, but it was also a direct revelation about the office of Abraham. And as a result of this informative dream, God instructed the king not to marry Sarah. God warned Abimelech that if he did not return Abraham's wife, God would punish him with death and the destruction of everything he owned.

In Abimelech's dream, confirmation of Abraham's true identity became revealed. God said to Abimelech: **Abraham is my prophet**. Not only did God tell the king who and what Abraham is, but he also explained the favor of the prophetic anointing, which rested upon Abraham. Herein is another parenthetical note: the prophet has favor not only for himself, but also for his family, his belongings, and his possessions. This is why God teaches through the word that people must be careful how they handle true prophets. Even if that prophet is in error (such as Abraham was), the fact still remains that Abraham was still God's prophet:

"...Touch not mine anointed, and do my prophets, no harm" (1 Chronicles 16:22/Psalm 105:15).

Abraham's storyline gives us secondary blueprints for the power of the prophetic anointing. But it also divulges certain privileges that are equally attached to this office. Additionally, it must be mentioned that the power of intercession is within a prophetic mantle. The intercessory gift associated with the prophetic office brings deliverance and an extension of life. God honors the prayer life of every righteous man. And a righteous prophet's prayer life is highly effective and never lacking in true privilege and power:

"...The effectual fervent prayer of a righteous man availeth much" (James 5:16b).

Thus, Abraham becomes the key to Abimelech's deliverance. Yes, a deliverance that came not only from Abraham's person, but also from his prayer life! And when Abraham prayed, God overlooked Abraham's faults and indicted a foreign king so he could realize that he was in the presence of a representative of the King of kings. No matter how bad the character of the individual called to be a prophet, God's favor and delight is always with that prophet!

This is why God's adamancy was pressed upon Abimelech while he dreamt such instructions. When he woke, it appears he immediately returned Abraham's wife. Scripture later explains the intent of Abraham's slightly truthful, but wholly given lie, which further shows that Sarah was in fact his half-sister. He described their blood relation as siblings because they had different mothers but the same father. Nevertheless, half of a truth is still considered a whole lie:

And yet indeed she is my sister; she is the daughter of my father, but not the daughter of my mother; and she became my wife. And it came to pass, when God caused me to wander from my father's house, that I said unto her, this is thy kindness which thou shalt show unto me; at every place whither we shall come, say of me, he is my brother (Genesis 20:12-13).

Despite Abraham's flaws, the word of God says that God considered Abraham's life to be the very definition of righteousness. The Apostle Paul declared that Abraham was the pinnacle of accounted righteousness simply because of his faith and not of his works (Romans Chapter 4). Thus, Abraham's life was more prophetic than his actual voice. He, like John the Baptist, was a prophet with no recorded prophetic word. And yet all prophetic honor is given unto him!

So the title, honor, and recognition as prophet are given to him because of his relevance to the prophetic cause of Christ. Abraham's testimony demonstrates that Christ's calling in your life is much bigger than any identity crisis you may have. If God never allows you to prophesy publicly, can you allow your life to become prophetic instead? And would this be enough if called upon you to be that type of prophetic instrument? For as it was with Abraham and John the Baptist, so it might be the same for you! This lesson teaches us that prophesying is more than just the movement of a man's mouth. It is also the movement of a man's life!

The Old Testament's Historical Progression of the Prophetic Voice

In my first book, *The New Prophetic Generation*, we discovered that the prophetic gene travels from a single individual and evolves among the Levitical families. The patriarch Jacob (or Israel) was the originator of this truth. Jacob passed the prophetic gene to his third born son,

Levi. And we must realize that the same family tree of Enoch and Abraham also came from Jacob and Levi. For it is in the family of Levi where the prophetic ministry is reintroduced once more.

Furthermore, the purpose of this gene coincided with the first national and pastoral leaders as they led the people of Israel through the exodus from Egypt during the 40 years of journeying through the wilderness. It was in the 4th Generation of Levi, under the leadership of Moses and his two prophetic siblings, Aaron [Exodus 7:1] and Miriam [Exodus 15:20-21]), that the first prophetic group and family was created:

"For I brought thee up out of the land of Egypt, and redeemed thee out of the house of servants; and I sent before thee Moses, Aaron, and Miriam" (Micah 6:4, KJV).

After Moses and his siblings' prophetic service, the prophetic ministry took a brief (and its first biblical) pause. But then the prophetic ministry entered once again within the next period of Israelite history. This period is known as the era of the Hebrew Judges (Judges 2:6-10, 16). The most famous of prophetic voices in this era was that of Deborah, a prophetess from Northern Israel (Judges 4:4-5). But not all prophets were known, in this era, by their given name (Judges 6:8). Yet, after this period there was another brief prophetic lull. And the prophetic established its second biblical pause.

It appears that the pattern of pauses within the prophetic is always for a reason. This method appears to be God's prevailing trend. Prophetic pauses are as if God reboots the prophetic ministry by producing a corresponding moment of silence before the next set of prophetic voices are heard. Studying Israelite history, along with prophecy, we discover that God shifted Israel by prophetic intervals every four hundred years. During the beginning stages of each four-century paradigm shift, there was a major flux in prophetic presence. But as the decline of the cluster of four centuries came to a close, the prophetic voice consistently and always took a rest. We see that this was done continuously prior to other generations and various Israelite historical eras (known as the Exodus and Wilderness Period [Moses]; the era of Judges [Samuel]; Kings [Elijah]; and even during the Captivity Periods [the 16 literary prophets of Israel]).

God gave the writer of 1 Samuel an inclination of how important prophetic vision is within every generation. Its presence is a hallmark reality. For it is surely missed when it is not present. It appears that silence protects the prophetic from being made common. This revelation is clarified when God sent the next shift after the period of the Judges. As the next prophetic leader, Samuel, was being born and developed. This is what the land was like with no prophetic vision:

***"...The word of the Lord was precious in those days; there was no open vision"* (1 Samuel 3:16b).**

This scripture explains that the final judge of Israelite history was none other than the Prophet Samuel. This period of transition, from the period of Judges, is known as the period of the Israelite Kings (1 Samuel 8:4-7). So the prophetic-generational leader Samuel was the new representative who ushered in a new prophetic voice and sound. It is also believed that Samuel was the cause of David's prophetic anointing. We learn that David was a prophet because it was the Apostle Peter who confirmed this as he preached his first gospel message on the Day of Pentecost (Acts 2:29-30).

The connection of prophetic unction could have taken place when Samuel anointed David to be king as he went to find David in Bethlehem (1 Samuel 16:13). This likely means that David was Samuel's prophetic apprentice and successor. The pattern of the prophetic father and son paradigm starts with Samuel and David (11th-10th Century of BC) and transitions with Elijah and Elisha (9th-8th Century of BC).

The prophetic father and son periods also consisted of one of the two greatest fluxes of prophetic activity in all Israelite history, meaning this period was when God released the relevance of prophetic groups and families. Samuel's guilds were known as the band of prophets. Elijah and Elisha's guilds were known as the sons of prophets. Thus, the manifestation of prophetic families and groups also shows the importance of prophetic presence as a community (1 Samuel 10:5-7; 1 Samuel 19:18-24; 2 Kings 2:1-18). And apostolically, I believe that this type of paradigm is something God is calling the church to create once again.

For this revelation is further supported by King David, who was the second king of Israel. David was prophetically under the supervision of the prophet, Samuel. And it was David who successfully created a similar paradigm for prophetic schools among Levitical families within the Tabernacle (1 Chronicles 9:22). The system both David and Samuel used was the logical three chief fathers of the known Levitical families: Gershon; Kohath, and Merari (1 Chronicles 6:1, 16, 31-48). But it would be Kohath that would flow the most, concerning the prophetic and music ministries combined.

Using the cycle of three, David assigned three praise and worship teams of prophetic musicians and singers from each of the chief sons of Levi (1 Chronicles 25). The musical and prophetic teams were all genetically related. It did not matter if you were good at music or not so great! Every Levitical family had their responsibility of not only various temple duties, but also worship assignments within both the tabernacle and temples.

The Doctrine of Prophecy

And even Solomon, David's son and kingly successor, would follow in his footsteps. Solomon reinstituted this paradigm when he created the temple instead of his father (2 Chronicles 5:11-14). Eventually the prophetic guilds seemed to dissolve as the prophetic voice returned to the singular voice instead of corporate demonstration.

This period of history contained the unfortunate pre-exiles and captivity periods. But it is the second greatest flux of prophetic activity within Israel. And within these periods, it is important to understand that there were two main captivities worthy of mentioning. One was the northern kingdom, which was composed of the first 10 tribes of Israel (that were taken by the kingdom of Assyria). And the other was the southern kingdom, which was composed of the remaining two tribes of Benjamin and Judah (that were taken by the kingdom of Babylon).

Before and during the two known captivity periods existed the emergence of a new prophetic expression known as prophetic literacy. Not only were the prophets speaking the word of the Lord. Now the prophets began to write the words of the Lord. Theologically we call these literary prophets either major or minor. The reason they are called major is because their writings are extensive compared to the Minor Prophets, who provided only incremental or small notations.

There were four Major Prophets: Isaiah, Jeremiah, Daniel, and Ezekiel. And there were 12 Minor Prophets: Obadiah, Joel, Jonah, Hosea, Amos, Micah, Zephaniah, Nahum, Habakkuk, Haggai, Zechariah, and Malachi. Collectively, the concluding 16 prophets spoke for God by writing during these two periods of Assyrian and Babylonian's pre-exilic, exilic, and post-exilic experiences.

Furthermore, it is important to dissolve the false teaching that there is a difference in any current prophet's ministry. We have people calling themselves Major and Minor Prophets in today's time, but there is no such thing! Again, the only reason we call those prophets major and minor is because of their writings. Never should this be used to specify ability, order, or personality. All prophets have the same ability to use the prophetic spirit to minister on whatever level God has given them to do so. Thus, the only Major Prophet is Jesus Christ and none other. And if we follow such vein, everyone else is considered a Minor Prophet in comparison to Him!

But in respect to order, each literary prophet had a given century he was called to serve. The Prophet Isaiah's ministry was in the 8th Century (740-697 BC); Jeremiah, the 7th century (627-586 BC); Ezekiel, the 6th century (593 BC); and Daniel spanned the entire 70 years of Babylonian captivity (Jeremiah 25:1; Jeremiah 29:10; Daniel 9:2). This means that Daniel's ministry covered a portion of the 7th and 6th centuries (605-536 BC), meaning Daniel was the oldest of the literary prophets and served the longest in this period of prophetic ministry. In fact, his service spanned 70-80 years.

In conjunction with the Major Prophets and the Minor Prophets, Obadiah and Joel operated in the same century as Elijah and Elisha (9th century BC). There were four 8th century Minor Prophets: Jonah, Hosea, Amos and Micah. Additionally, there were three 7th century Minor Prophets: Zephaniah, Nahum, and Habakkuk. There were two 6th century Minor Prophets: Haggai and Zechariah. Finally, there was one 5th century Minor literary Prophet: Malachi. Malachi is the final prophetic voice of the Old Testament (circa 400 BC).

This covers a timeframe of almost 700 years (1100 BC – 400 BC). Reviewing the Old Testament, prophets brings wisdom to the current practices of Christian prophetism. In other words, a prophet helps shape another prophet, and that help is necessary to the prophet's service. The best prophetic shaper, then, is a biblical prophet. As the Apostle Paul says, the spirit of the prophet is subject to the prophet (1 Corinthians 14:32). The unknown writer of Hebrews teaches us that we should mimic those of the faith and within the word of God. Thus, we can learn how God operates prophetically with this realization:

Do not drag your feet. Be like those who stay the course with committed faith and then get everything promised to them (Hebrews 6:12, Message Bible).

In conclusion, we can try to biblically epitomize the prophetic gift by following the Old Testament lineup: Enoch and Abraham, then Jacob and Levi. Moses, Miriam, and Aaron who are followed by Deborah and some unknown names among the judges. The prophetic then reestablishes with Samuel and David, followed by Elijah and Elisha. Then the prophetic voice becomes artistically expressed among 16 literary prophets (4 major and 12 Minor). Finally, the prophetic voice of old was sealed (for 400 years) after the prophetic ministry of Malachi. And now that we have been through the Old Testament's prophetic hall of fame, let's take a brief look at the New Testament lineup.

The Presence of Prophecy within Non-Biblical Years

But before exploring the New Testament's prophetic lineup, there is one more thing to discuss, and that's the possibility of prophecy within the period of what is called the non-biblical years. Theologically speaking, there are two known testaments of the Bible: the Old Testament and the New Testament. Between both testaments was a period called the intertestamental period. In this period, there were no formal canonized writings deemed acceptable by Jewish or

Christian theologians. However, historically speaking, it is a period that still had prophetic implications. Though it is theologically taught that the prophetic voice was silenced for 400 years, it is quite possible that the voice of the prophet was present during what are considered the non-biblical years (or the intertestamental period).

This is implied by the non-canonized writings (i.e. references to the Apocrypha and the scholarly works of Flavius Josephus, who is a known famous Jewish historian). From a biblical standpoint, we must ecclesiastically state that the official prophetic voice is silent. However, this does not mean that there were not any prophets used in the intertestamental period. Therefore, we likely conclude that the next cluster of biblical prophetic voices is only exclusively applicable based on the canonization perspective. This is why it is important to refer to the next set of candidates as New Testament Prophets instead of Old Testament Prophets. But there is a possibility of intertestamental prophets as well.

Prophetess versus Prophet

A commonality within Old Testament prophetism is the differentiation of male and female prophets (Exodus 15:20-21; Judges 4:4; 2 Kings 22:14; Luke 2:36-38; Acts 21:8-9). When now referencing the word "prophets," we must see this as a generalization instead of a gender classification. We must also note that male and female prophets are both mentioned within the New Testament as one title, compared to how they were mentioned in the Old Testament. This is because the prophetic office is non-gender specific and is under the New Testament's directive (1 Corinthians 11:4-5). It is no longer under the Old Testament's enforcements.

So it is acceptable to call a woman a prophet just as you would a man. The Bible declares that in the spirit realm, we have no case of gender (Galatians 3:28). Thus, if a woman wants to title her office as "prophetess," we must respectfully adhere and universally understand that "prophetess" is not greater or lesser in value to the word "prophet." Simply put, the words "prophet" and "prophetess" can be used among female candidates, if one desires.

However, the New Testament does not use such designations. The major point here is that every prophet, whether male or female, is still called by God to prophesize to his or her generation (Acts 2:17-18; Ephesians 4:11). And that generation is not about distinction of sex as much as it is about the development of people's spirit!

Who Are the Last Biblical Prophets?

The Irony of the First New Testament Prophetic Voices

And the main purpose for mentioning women in prophecy is because a woman is among the first three prophetic witnesses who reintroduced the prophetic ministry of the New Testament. The interesting thing about this is that the next three leading prophetic voices of the New Testament were likened unto the Old Testament prophetic first three (which was Moses, Miriam, and Aaron). Moses, Aaron, and Miriam were used in the period of the wilderness journey. In the New Testament, God used the next three to prophetically unfold Jesus Christ in the land of Canaan. For Palestine is synonymous with Israel. And Israel is synonymous with Canaan. Thus, just as we have three prophets ushering in the direction of Israel in the Old, we now have three prophets ushering in the direction of the church in the New.

This irony is a symbol suggesting how humanity has crossed over into a better Promised Land because of the arrival of Jesus Christ. This affirms the importance of remembering how the word of God declares every word to be established by the mouth of two or three witnesses (2 Corinthians 13:1). Thus, the three prophetic New Testament witnesses, Simeon, Zacharias, and Anna, are connected to the three prophetic Old Testament witnesses, Moses, Aaron, and Miriam. In the book, *New Prophetic Generation*, we discuss how Levi's son-ship of three is a prevailing number among prophetic ministry.

And among the first three prophetic witnesses of the New Testament, Zacharias (Luke 1:5-25) was the father of the famous John the Baptist. And Zacharias' main function in the prophetic was to usher in the understanding of how John's ministry would be in relation to the ministry of Jesus. In fact, Jesus and John are, by blood, cousins (Luke 1:67-80). But John and Jesus also symbolically connect us back to the paradigms of Enoch and Abraham, Moses and Joshua, Samuel and David, and Elijah and Elisha. What this lesson teaches is how God uses one prophet to announce another prophet's purpose within the earth. God establishes at least two prophets to support one major shift of the divine claims and transactions from heaven.

If God uses two, it is understood that there is also balance. But when God uses three, there is an even greater sense of spiritual urgency and relativity. We see this dualism of assignment with Zecharias' counterparts. Anna and Simeon's primary purpose was to see Jesus manifested in the flesh as confirmation that the Messiah had truly come (Luke 2:34-38). Their secondary purpose was to ensure that their prophetic ministry represented the culmination of the Old Testament prophetic ministry. As former prophetic harbingers of the old order, their assignment was to finish the age of the Old Testament and bridge the gap of the new age that

The Doctrine of Prophecy

we now call the New Testament. Their threefold chord cannot be broken. And their trifold witness confirms that Jesus was Christ.

Thus, Zacharias, Simeon, and Anna unanimously signified the true ending of the former prophetic order and testament. Additionally, after their trifold witness, Jesus came and sealed the revelation that now is the presence of a new prophetic generation and regime (Matthew 1:1a; Revelation 19:10b). For three prophets opened the prophetic generation of the past. And three prophets now open the present prophetic generation that is certainly going forward into the future. Any who are called "prophet" in today's time must respect these chief positions in both the old and new orders.

The Convergence of a New Prophetic Generation, Covenant and Dispensation

The inception of the new prophetic family was summoned once again at Pentecost. The Apostle Peter mentioned it during his sermon that led 3,000 Jewish souls to Christ (Acts 2:16-18; Joel 2:30-31). During the age of the early church (Acts 13:1; 1 Corinthians 12, 13, 14), the churches of Antioch and Corinth increased in heavy prophetic activity (Acts 13:1 and 1 Corinthians Chapters 12-14). Additionally, the churches of Ephesus, Thessalonica, and Rome also had prophetic presence with the number of churches increasing there as well (Ephesians 4:11; 1 Thessalonians 5:20; Romans 12:6).

And another noteworthy thing to mention is the massive usage of the given names of the prophets in the Old is dramatically different within the New Testament writings. Names such Silas (Acts 15:32) and Agabus (Acts 11:28, Acts 21:10) are briefly mentioned in the New Testament. However, after their presence, we see less classification of "certain prophets." Eventually, the Apostle Paul commanded a corporate mandate through several of his dissertations, especially when teaching about spiritual gifts in his letters to the churches of Corinth and Rome (1 Corinthians 14:1, Romans 12:6).

Thus, the New Testament church age flowed very differently than the Old Testament church of the wilderness. This was because the prophet had to have proper prophetic tonality. And their message and mission dramatically changed when the Old Testament voice was translated into a New Testament sound. It is clear that this sound is to remain in the earth as long as the church is there too.

But there is a more systematic reasoning for why the sound has changed (Acts 2:1). And that reasoning is because of the relevance of covenants and dispensations. For covenants and dispensations both play vital roles in the ministry of Hebrew and Christian prophetism. Theologically, we are taught that there are seven covenants and seven dispensations.

A covenant is the set agreement God makes within a specific generation among a specified generational leader, who is given the assignment of leading God's people. The seven covenants of the Bible are called the Adamic (named after Adam), Edenic (named after Eden), Noahic (named after Noah), Abrahamic (named after Abraham), Mosaic (named after Moses), New (named by God to suggest Jesus Christ, which is the equivalent of the New Testament), and the Davidic (named after David).

This covenant is to confirm Christ as the final king for the world since the golden age of Israel was more conducive to David's leadership and rule. Thus, this covenant is removed from the historical lineup and placed prophetically at the end of time, history, and reality. God will fulfill this covenant when Jesus returns to the earth to complete the purpose of days. This, then, is the reason Peter says we are in the last days. Until the days have ended, the prophetic is aligned to these seven covenants until they are all fulfilled.

And, equally, there are seven dispensations. A dispensation is different from the purpose of a covenant. For a dispensation is a set of conditions, benefits, and allocations that God administers within each specified covenant. If the dispensation is not adhered, then the covenant is eventually dissolved or suspended.

The seven biblical dispensations are:

- **The Dispensation of Innocence** (worked with the covenant given to Adam)
- **The Dispensation of Environment** (worked with the covenant concerning Eden)
- **The Dispensation of Human Government** (worked with the covenant given to Noah)
- **The Dispensation of Promise** (works with the covenant given to Abraham. This covenant is still active).
- **The Dispensation of Law** (works with the covenant given to Moses. Some of this covenant is also active as well. But through the Gospel some portions of this dispensation and its covenant are discontinued).
- **The Dispensation of Grace** (works with the covenant given to Jesus Christ. We are presently in this time period).
- **The Dispensation of the Fullness of Times** (will work with the covenant given to David. This dispensation and covenant will be fulfilled at the end of Great Tribulation).

The Doctrine of Prophecy

The Apostle Paul reveals that the church (of every age and generation) resides within the dispensation of grace (Ephesians 3:2). This also means that the church age is under the New Covenant. The New Covenant compares to the dispensation of the law, which was under Moses' administration, or under Moses' covenant, which God had given to him. We epitomize his covenant with the manifestation of the Ten Commandments, but we come to learn that the ten laws became 613 laws, and now those laws have evolved into thousands.

But, as the Bible declares, we are no longer under the law. For Christ has come to fulfill the law, and since the law is fulfilled, we are to take up the teaching of Christ. It is the teachings of Christ's gospel, and the words of his apostles and prophets that we move from the mountain of Sinai to the mountain of Zion. Here is the symbolic purpose of the Day of Pentecost (Acts 2:1). It commemorates the act done on Mount Sinai, 50 days after Israel was delivered from Egypt. But now that this covenant has ended, we who face Mount Zion, by way of Pentecost, are under the prophesied New Covenant of Jesus Christ.

And the prophets Jeremiah and Ezekiel prophetically explained how God would provide this new covenant (Jeremiah 31:31, Ezekiel 37:26). Also, the unknown apostolic writer of Hebrews confirms this when he intricately states how Jesus released the new covenant after his atoning work at Calvary (Hebrews 8:8, 13; Hebrews 12:24). For now, the goal of the church age prophet is to usher forth the believer to Christ (1 Corinthians 14:22) by way of grace and under God's new agreement (i.e. covenant).

This covenant is not as serious as the old. It also has a different voice. Thus, the prophet must match the dispensation and covenant in which he presently resides. Any other tonality is suggestive of another covenant and dispensation. And that type of behavior and transaction is inappropriate and illegal.

The goal of the Christian prophet is therefore to minister abundantly, rather than to attempt to send people to hell and speak damnation, fire, and brimstone. The prophet is still a righteous judge, but in the spirit of Jesus Christ and not the spirit of a misunderstood prophetic voice. This is the difference between the Old Testament prophet and the New Testament prophet. One was under Moses' ministry. The other is under Jesus' ministry.

What this further explains is how Christian prophets are the twin siblings of the office of the Evangelist. Since New Testament prophecy is for believers rather than unbelievers, the gospel of Jesus Christ must be presented first to the unsaved, then prophesying is allowed afterwards. For the New Testament and church age prophet will be collected with the body of

Christ during the Rapture (1 Corinthians 15:51-53). And it is every spiritual leader's assignment to help populate heaven.

The prophet now has new orders. Speak the truth. Prophesy the truth. But make it all applicable to Jesus Christ! The New Testament later-day prophet is about preparing the bride of Christ for the unknowing date of Jesus Christ's return. We are now striving to become part of the prophetic hall of fame of yesterday with our prophetic counterparts of the early New Testament church. Now I must ask: Do you belong in this lineup?

The Very Last Prophetic Voices of the New Testament Era

The next era in which this unique voice will commence is in the period called the Great Tribulation. The revelation of the Great Tribulation was given to the prophet Daniel during the days of the Babylonian Captivity (Daniel 9:20-27; Daniel 11:36-45; Daniel Chapter 12). This revelation exists in a period of about seven years before the millennial (1,000 years of) reign led by Jesus Christ. It marks the period where God prepares the world for the last days. It also ushers in the return of Christ and His establishment of mankind's dominion, which was lost with Adam when he fell by transgression in the Garden of Eden.

The first three and a half years will be a pretention of peace. However, at the end of the first three and a half years, the next period will arrive in which the antichrist will make war with the world. This will be the time when the last prophetic voices will emerge. The primary purpose of this period is to establish the last gathering of Gentile and Jewish unbelievers predestined to become believers.

But the primary presence of these last two prophetic voices will be to the completion of God's promises made to Abraham and the covenant that He made with him. Thus, the presence of the last two prophetic voices will take on a more Israelite tonality and mentality. For it was pre-established for the sake of redeeming a remnant of 12,000 tribulation souls within each tribal-nation of the scattered people of Israel (Revelation Chapter 7) that for this reason these prophets will manifest. This is why, at the end of the church age, the Old Testament tonality of the prophetic will seem as if it has returned for one final sweep. Remember, though, that this prophetic hybrid voice will have the Old Testament understanding as well as New Testament clarification.

This implies that the church cannot dissolve the need for prophetic ministry any more than Israel can. So the final prophetic voices will end with two unique prophets who will minister similar to Elijah and Moses' prophetic ministries. Their last utterance will have the Gospel, but with a twist of gloom to it. For Jesus will send these two prophetic voices as a means of calling Israel unto repentance. But their prophetic assignment will be administering the gospel to Israel so that they might find a relationship with God through Jesus Christ. For Jesus Christ must be acknowledged by the Jewish people as the true Messiah. So these last two prophets will evangelize and prophesize within the earth for the very last time:

And I will give power unto my two witnesses, and they shall prophesy a thousand two hundred and threescore days, clothed in sackcloth. These are the two olive trees, and the two candlesticks standing before God of the earth. And if any man will hurt them, fire proceedeth out of their mouth, and devoureth their enemies: and if any man will hurt them, he must in this manner be killed. These have power to shut heaven, that it rain in the days of their prophecy; and have power over waters to turn them to blood, and to smite the earth with all plagues, as often as they will. And when they shall have finished their testimony, the beast that ascendeth out of the bottomless pit shall make war against them, and shall overcome them, and kill them. And their bodies shall lie in the street of the great city, which spiritually is called Sodom and Egypt, where also our Lord was crucified. And they of the people and kindreds and tongues and nations shall see their dead bodies three days and an half, and shall not suffer their dead bodies to be put into graves. And they that dwell upon the earth shall rejoice over them, and make merry, and shall send gifts one to another; because these two prophets tormented them that dwelt on the earth. And after three days and an half the Spirit of life from God entered into them, and they stood upon their feet; and great fear fell upon them which saw them. And they heard a great voice from heaven saying unto them, Come up hither. And they ascended up to heaven in a cloud; and their enemies beheld them (Revelation 11:3-12).

This clearly teaches that the truth of the prophet's mantle will always remain in the earth. This revelation does not dissolve until the final two prophetic voices of the Great Tribulation, which further shows how God strategically uses each mantle distinctively within each generation. However, this also demonstrates how a prophetic mantle can shift its usage. The adaptability of a prophetic mantle is, then, determined by the specific era, dispensation, and covenant it is therefore needed and used.

For it is equally the church's responsibility to use the Old Testament prophetic mantles until the Lord's return for his Holy Church. Herein is the connection of the past to the present, as well as the present to the future. And if you are part of the church, then you have a right to become part of its prophecy. For the connection of prophesying now is just as applicable to prophesiers back then. Therefore, you must learn from some of the prophets of the past in order to become a greater prophet of the present. This is certainly about the advancement of prophecy, generationally, towards the future! The question at hand is: Will you become another great representative?

CONCLUSION OF LESSON 1:

...Because there are two forms of discipleship. The first is instructional and exists through a formal class and teaching. This form is what we call didactic discipleship. The other form is what we call demonstrative discipleship. This is when you observe the actions, behaviors, and visual abilities of someone else to learn various techniques from them.

Simply put, if you want to be a great singer, you have to study and learn from other greater singers. If you want to be a great writer, you have to study and learn from other great writers. So if you want to be a great prophet, you have to study and learn from other great prophets.

The prophets most proven in their greatness are not those who have come before us according to our generation. Instead, the prophets God has undeniably proven, because of their memorialization within the word of God, are those most proven to have the best greatness. And if a prophet does not study biblical greats, they will be unable to obtain their own prophetic greatness. This is why I took this comprehensive journey in identifying the biblical prophets from A-Z. Now it is up to you to return to the Bible for a more intensive study. For this is the sake of your own success of serving Christ within His prophetic ministry.

My personal testimony is I, too, am confirmed to be a prophet. But after my confirmation, I went and creatively studied every word that was applicable to prophecy. This same journey I now encourage you to take. The exercise is simple. Create a topical study of all the derivatives of prophet, prophets, prophetess, prophecy, prophesy, and prophesying. The goal here is to memorize all biblical references applicable to your ministry before you attempt to advance in prophetic servicing.

If you follow this prescription, you will discover a prophetic pathway that will carve out your own distinction prophetic destiny. These pages contain what we call the "word of life," in which God has strategically placed the great hall of fame concerning biblical prophetic producers. But now it is your turn to take up such a mantle. For you are called to do this in your own unique way.

CHAPTER 2

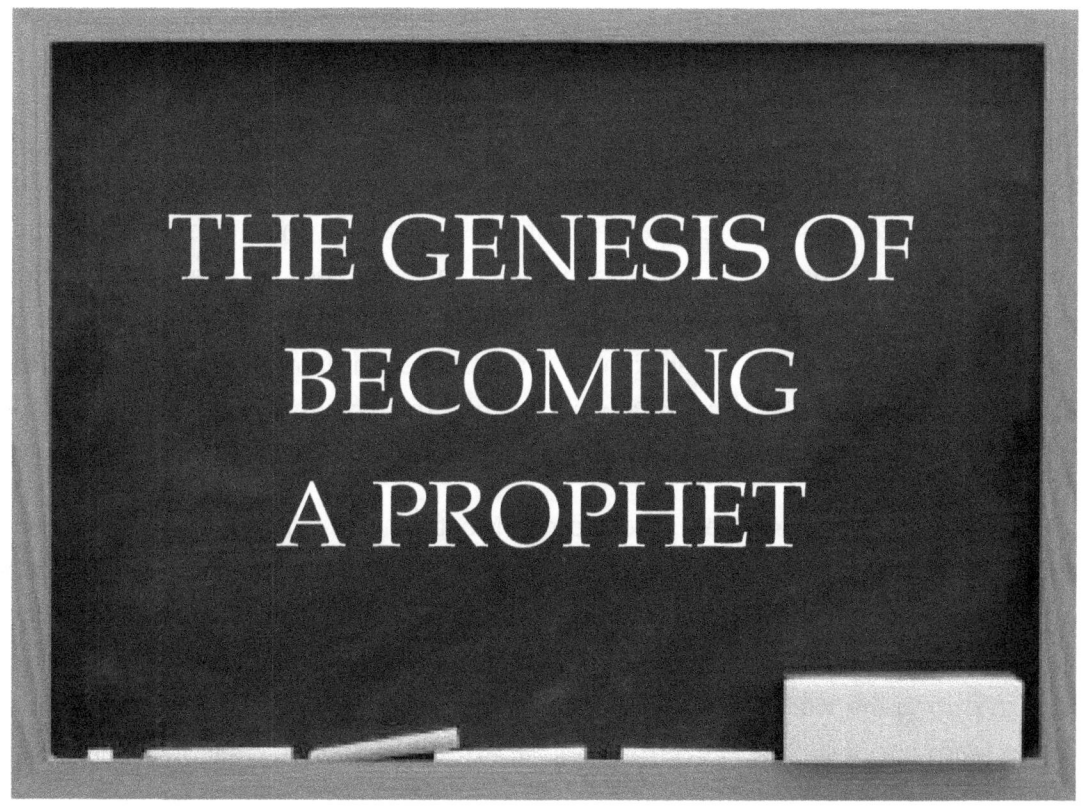

What is a Prophet?

"And He gave...some prophets..." (Ephesians 4:11a)

His Foundation Begins with Naturalness

No one serving as a soldier gets involved in civilian affairs—he wants to please his commanding officer (2 Timothy 2:4, NIV).

Now it's time to get even more specific. There is a logical way for you to become a prophet. In this lesson (or chapter), we will discover the purpose of the prophet, the nature of the prophet, as well as how to become properly aligned in your prophetic work. As all things have specific periods, before you decide to accept the calling of the prophet, you must make sure that your calling is similar to the genesis of every prophet.

And we often overlook one major component when studying the prophetic. It is an important part, though we often take it for granted. We forget that prophets are human beings first and prophets second. They are given an entirely natural life and are born into a traceable family and bloodline. Thus, their initial beginnings are shaped by their environment and distinctive upbringing. However, what truly transforms them is the divine summons of God, which He gives to the prophet at an appointed time. Until such time, they are allowed to remain a regular person, living an unknown space while living in this known world. This is why a prophet is not spiritual first. His foundation begins with natural living.

All prophets are called from the womb. Most of the time, they are allowed some reasonable portion of a natural and normal upbringing. But at the appointed time the prophetic anointing may require the prophet to put his childhood on hold. This was possible in the cases of Samuel, Jeremiah, John the Baptist, and even Jesus. As we know, each of their anointings were given prior to exiting the womb. But their natural living still encompassed a period in which they were able to learn about life. I believe that God allowed this so that their spiritual living would not become imbalanced.

Eventually, during some part of their life, God interrupted their natural living to begin a prophetic emergence and evolution. This process is never a full divorce from the prophet's naturalness. However, prophets must learn how to shift between both worlds. The best way to help describe this vacillation is to compare it to a marriage between the super and the natural.

Thus, it is advisable that the prophet always uses the natural as an anchor. In doing so, they operate within the supernatural realm like an eagle using its keen eyesight to search for prey from the highest heights. With precision, an eagle flies down and grabs his prey but then accurately returns back to the heights until he reaches his nest to digest what he has captured.

This is similar to how a mantle becomes active among the true prophetic oil from God. The anointing will catapult you up into the heights of heaven, but you cannot stay there forever! Eventually, you must come down and rest. For even an eagle has moments of rest on a branch before he takes flight into the heights again. In the same manner, the prophet must realize that his process within both worlds is the same.

Another perfect analogy is civilian living versus military living. When you join the army, civilian life never is the same. Every now and then you might join civilian life to visit family and friends. But for the most part, you are property of the particular military branch you've joined. So, when your commander gives you orders, everything else becomes secondary. This means that if you're deployed in the states or out of the country, you cannot resist your commanding officer.

And if you are truly a soldier bred for military service, then you will adhere to what is asked of you. This is because the military reconditions its officers to be prepared to abruptly stop whatever he is doing in his civilian life. And civilian life is equivalent to a prophet's natural life. Everything changes once God calls the prophet from his naturalness into his supernatural responsibility. This certainly takes dexterity of mind and heart, and it comes with its own particular challenges.

Staying with the military analogy, the newly inducted prophet receives his rank within the spiritual army of the Lord. As one becomes a private, with the possibility of one day becoming a general, so too does a novice prophet grow into a seasoned prophet. Just as the military official knows that he is a hybrid of civilian and military realities, a prophet must also work under the same guise of the natural and the supernatural realms. He is both natural and spiritual. He is a natural-civilian when he is needed and he is spiritual-military when he is needed.

And when joining the army, one's entire life becomes about the art of war and military living. You have orders. You have superiors. You have missions. And you have rankings to matriculate. This is why a prophet must respect the experience of being a licensed minister, first (Acts 12:5) and then an ordained position of an elder later (Titus 1:5). Just as the military processes you, so, too, does the church process you. It is every soldier's responsibility to pick which military branch for which he wants to serve, but with the realization that once he has chosen that branch, his service is for a lifetime. In the same vein, it is the prophet's responsibility of finding a church home where he or she will faithfully serve and develop into a credential man or woman of God. And with the same mindset, he, too, should remain faithful to that branch until the fullness of his elevation has occurred.

The Doctrine of Prophecy

This example further serves as a map of what happens to the candidate called of God, both in the world and in the spirit realm, particularly for the Lord's service, which is known as prophetic service. Or, as I said before, this is known as the ministry of prophetism. Simply put, when you are a prophet, your entire life will go through constant changes. You have to accept the random orders of God. You will have to forsake all that you may desire and know. Everything that you are comfortable with will become uncomfortable the moment you hear the divine call. This is like being drafted into the military instead of choosing to enlist.

Yes, prophets are special human beings who are called at a particular time in their lives. In fact, it is the prophet's sole foundation. The prophet's subsequent calling usually is shaped by this major premise, which is why the prophet is called a supernatural officer of God. But the root word in supernatural is the word "natural," meaning that his foundation in being natural will allow him to be successful in his supernatural endeavors.

Using the concept of the five-fold offices described in Ephesians Chapter 4, apostles would be equivalent to the office of generals according to the military analogy mentioned earlier. Here, prophets would be colonels. Lastly, teachers are like majors. However, before you can become a general you must become a private. I cannot over emphasize this enough!

In like manner the prophet must start as a licensed minister. In time, with maturity and under the right supervision, his elevation should bring them to the office of elder. For no one joins the army at the status of a general. This is why you are certainly called to start at the bottom and work your way up (in time). Thus it is advisable that a novice prophet becomes a student of his natural life first, and then a student of basic biblical information when his life begins to change. This format is the best policy to ensure sanity in your prophetic office.

If this humble behavior is active when the novice and apprenticeship phase of the prophetic is present, it is certain that a healthier career in the prophetic will occur. The prophet is advised to grow organically. Thus, a prophet is born first to serve as an insubordinate within the military position of the army of the Lord.

Surely, a prophet's importance is based upon the assignment within a kingdom reality. We certainly do not need any more people attempting this office with the mentality of a mere "church going" point of view. No, we need the emerging prophetic candidate to understand that he plays a highly critical role in God's encampment. Since prophesying is an important assignment, the candidate should not mind operating with patience until it is time to be received as a confirmed prophet. The Apostle Paul puts it in this perspective:

"And God hath set some in the church, first apostles, secondarily prophets, thirdly teachers..." (1 Corinthians 12:28a, KJV).

Again, I must stress that the key word in supernatural is the word "natural." After one's acquaintance with his or her naturalness, in time God will elevate the individual to a supernatural "birth." In the Bible, Jesus told Nicodemus that a man must be born again (John 3:3-8). He went further to say that this second birth must be born of water and of the spirit. We know that water is a symbol for the word of God (John 15:3). Certainly the spirit refers to God's Holy Spirit (or Holy Ghost). This type of second birth is what we theologically accept as salvation, which is authenticated by faith through grace (Ephesians 2:8). Once the individual has received salvation the process then confirms that a believer must receive the baptism of the Holy Ghost. For it is the Spirit's baptism that takes the believer out of the world and places him into the realm of spirit (1 Corinthians 12:13). There, every believer is given license to see angels and demons, and is able to gain understanding by discerning the ways of the Spirit of God.

Naturally speaking, every first birth is surely deemed natural. Then one's second birth, with the means of Christ, is deemed supernatural. So in our Christian belief, a man must have two births within his lifetime in order to be validated in any candidacy concerning a supernatural assignment. This is the fundamental reality for one's true acceptance within Christian prophetic service. A Christian prophet is not truly accepted by God until he has fully discerned the difference between his two births. Again, both births are required. One is natural and the other is supernatural. If you have not received your second birth, please review the following scriptures:

"Then Peter said unto them, Repent, and be baptized every one of you in the name of Jesus Christ for the remission of sins, and ye shall receive the gift of the Holy Ghost" (Acts 2:38).

"That if thou shalt confess with thy mouth the Lord Jesus, and shalt believe in thine heart that God hath raised him from the dead, though shalt be saved" (Romans 10:9).

Now that we have reviewed the plan of salvation, which is the means of the second birth, let's return to the analogy of birth. When a woman is going into labor, the sign of such labor occurs when her water breaks. In the same vein, the prophet must have a foundational reality of natural existence with the breaking of the prophetic womb. Of course, this is indicated by two witnesses: the Spirit of God and the word of God. If this does not occur, the prophet's supernatural birth will be deemed illegitimate and certainly corrupt.

God has never recklessly chosen any of his prophets, whether Jewish or Christian! No, a prophet's calling is divine and deliberate; it is predetermined by an almighty God before that prophet's first birth. This is why a prophet must never let go of humanity while attempting his journey into the depths of spirituality.

It is very important for the success of a prophet's duration in ministry. In fact, some prophets face a spiritual and personal identity crisis because of this simple but necessary balance. We heard how Moses struggled with this assignment. We have also seen how Abraham's flaws could have overshadowed his assignment. And we even have proof that David's sins of sexual promiscuity could have aborted his assignment. But despite problems in a prophet's life, his naturalness is connected to the uniqueness of his prophetic assignment.

This is one of the hardest concepts to grasp for overly spiritualized people attempting to perform prophetic works. They cannot fathom why God may have selected them, or anyone else for that matter. But herein resides an important point: the natural life and supernatural elevation, combined within the prophet, create an ultimate weapon for God. In the case of Jacob, who was wickeder than his twin brother, Esau, God used the life of Jacob to bring about the lives of Israel. God's choice was not based on anything that Jacob had done. Instead, God's choice was based on his will alone:

"…To Rebecca, also, a promise was made that took priority over genetics. When she became pregnant by our one-of-a-kind ancestor, Isaac, her babies were still innocent in the womb—incapable of good or bad—she received a special assurance from God. What God did in this case made it perfectly plain that his purpose is not a hit-or-miss thing dependent on what we do or don't do, but a sure thing determined by his decision, flowing steadily from his initiative" (Romans 9:10-11, The Message Bible).

Yes, prophets become God's secret weapons within the earth! And the weaponry is found in their anointing. But it is also found within their distinct personalities. This is why they are strategically deposited within a natural experience first, and why it further explains the necessity of God's unique design about a prophet's natural makeup. One's location of birth, nationality, cultural influences, demographics, and societal origins all play vital roles in a prophet's ministry.

These factors also explain the reason why a prophet's creation is not experimental. Neither is the life of a prophet haphazard. Thank God it is not a catastrophe! The concept of the supernatural destiny emerging from the prophet is like a person in a layover at the airport. It is true that some of that time, concerning God's waiting, God wants the prophet to experience certain measures of humanity. But, when the appointed time emerges, there is always clear purpose. And that purpose is always to carry out God's agenda. Then the layover can end and the flight to the skies can resume.

For God, the almighty, has a method of releasing His mind and His will incrementally within the earth. And just like humans feel the need to share, God, too, functions with the same modus operandi. The scripture teaches that knowledge and the manifestation of prophesying come in increments (1 Corinthians 13:9). But even within these increments, nothing happens without a prophet's presence. And so a prophet can only share when God reveals such increments by way of a prophet's spirit:

Surely the Lord God will do nothing, but He revealeth His secret unto His servants the Prophets (Amos 3:7, KJV).

So prophets are created and manifested at the exclusive discretion of God. But their natural origins come from a traceable point of reference. Some Hebrew prophets are considered to have come from the tribe of Reuben (i.e., Joel), others from the tribe of Simeon, (i.e., Habakkuk, Zephaniah, and Nahum), and others from the tribe of Judah (King David; Isaiah; Daniel). Additionally, some were from the tribe of Ephraim (i.e., Micah) or the tribe Issachar (i.e., Hosea).

But the most traceable are those from the tribe of Levi (i.e., Moses, Miriam, Aaron, Samuel, Jeremiah, Ezekiel and Zechariah). In fact, some even say that Elijah was a descendent of Aaron, making him of a Levite origin as well. For even John the Baptist and Jesus Christ were from Levi's sons by way of Aaron (Luke 1:5, 26, 35-36), which is confirmed in the relationship of Mary and Elizabeth, who were cousins, making John and Jesus kin as well.

Though some sources are not all fully confirmed, there are many more speculations (internal and external from the bible) concerning the prophet's earthly origin. Whether the Bible lists the family history of the prophets (some are and some are not), each prophet starts from a natural starting point and then progresses spiritually. This is why the validity of this perspective stands firm.

For a natural reality is central to the survival of one's prophetic existence. If the prophet has no connection to his origins, then he will likely become unsuccessful in prophetic ministry. This is why it is so necessary to combine humanity with spirituality. If God wanted an absolute spiritual being, he would have bypassed the idea of a human prophet altogether. And he would have chosen only angels.

Instead, God designs a vessel that is more tangible and traceable. This means that we have some of the earth and some of eternity within us. For God extracts portions of the prophet's assignment from the ministry of angels, but God takes the other half of our assignment from the loins of men (meaning our parent's union). Here is a more creative explanation of what is a prophet: the prophet is a composite of man with ministry. And never will the prophet be ministry without being a man.

I cannot stress this enough! This has an utmost of urgency! Humanity must be the first prerequisite of any prophet's identity. For Jesus himself was a man, and yet he was God (1 John 4:2). Adam was made of dirt and water from the earth before God breathed life into him (Genesis 2:7). And so it is with any aspect of God's decision to choose human vessels, meaning that even prophets mimic the same factors in that they are both human and divine. Their humanity is just as important as their spirituality.

And with this dualistic design, the prophet will constantly vacillate between two worlds. One realm will be on the behalf of God, who is complete spirit; the other will be on the behalf of man, who is composite of both spirit and world. This is why a prophet's ministry must become balanced in the conceptualization of walking between both natural and supernatural realms. If a prophet is only focused upon his supernatural identity, then his humanity will greatly suffer and could possibly lead to dire consequences, even mental illness.

The old saints used to say it in this manner: "You are so heavenly bound that you're no earthly good." This old-time mantra expresses the importance of balance. When there are imbalances between the spiritual and natural, there will soon be problems that lead to disorder. A prophet who is not grounded as a human being will thus become *that* prophet notoriously known for moving towards false balances in his prophetic ministry:

"A false balance is abomination to the Lord..." (Proverbs 11:1a, KJV).

"...And a false balance is not good" (Proverbs 20:23b, KJV).

Thus, prophets must never be embarrassed by their upbringing, struggles with sin, or family history. Regardless of a prophet's disdain for his family, history, and various shortcomings, a prophet must work towards ministerial realization and true deliverance. God is the supreme decision maker regarding the truthfulness of any prophet's humanity. God predetermines which family is responsible for producing and preserving each prophetic conduit. God has also dispensed precise measurements of grace and mercy to abound with each true prophetic vessel:

"Great deliverance giveth He to his king; and sheweth mercy to His anointed..." (Psalm 18:50a, KJV).

"...Where sin abounded, grace did much more abound" (Romans 5:20b, KJV).

The stabilization and realization of both worlds are the keys to God's consistent manifestation and maintenance of a healthy prophet. So, regardless of sin, the prophet's gift and calling is without repentance (Romans 11:29). And just because the prophet can find prophetic unction does not qualify him to truly ascertain salvation (Matthew 7:21-23). It is important that both births – first (natural birth) and second (supernatural birth, which is expressed through the Salvation of Jesus Christ) – must become part of the prophet's total DNA.

This means that prophets have no excuse when accepting the entirety of their call. Secondly, it also means that prophets should grow in leaving their sinfulness and former lives behind as they progress more in Christ and their Christian work. For in Christ, the prophet's identity is fully clarified. Surely, it is in Jesus Christ that the prophet's ministry is legally covered.

Now, the Lord Jesus' birth is a rare exception. His unique birth reveals that God was made like man to save man. This is why Jesus is the master of all true prophets, both Jewish and Christian alike. After all, the source of prophesying is Jesus Christ! And it is recorded in God's word that the spirit of Christ is in all true prophets, past, present and future (1 Peter 1:11). Though man is made slightly lower than the angels, a prophet's birth is never greater than God's existence. With this same regard, a prophet must understand the truism of his human limitations before trying to ascertain any supernatural assumed possibilities. Are you walking in your humanity as much as you desire your divinity? If you are, then you are establishing not only balance, but also the greatness of the realms of prophetic blessings. For with that balance, the proper matriculation of your own prophetic ministry will continue to grow even more unto God's perfect day (Proverbs 4:18)!

His Spiritual Elevation is Based On Prophetic Relevance

Now that we have clarified the necessity of the natural, let's move forward with the supernatural. For it is the prophet's spiritual ministry that makes the prophet unique and provides a prophet with the extraordinary proportions of prophetic power. This is why a prophet is viewed as a special gift from God to man.

The specialness surrounding the dynamics of a prophet's natural birth, coupled with the prophet's divine ability to perform supernatural works, makes a prophet certainly above average.

In some sense, the prophet becomes like Superman. He is part Clark Kent, whose development is from the earth, and part Kal-El, whose origination is from Krypton.

Superman's storyline is a great analogy for the supernatural life of a prophet. This is because Superman was given human identity to help conceal and protect his extraterrestrial origination. Together, both realities help him assimilate into the world. But his dual identities as Clark Kent and Kal-El must also remain balanced. Furthermore, it is the same with the prophet of God. Again, if you subtract one from the other, you lose the true identity of the prophet.

So God always adds a twist to the emergence of his prophets. The prophet is strategically born to reach certain regions, cultures, and people. If this were not so, then Jeremiah would have not been born of priestly parents, and Isaiah would have not been born close to Israelite royalty. Even Jesus, who was born poor and working-class to a stepfather and a very young and inexperienced mother would have rather been born among the top Israelite echelon of his day.

But these anomalies within each prophetic birth, naturally and supernaturally speaking, confirm God's sovereignty. Again, the prophet's manifestation is at the discretion of God alone. Every prophet's DNA, destination of birth, family, storms, struggles, and generational curses become part of a series of blueprints and genetic mapping necessary in the creation and totality for the gift we call the prophet! This is why a prophet is created naturally, as well as why a prophet is elevated supernaturally:

"The word of the Lord came unto me, saying, before I formed thee in the belly I knew thee; and before thou camest forth out of the womb I sanctified thee, and I ordained thee a prophet..." (Jeremiah 1:4-5a).

This may seem like we are going backwards, but we are not! Yes, a prophet is a supernatural being. But a prophet does not become supernatural first. He becomes natural first. Of course, in the realm of God things always take on a spirit form first. In the same way, we must look at the spiritual formation of the prophet to understand the fluidity of supernatural reality within the ministry of the prophet. Thus, God intricately wraps flesh around a special spirit. It may look as if it is just the union of two extreme but plausible genetic codes from the composites of mother and father.

But a certain male and female become each prophet's parents for a reason. For example, Enoch's and Abraham's parents were chosen by God for a specific purpose, because the generations born from them became highly significant in the history of Israel. This is why genetic makeup is very important in God's shaping of every prophet's personality. For the prophet's soul is uniquely crafted from the composites of his mother and father's DNA. But it is also contained in the unique and yet dualistic soul and spirit of each prophet.

This impartation is exclusively in the hands of God! For the prophet's existence starts prior to his natural conception because the prophet's life chiefly begins in heaven. Though the prophet's full conception occurs within a womb, the sanctification of a prophet is conducted differently than others. For the prophet truly receives an initial deposit of sanctification before exiting the womb. While others have to acquire this apprehension through an external reality and process of deliverance. Of course, this process usually happens after exiting of the womb, when one receives salvation through Jesus Christ.

Even though a prophet is given an internal and external anointing in the womb, he, too, must still become a recipient of salvation. John the Baptist, even with his prophetic ability, which was given before he met Christ (Luke 1:13-15), still submitted to the presence of God in Christ (John 1:29-34). So, if John was anointed and submitted to Jesus, then it behooves us to do the same!

When Jesus came to the famous baptismal scene, he first told John how he had to fulfill all righteousness (Matthew 3:13-17). John was anointed before coming out of the womb in order to properly handle the prophetic assignment of forerunning for Jesus. Never was this preordination and sanctification a means of justifying the prophet does not have to come into compliance to the things of God, or the ways of God found in the Lord's church. But John could not leave the earth without fully receiving salvation, which is only accomplished through believing in the testimony of Jesus Christ:

The next day John seeth Jesus coming unto him, and saith, Behold the Lamb of God, which taketh away the sin of the world. This is he of whom I said, after me cometh a man which is preferred before me: for he was before me. And I knew him not: but that he should be made manifest to Israel, therefore am I come baptizing with water. And John bare record, saying, I saw the Spirit descending from heaven like a dove, and it abode upon him. And I knew him not: but he that sent me to baptize with water, the same said unto me, upon whom thou shalt see the Spirit descending and remaining on him, the same is He which baptizeth with the Holy Ghost. And I saw, and bare record that this is the Son of God (John 1:29-34, KJV).

So the reason for this special status prior to the exiting of the womb is that God's unique assignment is placed upon the prophet's life for the advancement of God's kingdom. The reality surrounding a prophet's procreation is the means of lawfulness. This is important when studying the prophet's emergence. But theologically and scientifically speaking, it does not seem lawful enough. Remember that there is always a twist in the birth of a prophet.

And the confirmation of such supernatural evolution is frequently testified throughout scripture. David's prophetic purpose is shared in one of the most sinful moments of his life. This sinful moment was during his repentance from the sin of adultery with Bathsheba:

Behold, I was shapen in iniquity; and in sin did my mother conceive me. Behold, thou desirest truth in the inward parts: and in the hidden part thou shalt make me to know wisdom (Psalm 51:5-6).

Even though man is born into sin, God anoints the prophet both internally and externally! And David, who was called to become king after Saul, was one who had such an anointing prior to his earthly existence! Additionally, the Apostle Peter was the voice that blatantly confirmed David as a prophet of God (Acts 2:29-30). The King-Prophet David would often testify about his own spiritual experience with God's internal and external anointing, saying:

For thou hast possessed my reins: thou hast covered me in my mother's womb. I will praise thee; for I am fearfully and wonderfully made; marvelous are thy works; and that my soul knoweth right well. My substance was not hid from thee, when I was made in secret, and curiously wrought in the lowest parts of the earth. Thine eyes did see my substance, yet being unperfect; and in thy book all my members were written, which in continuance were fashioned, when as yet there was none of them (Psalm 139:13-16).

Here we have confirmation that a calling is not based on the person. Rather, it is based on God. Even though the spirit of the prophet is wrapped in the personality of the prophet, the soul and spirit of the prophet are uniquely combined with the flesh and given a predetermined genetic makeup for the specifications of a unique ministry. And this ministry cannot be invalidated even when the prophet has defects in character and ethics. However, this also does not excuse a prophet's behavior. What it does do is show that God can use anyone He so chooses.

David later received his external anointing. It was given to him when Samuel came to anoint him in the presence of his father and brothers (1 Samuel 16). But when David had sinned with Bathsheba, it was his internal anointing that was implied. In other words, as he repented for his sin of adultery with Bathsheba, David could sense that God had given him something special, not just over his life (i.e. one's anointing), but also within his life (i.e. the Spirit's filling). This is why God anointed twice. And we, too, need to be anointed twice!

Another example of this type of double anointing is the Apostle Paul. Even the Apostle Paul wrote of a similar experience in his epistles. There, Paul wrote as a man who understood the specialness of life and intimacy with the Spirit, which only happens to certain individuals prior to their birth. Paul understood that it is God who gives all his messengers a unique intimacy with his spirit and word, as well as with their own natural estate. Paul spoke of this very same concept, like Jeremiah, as he wrote to the churches of Galatia:

But when it pleased God, who separated me from my mother's womb, and called me by His grace, to reveal His Son in me, that I might preach Him among the heathen; immediately I conferred not with flesh and blood (Galatians 1:15-16).

Therefore, apostles and prophets should be considered a special breed. Even within their distinct fickleness and frailty. For their true ordination happens first inside the womb, in which "the super" and "the natural" reside. It was there that God spoke the prophet's spirit into existence. Then he placed that spirit within a mortal body located in the womb of his earthly mother. And the prophet is now a mixture of spiritual and natural combined.

The prophet is a composite of mess and messages. He is a composite of greatness and the potential for great failure. But regardless of these conflicts the prophet is destined to speak for God! This began before salvation! And it was validated in his pre-born sanctification. This is not an easy fact to digest. For I know that this concept does not assist the theology of salvation at all!

It is hard for theologians to conceive that a portion of a prophet's creation is done in the heavens, prior to the final portion that materializes on earth. This concept goes beyond all logical thinking and theological acceptance. However, Jeremiah's testimony confirms such phenomenon, and Paul's theology confirms, too, that a gift is without repentance (Romans 11:29). And a prophet is greater than his setback and his sins.

By now I hope you have gotten the point, but just to drive the thought onward, let us use another example. This example speaks about Moses. For Moses' initiation into the prophetic phenomenon happened during a unique period within his life. After he slayed the Egyptian and fled Egypt, his goal was to live obscurely. No more palaces and pomp were in his view! For a brief moment, when he fled into a foreign land and met and married Jethro's oldest daughter, Zipporah, it appeared that life and God would grant his desires.

The Doctrine of Prophecy

Eventually, from their union they had a son. But just when Moses seemed to have reached a season of rest and contentment, God sent a divine interruption. For Egypt's affliction upon Israel was far greater than Moses' personal desires. And like the civilian who is drafted into military living, Moses received his deployment orders for prophetic service, which took him back to Egypt where he had fled:

And Moses was content to dwell with the man: and he gave Moses Zipporah his daughter. And she bare him a son, and he called his name Gershom: for he said, I have been a stranger in a strange land. And it came to pass in process of time, that the king of Egypt died: and the children of Israel sighed by reason of the bondage and they cried, and their cry came up before God by reason of the bondage. And God heard their groaning, and God remembered his covenant with Abraham with Isaac, and with Jacob (Exodus 2:21-24).

We must now mention that God made Moses Jewish. God also made Moses a descendent from a strong Levitical prophetic family line. This teaches a very important lesson: the prophet is God's property. When the greater purpose of Moses' existence is unveiled, it reveals the necessity for Moses to return to Egypt and aide in Israel's pending deliverance. God interrupts Moses' quiet life with Zipporah and his son for the purpose of awakening his prophetic assignment. And when God came to collect his prophetic property, there was nothing Moses or anyone else could do about it. Not even the candidate himself!

Moses was not just a man who was a Levite born and raised in Egypt's royal family, or a fugitive on the run – he was, above all, God's prophet! And it was evident that his prophetic duty was now operative. If Moses had not reported for prophetic duty, he would have been guilty of being AWOL.

The truth about compliance is that every spiritual officer of God is hardwired to obey the commandments of his superior officer. And we surely know that God is our superior officer. My question to you is this: are you reporting for duty? Because the truth is, you are either on duty in the spirit, or you either are off duty in the spirit. And your compliance determines the truthfulness of your current prophetic shift! No man can determine the hours he must set serving God. Only God can do that! For when you are on duty, you are fulfilling your prophetic birth! In so many words, it is like the water of the spirit realm had broken and prophetic labor had commenced.

Moses is a great example of this. He was supernaturally born on the backside of a desert to save a people in a massive land filled with affliction. He was preordained to reach this date of revelation. Not because he wanted to, but because he was called as a prophet. And in God's eyes, Moses possessed the right makeup to handle this assignment, which is amazing! God can take fugitives and make them forging leaders! Not only did Moses become our first major prophet, but he also became our first prophetic pastor of the largest mega-church that the world will ever know:

"And the Lord said, I have surely seen the affliction of my people which are in Egypt, and have heard their cry by reason of their taskmasters; for I know their sorrows; and I am come down to deliver them out of the land of the Egyptians, and to bring them up out of that land unto a good land and a large land flowing with milk and honey..." (Exodus 3:7-8a).

"Now therefore, behold, the cry of the children of Israel is come unto me: and I have also seen the oppression wherewith the Egyptians oppress them. Come now therefore, and I will send thee unto Pharaoh, that thou mayest bring forth my people the children of Israel out of Egypt" (Exodus 3:9-10).

The point to all of this is this: The prophet only awakens when the need for the prophetic anointing becomes relevant. The predetermined conversation with the spirit and soul of the prophet before he was placed in his mother's womb will reactivate itself. And the consciousness of the prophet's purpose will overtake the civility of the prophet's desire to remain comfortable. Thus, his elevation shifts from a natural agenda to a supernatural one. Yes, his awareness does not occur until the destined date of purpose reaches its relevance.

Until then, the prophet is like a secret agent placed into a sleeper cell that is hidden in an unknown part of the world. In like manner, when God is ready to activate a prophetic anointing, only then can one become truly prophetic. Prior to such activation, life is usually filled with reasonable portions of normalcy and natural civility. Yes, the spirit of the prophet is only relevant when the need for the prophet is made evident. If you find your relevance, you, too, will find your prophetic importance! But are you ready for such duty? Once you sign up for the spiritual service of God, there is no turning back unless you are honorably or dishonorably discharged!

His Assignment is to be a Messenger of God

"If any man speak let him speak as the oracles of God..." (1 Peter 4:11a).

The word "oracle" has many connotations. There are three primary understandings we must review. The first is in regards to the Tabernacle and Temples of Israel. These edifices of worship are where God spoke to Israel, his people. There were three known rooms within both the tabernacle and temple: the Tent of Meeting (front porch), the Holy Place (the location were

The Doctrine of Prophecy

sacrifices were made), and the Holy of Holies (the restricted place allocated for only the High Priest's presence to enter there once a year).

The place known as the Holies of Holies was considered the place where the oracle of the sanctuary resided (1 Kings 6:31; Psalm 28:2). And the oracle of the sanctuary was like a voice box placed strategically within the house of God. It was the deepest place within both the tabernacle and temple structures. This is why only a few were allowed to enter into the Holy of Holies.

The separation of the Holy Place and the Holy of Holies is called the veil. When Jesus died on the cross, the Bible says that the veil was torn into two pieces (Matthew 27:51). From the top to the bottom, this veil was ripped as a symbolic act of God whereby all true worshippers may go further into the Spirit, by way of God's presence. But not everyone was able to handle the depths of worship, even though everyone was given this new privilege through Jesus Christ (John 4:24, John 9:31). But as the scripture says, many are called, but few are chosen. This means that all have the same rights and privileges but not all will use the divine rights, such as greater worship and greater intimacy with God. And this is why the prophet is still needed.

So the prophet becomes the human voice box set deeply within the house of God. Not everyone is allowed to be in this office (1 Corinthians 12:29). Some are prophets, while others are only prophetic at random moments. But when one is a true prophet, he operates as an oracle. His operation places him deeply within the spirit realm. And he ministers from the depths of the most strategic places of God's heart and will. These strategic places can be likened to the deepest moments of corporate worship within any modern house of God.

Thus, the prophet, who is the human oracle, is a place and a person to whom God speaks in his church. For the prophet is still his current manifestation of a greater realm of authority given by God to minister unto his people. Therefore, we need the prophet to speak for God unto us, just as the oracle of God's voice spoke through the tabernacle and temples. The moment of oracle is when the Shekinah glory rested inside the Tabernacle instead of in front of it (Exodus 40:34-38). This is why the prophet stands before us. He is there to bring God to us, and us to God!

The second reference about the oracles of God was of a priestly understanding. Generally speaking, the word "oracle" also means the Holy Scriptures (Hebrews 4:12; Acts 7:38). Whether the word of God is spoken as prophetic or evangelistic, or in the form of *logos* or *rhema*, all words of God are induced in an oracle-like manner. For they come from the most sacred place in the spirit of a man. God has made man's spirit and God's spirit one through salvation:

"...He that is joined unto the Lord is one spirit" (1 Corinthians 6:17, KJV).

Even though a priest was a position of spiritual purpose within the Old Testament, he, too, was a recipient of the anointing of God. Though his spiritman may have not experienced what we can now experience, his positioning in God was certainly led by the Spirit. God had placed his anointing on two main items used within the priest. It was there that the priest would be spiritually connected to God. And when a man would inquire "by the oracles of God," it was also by the means of the *urim* and *thummim*. These two properties were located on the top of the breastplate of the High Priest's garment. And the name of the high priest's garment was called the holy ephod. From there, the High Priest would speak for God, but through the context and contents of the law of God.

It was said that the High priest was the highest of all priestly representatives among the people. For only priests could access the inner courts of the most holy place. But the High Priest (who was a descendent of the sons of Aaron) had fuller access and privileges throughout the sanctuary.

And with this accessible responsibility, the High Priest also had to be a great student of the law of God. This was the means of any priestly utterance that were applicable extractions of the law. For when a man would inquire through the *urim* and *thummim* experiences, the prophetic would not only be priestly, but would also become word-based as well. The parallelism to this revelation is simply in the necessity of the prophet knowing how to preach and teach God's word. This, then, is the reason why a prophet must become an elder of doctrine so that his prophetic ministry can have a higher purpose. Because all prophets must thoroughly know the word of God so that they may rightly know the non-written word of God!

Jesus taught the disciples that when the Holy Spirit (or the Comforter) would come, it would be the Holy Spirit's job to bring all things back to a disciple's memory (John 14:26). Jesus also explained how the Holy Spirit would guide us to all truth, and that it would be the Holy Spirit's assignment to speak through every believer as a direct representative of God (John 16:13). Thus, the oracle of God is a human amplifier. In like manner, the prophet is assigned to be a literal conduit through which God can flow by his word unto his people!

This is why it is important that the prophet picks the suitable word of the Lord in forth-telling moments as well as in foretelling moments. The more word-driven a prophet operates according to the canonized word (or the Holy Bible) the better the prophet will prophesy. For the word of God, which is written, shall stand forever (Isaiah 40:8). This is why the prophet is encouraged to discern the will of the Lord before speaking prophecies. The more God's word is inside the prophet, the easier God's word can flow from the prophet!

Thirdly, the word "oracle" also means "the word of the Lord" (2 Samuel 16:23). The phrase "the word of the Lord" refers to the prophetic word of the Lord that is not necessarily found in the Bible. Usually, this type of prophetic word is spoken directly by one who carries the prophetic office. Herein reside a greater vocal ministry of the prophet and the purposes of God that elevate the prophet to the position of primary speaker within his tabernacle, temple, church, and kingdom.

If the prophet is spiritually tone-deaf to this type of word from God, then the relevance of direction from the word of God becomes hindered within the lives of God's people. For it is the prophet's primary responsibility to be the representative of God's voice within God's sanctuary. And it takes a strong prayer life and the gift of discernment to recognize when the voice of the Lord, through the word of the Lord, has come in the form of one of God's prophetic workers.

Prophets are sanctuary gifts first and foremost rather than secularly assumed instruments for kings, ungodly kingdoms, and marketplaces. This is why the doctrine of prophetism starts with the increase of one's biblical understanding. Once a person increases his biblical understanding, he can then pray to God for understanding to turn into proper knowledge, understanding and wisdom. As Solomon exhorted, "in all thy getting, get an understanding" (Proverbs 4:7).

It is the prophet's job, then, to know the voice of the Lord. Like a musician must learn ear training, so must the prophet of God become trained in his ability to spiritually hear God. There are three things that I have prayed for throughout the duration of my prophetic ministry. I pray to God that I might hear, see, and operate clearly, accurately, and soberly!

When these three things are not in motion, the soundness of the prophetic voice will become indistinct. If such prophetic convolution manifests, then confusion will result. Like the oracle, the prophet must have the right answer at the right time. Or the wrong verdict will cause the wrong action to be made within the house of God among the people of God:

For if a trumpet give an uncertain sound, who shall prepare himself to the battle? (1 Corinthians 14:8, KJV).

His Governmental Authority is Given By God:

"My Times are in Thy Hand..." (Psalm 31:15a).

It is true that natural births are uncontrollable. Even with modern technology, the cycle of natural birth can only be monitored. But the power of birth comes organically through the makeup of the mother's body and the invisible providence of God. In the same vein, never does God place a prophet's birth entirely in the hands of the prophet. For his supernatural birth is just as uncontrollable as one's natural birth.

When the prophet is elevated from natural to supernatural, there will always be a major shift within the earth's realm! Regardless of a prophet's specialty in prophetic ministry, there must be a legitimate means of natural genesis. Everything has its proper time – even the ministry of every prophet! And this same symbolism can be applied laterally to the prophet's formal ceremony of ordination:

The Spirit of the Lord is upon me, because he hath anointed me to preach the gospel to the poor; he hath sent me to heal the brokenhearted, to preach deliverance to the captives, and recovering the sight to the blind, to set at liberty them that are bruised, to preach the acceptable year of the Lord (Luke 4:18-19).

Looking further at the comparison of natural births to supernatural births, some births may have inordinate dates. For example, when a baby is born early we term them premature. Other births that occur, at or after the calculated date, are termed full-term. But whether a baby is premature or full-termed, the risk factors of birth will always face the possibility of death. It is medically known that birthing and delivery can sometimes be complicated. So it is the same with the supernatural birthing of God's prophets!

There is always the threat of prophetic life when the earth shifts and creates the entrance of a prophet. Every time a prophet is born expect the threat of annihilation to complement a prophet's coming forth. A prime example of this is when Moses was naturally born and Pharaoh decreed that all newborn infants of the Hebrews were to be annihilated (Exodus 1:22). Subsequently, when Jesus was born, Herod commanded a similar massacre (Matthew 2:16). Thus, the prophet must expect high risk factors surrounding his natural and supernatural birth. You, too, can look back and see all of the plots and plans to wipe you out! This is why in some cases it has been very hard to live. But even in the face of this attack, the prophet must understand that God has a plan to make an escape route for the prophet's survival!

But the prophet has no choice. He is called to exceed fear and death so that his ministry may emerge. In scripture, we find too many glimpses of possible threats during the duration of a prophet's lifespan. Simply put, the first lesson in prophetism is that you do not own you! When God is ready to use you, it will behoove you to move when He calls. Paul teaches us that military life will come with heavy battles. But we must endure them as a good soldier. And every soldier is trained for survival even in the face of death. This is why Paul exhorts Timothy to endure his life's situations as a good military officer of God:

"Thou therefore endure hardness, as a good soldier of Jesus Christ" (2 Timothy 2:3, KJV).

This is why Moses' testimony again gives us a classic illustration of this context. At the age of 80, God came to Moses in the form of a burning bush, and Moses' prophetic life was born (Acts 7:17-34). Even throughout Moses' ministry, there were times when he had to walk through fires, experience floods, and see lightning flashing. But these circumstances never could overtake the major premise of the prophetic work inside him. This teaches us another important lesson: Life will be hard for the prophet, but the prophet is designed to endure such afflictions. For his assignment is always greater than his comfort or discomfort. Here, then, is the first concern that a prophet must face:

By faith, Moses, when he was come to years, refused to be called the son of Pharaoh's daughter; choosing rather to suffer affliction with the people of God, than to enjoy the pleasures of sin for a season (Hebrews 11:24-25).

Prophets are messengers of God, born with a natural life that is also supernaturally special. So it behooves the emerging prophet not to resist or reject his place of natural birth and lineage. Regardless of how hard the starting points of his life may have been, or even the details surrounding such difficulties he currently endures, it is indeed the first place one must start in order to understand why a prophet is born.

It is also the same place that each prophet grows in his governmental power, which is given him by God. For it appears that each storm a prophet's life must weather, truthfully becomes the prophet's power source to perform prophetically. Paul said the power of Christ is strongest when we are at our weakest (2 Corinthians 12:9). And Jesus teaches us that after the Holy Ghost comes upon us, we shall receive power (Acts 1:8).

This explains how there is also another level of power called authority. This same authority is what Jesus taught to us through the words found in Mark 7:29. One form of divine power is called *dynamis (doo-nee-mus)* power. The other form of power is called *exousia (x-soo-*

sea-ah). We need both might (*dynamis*) and authority (*exousia*) as a prophet of God. And these forms emerge strongly in the midst of our hardest moments because this is where the greatest relevancy of a prophetic ministry resides.

This is why David said "God has my time in his hands." It doesn't matter if you're a priest like Jeremiah, a royal dignitary like Isaiah, sons of farmers like Amos and Elisha, or even a displaced soul like Moses. When it is time for the prophet's emergence within you, God surely comes and collects. This is why God has given prophets a brief period of normalcy within their humanity! But eventually time will be up! The prophet of God will have no choice but to come forth! This is when he will have to dismiss civilian life in order to speak on behalf of God.

And never does the submitted and committed prophet want to displease God. For again, he is subject to his commanding officer, Jesus Christ! Christ has predetermined his life and death. He has predetermined his civility and ministry duration. And he has predetermined his time on earth. It is with that time that he is able to walk in the power that God has given him. He is to take that same power and authority and influence the church and kingdom. Truly all power comes from the endowment of the Holy Ghost. However, it does not come from might, or any other power. Surely, it comes from the timing of God's spiritual power (Zechariah 4:6). And the power of your pain to be born prophetically will certainly assist with this revelation!

His Identity is a Composite of Ancient and Ascension Gift:

The final working definition for the contemporary prophet is a combination of Old Testament and New Testament references. The best summary is found in the book of Ephesians. When Paul taught the churches of Ephesus about the ascensions of Christ, he revealed the release of Christ's new order of prophets: This is why it says:

"When he ascended on high, he led captives in his train and gave gifts to men." (What does "he ascended" mean except that he also descended to the lower, earthly regions? He who descended is the very one who ascended higher than all the heavens, in order to fill the whole universe" (Ephesians 4:8-10).

Since the prophet is mentioned in the Old Testament, it is important to understand that the prophet is the most ancient of all spiritual gifts. But now the prophet has also evolved significantly since the first prophet was mentioned in the Old Testament. And the prophetic assignment, although under a different dispensation, remains primarily the same regardless of its variations. This is why the prophet is called a supreme gift among the primary three Old Testament gifts (and those gifts are pastor, teacher, and prophet).

Though prophet, pastor, and teacher are Old Testament gifts, they also are now noted among the five-fold ascension gifts (Ephesians 4:11). We call these gifts "ascension gifts" because the functionality of purpose has slightly changed since Jesus' resurrection and final ascension into heaven. It would be on his ascension day (40 days after his resurrection – Acts 1:3, 9-11) that the finalization of these gifts would shift from Old Testament functionality to a New Testament reality.

Now, the New Testament Prophet and the other four gifts mentioned, speak only about the cause of Christ. Though ancient prophetic perspective was speaking for Jehovah, Elohim, and Yahweh, it is now speaking for the God we call Jesus Christ. Jesus Christ, God the Father, and the God of Israel, which is the same God of Isaac, Jacob, and Abraham, comprise the one God (Deuteronomy 6:4; John 10:30). And every man who believes in Jesus must accept that Jesus is the current manifestation of God, the God of Israel and the God of the Christian alike.

And it is the manifestation of Jesus Christ (as God), who has realigned and reestablished the prophetic office to become a part of the five-fold team. It is the Spirit of Jesus' that replaces the prophet's voices of yesterday by making them relevant for today. This was done strategically the moment Jesus was resurrected. And it was not completed until the moment Jesus finally ascended back into heaven. This is why God still gave the prophets to the church and the world.

So God releases the manifestation of this new prophetic order and generation using a divine strategy. The divine strategy started the moment Jesus gathered the redeeming saints of old from the depths of the earth. This means that all former Old Testament believers such as Abraham, Isaac, Jacob, David, to name a few, were redeemed on the day Jesus resurrects.

But Jesus did not stop there. Anyone who had recently died in the timeframe of Jesus' earthly life and death, and who also truly believed in God, was also resurrected and taken into heaven as well:

And the graves were opened; and many bodies of the saints which slept arose, and came out of the graves after his resurrection, and went into the holy city, and appeared unto many (Matthew 27:52-53).

And the location they were taken to after Jesus resurrected them was certainly a major part of the strategy! This place was the strategic place that we must mention before moving forward. It was a place that was given two names. The first name was the Bosom of Abraham (Luke 16:22), and the second name was Paradise (2 Corinthians 12:4). The Bosom of Abraham was the former holding pattern and space that represented the hope of redemption for Old

Testament saints. Subsequently, Paradise was the new holding pattern and space that represented the New Testament hope of redemption for all who became a believer of Jesus Christ. In essence, Jesus was redeeming the old while merging it with the new.

This is why we accept the fact that the Bosom of Abraham and Paradise are now one location within a certain realm of heaven. The writer of Hebrews also calls this place "The Great Cloud of Witnesses" (Hebrews 12:1). It was Jesus who revealed the names of both places. Jesus revealed the name of the Bosom of Abraham, and he used a parable about a rich man and poor man who both go into the depths of the earth upon their deaths. One man would die and find himself in hell (which is the Hebrew word for *Gehenna*, or the place of suffering). The other man, who was faithful to God, was carried by the angels into the place known as the Bosom of Abraham, which was *Hades*, a Greek word meaning "the land of the dead":

And it came to pass, that the beggar died, and was carried by the angels into Abraham's bosom: the rich man died, and was buried; And in hell he lifted up his eyes, being in torments, and seeth Abraham afar off, and Lazarus in his bosom (Luke 16:22-23, KJV).

The second name of this place was mentioned at the cross. Before Jesus died he had a dynamic conversation with another individual being crucified at the same time. This individual was guilty of his sins in contrast with Jesus who was not guilty at all. It was the sin of theft that brought the thief to be crucified on a cross, right next to Jesus. As the thief spoke with Jesus, he explained to Jesus that he wanted redemption, for the thief refused to die in condemnation and eternal judgment (Luke 23:39-43). When Jesus accepted this man's heartfelt request, he mentioned the name of the place that he and Jesus would both travel to upon their physical death:

"...Verily, I say unto thee, Today shalt thou be with me in paradise" (Luke 23:43b, KJV).

It would be this very place that God would take and presently make a new temporary location in heaven. The Bosom of Abraham (also called Paradise) was taken from the depths of the earth into the 3rd dimension of heaven. When Jesus took the keys of death, hell, and the grave into his theocratic control, he also freed the deceased citizens of the Bosom of Abraham (also known as Paradise) (Luke 16:22-26). The Bible says that there was an invisible gulf between both dimensions in the depths of this location when it was first placed beneath the earth:

"...Between us and you there is a great gulf fixed: so that they which would pass from hence to you cannot; neither can they pass to us, that would come thence" (Luke 16:26b, KJV).

The invisible gulf dividing Paradise (or the Bosom of Abraham) was removed by the power of Christ and his resurrection. Now hell is full and reserved for all unbelievers because of the resurrection of Jesus Christ. The prophet Isaiah saw this prophetically happening even within his lifetime:

"Therefore hell hath enlarged herself, and opened her mouth wide without measure..." (Isaiah 5:14a, KJV).

But we know that hell is not the final resting place of the wicked. We know that place is called the Lake of Fire and Brimstone (Revelation 20:14). When Jesus finishes his testimony, hell and the last enemy (death) will all be tossed into this final place of judgment. But for the believer that dies in Christ, or is raptured during the experience of Christ's collection of the church, he will return with Christ and all those he had gathered from the depths of hell on the day Christ is resurrected. These citizens of Paradise will become the citizens of the New Heaven and Earth during and after the millennial reign of Jesus Christ.

So, though a man's body goes into the grave, his spiritman and soul goes upward instead. This is what David meant when he said prophetically and with confidence in God:

"...My flesh shall rest in hope: because thou wilt not leave my soul in hell..." (Acts 2:26b-27a, KJV). So it is called Paradise because to be absent from the body is to be present with the Lord (2 Corinthians 5:8). And Paul explained the initial formation of this place as he mentioned Jesus descending and ascending (or going up and down) from hell to heaven, and then back to the earth again. This constant ascending and descending was spoken of briefly, shortly before Paul explained the purpose of the five-fold gifts:

This is why it says: "When he ascended on high, he led captives in his train and gave gifts to men." (What does "he ascended" mean except that he also descended to the lower, earthly regions? He who descended is the very one who ascended higher than all the heavens, in order to fill the whole universe" (Ephesians 4:8-10).

This also explains the phrase in Ephesians, which says that Jesus led the captive out of captivity. This particular moment of leading the captive refers to when Jesus removed the door of hell and took Abraham, and everyone there, out of hell and into heaven. Of course, it is strange to hear that Abraham was in hell. But we now understand that the text means that Paul and Jesus refer to the other side of hell. This strategy was synchronized with a greater realization. From these very moments Jesus supernaturally awakened the wombs of present and future mothers destined to carry the souls of his New Testament prophets.

And, as a conquering king who wins a conquest and distributes spoils (i.e. gifts) to his people, upon his return to his own kingdom, Jesus distributed the gift of the office of prophet to the Kingdom and the world (Psalm 68:18). The prophet then had new orders: preach and prophesy! Save souls while confirming souls under the Gospel of Jesus Christ! This is the New Testament's primary purpose, and even the purpose of the other five-fold gifting mentioned in Ephesians 4:11.

For the greatest portion of the supernatural awakening of every prophet happens on the moment he received the Gospel of Jesus Christ. Whether the process is difficult or peaceful, a prophet never compromises his message or assignment. The prophet will never relinquish his duties for the sake of sin and a season of pleasure (Hebrews 11:25). He is trained to overcome the severity of such circumstances and develop himself to ensure that the grace and Gospel message reach the intended recipient regardless of the obstacles during his journey.

The Doctrine of Prophecy

CONCLUSION OF LESSON 2:

This is the truth behind real vision. For the true definition of prophetic vision comes from the prophet's functionality. And the greatest portion of a New Testament prophetic functionality is one's fluidity with the Gospel of Jesus Christ. Every prophet must be a preacher of the Gospel. One may be a lover but never a fanatic of the Old Testament. For the law is not most prevalent. Faith, through grace and the hearing of the Gospel, is the utmost. Here, then, is our chief assignment concerning prophetic ministry:

But before faith came, we were kept under the law, shut up unto the faith which should afterwards be revealed. Wherefore the law was our schoolmaster to bring us unto Christ, that we might be justified by faith. But after that faith is come, we are no longer under a schoolmaster (Galatians 3:23-25, KJV).

This is why a prophetic-private (or a beginner prophet) must go through prophetic boot camp. Prophets must be clear on their prophetic orders and mission. The prophetic officials are called upon to defeat the error of New Testament teachings. They are called upon to combine the wisdom of the Old Testament prophets with the knowledge of the New Testament teachings of the first prophets of the new covenant.

Modern prophets are the combatants of erroneous traditionalism, dogmatic doctrines that are made of men and not of God, and the excessiveness of denominationalism that drowns out authentic Christian Faith. For where there is true prophetic vision, the people will not perish. But where there is untrue prophetic vision, the people suffer. And true prophetic vision comes to correct a wrong.

This is why a prophet is the receiver of such vision. The prophet is God's messenger of what is wrong within the world, the kingdom, and the Lord Jesus' church! The prophet is sent not only to speak about what's wrong, but also to proclaim how to dissolve wrongs while abdicating for what is right! Moreover, the prophet speaks the mind and mouth of God to correct such wrongs. And if people are receptive, they will remain within the will of God. But if they are unreceptive to the prophet, they will reap unfortunate consequences.

Remember: a prophetic birth has to happen at the right time because it is for a specific reason. Once there is prophetic legitimacy, the authentic and proper prophetic can manifest. When the prophet's birth is legitimate and authentic, eventually a prophet's spiritual awakening can bring spiritual change. But the time and date of such awakening is solely in the hands of God and is usually during a pivotal part of the prophetic agenda.

In other words, the current prophet is established to suffer for the cause of God. More specifically, he must be willing to suffer for the cause of the Gospel! For it is Christ that has commissioned him, and it is Christ who speaks through him. And if the Spirit of God, which is also called the Holy Spirit (or Holy Ghost), is with the prospective prophetic voice, then it is the same Spirit of Christ that signifies the prophets of old as well.

This is our working definition of a true prophet of God, one who gives up life, as he knows it, in order to serve God. Just as the former prophets of old did, now the new prophets of today must also do. They are the current representations of an ancient gift. But this also includes the ascension. What a legacy! The assignment of yesterday, but with the heart of today! The New Testament Prophet is a carrier of both Testaments and worlds.

The implication of the prophetic assignment certainly means God knows what is best for the earth. He has all suitable answers, answers that are powerfully hidden in the secret will of God. These secrets can only manifest through the ministry of the prophets of God. But what an amazing concept. God uses a mortal to talk about the immortal. God uses a mere man to speak as a mighty man of God. God makes the prophet like a best friend who reveals approved secrets.

This is why the prophet passionately proclaims what God wants. This is also why he is labeled as an oracle of God. Through the human and divine, the mouthpiece and the voice box, the prophet releases the proper content, context, and flow of God's word. How much of God's word are you hiding in your heart so that you can have the proper prophetic flow of God when serving the lives of God's people?

For God is awesome enough to create such an assignment within the world, and the prophet has a great responsibility of following through with this assignment. But he is also a divine revelator, where God can release hidden truths that only God knows, for nothing will take place within the earth without the presence and ministry of a prophet: (Amos 3:7)! This is why we need the prophet to go deeper within worship, deeper in study and deeper in prayer.

For this elaborate explanation helps set the parameters of the dos and do nots of understanding what a prophet's functionality is truly about. If the prophet remains humbly connected to who he really is as a human being, he will not lose the sensibility of compassion, which is a necessity in order to walk in the spirit of Christ, or the spirit of prophecy.

Furthermore, if you review the concept of the doctrine of Election, you will discover how God chooses imperfect people to do a perfected work (Romans 9:11). In like manner, God has chosen imperfect men and women throughout the ages to carry forth an office that has a legacy of thousands of years behind it. But this office also has the responsibility of forging even more creative expression from it, and this is required until the Lord has completed his full assignment.

For it is in sobriety that the power and the authority of a prophet truly exist. As long as there is a problem in the world, the church, and even the Lord's kingdom, there will always be a need for a prophetic voice. The simple ministry of a prophetic voice is always sent to convey, through whatever form is applicable, that God is God. It is a marvelous revelation that God has made man a little lower than the angels, and yet has elevated certain men to imitate these angels. This is the purpose of our presence. And in this, we are given great access to the spirit realm just as the angel has access to both heaven and earth. For the prophet must learn that this privilege is something never to be played with or taken out of context.

Therefore, it is very important that the true prophet strays away from those who operate recklessly and lack proficiency and true purpose. For these five points are here to admonish one's independence and interpersonal development. If one operates his natural foundation, spiritual elevation, assignment, governmental authority, and true identity, then that prophetic individual will greater glorify the Lord our God.

CHAPTER 3

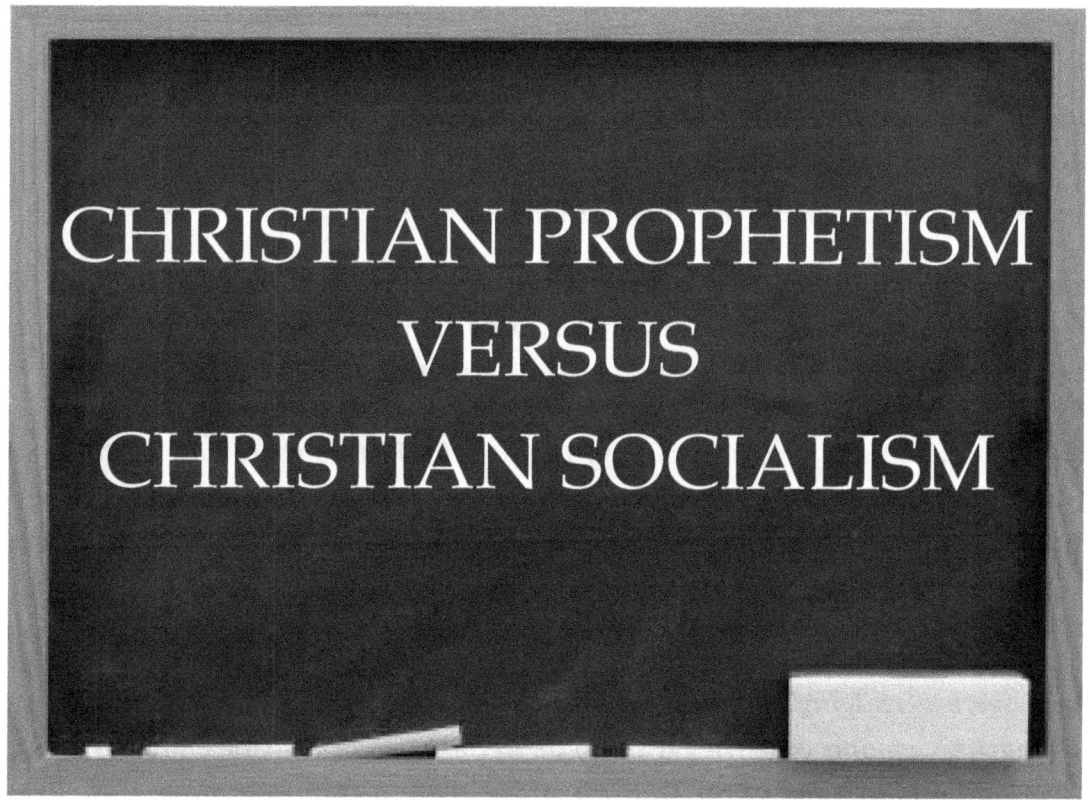

When is the Prophet Most Needed?

But there were false prophets also among the people, even as there shall be false teachers among you, who privily shall bring in damnable heresies, even denying the Lord that bought them, and bring upon themselves swift destruction (2 Peter 2:1).

The Ministry of a True Prophet Counterattacks the Manifestation of False Prophets

Beyond the prophet's ability to convey the voice of God into the ears of men, the prophet's main goal is to rebuke prophetic errors, disorders, and prostitution. For there will be times when the prophetic is misrepresented. And it takes a prophet to correct things done in the name of a prophet. But the greatest war against the true presence of prophecy is the presence of false prophets.

When there are severe infections of false prophetism, God sends true prophets. Thus, the prophet is primarily needed to handle the false prophets who attempt to sway the Lord's people and kingdom from knowing the mind and will of the Lord (Ephesians 4:14, 16 and 5:17). The Apostles worked right beside the prophets. They exposed the truth. The enemy created false counterparts to distract the people of God from the true men and women of God:

But there were false prophets also among the people, even as there shall be false teachers among you, who privily shall bring in damnable heresies, even denying the Lord that bought them, and bring upon themselves swift destruction (2 Peter 2:1).

But there were also false prophets among the people, just as there will be false teachers among you. They will secretly introduce destructive heresies, even denying the sovereign Lord who bought them—bring swift destruction on themselves (NIV).

Let's review this same text in one final translation:

"But there were also lying prophets among the people then, just as there will be lying religious teachers among you. They'll smuggle in destructive divisions, pitting you against each other—biting the hand of the One who gave them a chance to have their lives back. They've put themselves on a fast downhill slide to destruction…" (The Message Bible)

Just as false prophets were present in the Old Testament, they were present in the early New Testament church as well. In fact, they even will be present now all the way into the Great Tribulation. For every era must have a prophetic resolution in it to combat the wrong prophetic presentation of each generation. This is primarily why the ministry of a true-prophet is still presently active and necessary. For it takes a true prophet to combat the presence of a false prophet. Scriptures show whenever there is a true prophet, the devil always creates multitudes of false prophets (Jeremiah 23:9-32). It is the strategy of the enemy to attempt to drown the presence of an authentic prophet by having so many assume the title of prophet.

This teaches a very clear reality: ministry can be very competitive. Please understand and know that this competition is not between flesh and blood. It is between light and darkness and good and evil. This is the real competition and the greatest prophetic dilemma. Jesus himself says that many will come in his name attempting to deceive the very elect:

For false Christ's and false prophets shall rise, and shall shew signs and wonders, to seduce, if it were possible, even the elect. But take ye heed behold, I have foretold you all things (Mark 13:22-23, KJV).

The Apostle Peter, too, prophesies about this potential infection of prophetic error that will enter the church. Peter saw a day when false prophecy would invade the local church as a means of undermining the universal church's mission and message, which was about Jesus Christ's crucifixion and subsequent resurrection. But Peter also taught that God always reacts and responds to the high rise of false prophets! And the strategy is very simple! God ordains the emergence of more true prophets to counterattack the presence of false prophets. For further study, please review these moments in Scripture:

- **The prophet Elijah contests the large number of false prophets of Baal: 1 Kings 18:20-40.**

- **The prophet Jeremiah contests the large number of false Samarian and Judean prophets: Jeremiah 23:9-32 (11, *13, *14, 16, *21, *25-26, *28, *30-32).**

- **The false prophetess Noadiah and the compromised prophet Shemaiah were both used to discourage Nehemiah and the children of Israel from rebuilding the walls of Jerusalem: Nehemiah 6:10-12, 14.**

The Bible also declares that there is nothing new under the sun. The strategy of the devil is the same in every generation. False prophets existed in the past, false prophets exist in the present, and there will be false prophets in the future. One of the major false prophets of the days of John the Apostle was one among the churches of Asia. And just as a true prophet can take on the mantle of a former true prophet, this false prophetess took on the mantle of a former false leader. This false leader was formerly known as Jezebel! And a similar spirit like Jezebel infected the church in Thyatira (located in the Asia Minor): Revelation 2:20.

This fight is not about denominational differences. No, we have even bigger issues and fires to put out! We now have to prepare ourselves for the undeniable truth that the enemy will continuously send his demonic hordes that will try to silence the testimony, name, and source of Christianity, which is Jesus Christ. But the good news is there is no failure in God. And no demon in hell or earth can match the power of God. But we who are of God must stop the civil wars and family feuds among God's Holy churches. Yes, the falsity in prophetism is one of the biggest battles that transcends across times, denominational barriers, and other obstacles. This is the biggest dilemma that we all must unite to fight. And we must stop being distracted.

Thank the Lord, for the Apostle Paul, who teaches the "One Lord, One Faith, and One Baptism" paradigm (Ephesians 4:5). For the fight is not Christian against Christian. The fight is Christians against the devil, who seeks to remove the name of Jesus from the hearts of men and to prevent the name of Jesus in reaching potential hearts. The Prophets and Apostles foretold of these times. It was also prophesied that doctrinal corruption would manifest. We were even biblically forewarned through prophetic means that the spirit of legalism would try to overtake our congregations as well. Here, then, is our true battle: the spirits of consumerism, materialism, sexism, classicism, and capitalism! These spirits attempt to plague the church of its truest nature. And true nature is divine order and fluidity in Christ Jesus:

For the time will come when they will not endure sound doctrine; but after their own lusts shall they heap to themselves teachers, having itching ears; and they shall turn away their ears from the truth, and shall be turned unto fables (2 Timothy 4:3-4, KJV).

Not only should we remain in a state of alert, we must also arm ourselves with the reality that it will take certain divine medicines to cause such prophetic cures from the manifestation of these demonic illnesses. For these greater infections are wrapped into the subject matters like new age mysticism, divination, and other spiritual perversions. They have come like a tag-team. And they are here to compete with the power of God. A famous illustration of such warlike reality is mentioned in the Book of Acts:

And when they had gone through the isle unto Paphos, they found a certain sorcerer, a false prophet, a Jew, whose name was Bar-jesus (Acts 13:6).

Again, history certainly repeats itself in cycles. God is the same yesterday, today, and forevermore (Hebrews 13:8). And even now, the enemy is continuing his reproductive counterattack and demon-like mimicking. This has been the same attack down throughout the ages! We say it with this saying: he is doing the same ole tricks! So he doesn't have any new tricks up his sleeve! Therefore, we should expect false prophets to come and draw the people from the church and God's kingdom. This is why false prophets have come. They have come to attempt division and demonic conquering.

When John was instructed to write about different spirits and sights that he saw, one of his visions included a demonic trinity in the form of frogs that represented the presence of the beast, the serpent, or dragon – Satan himself – which is the motivator of the false prophet. These demonic and false spirits will be used to falsely prophesy even in the days of the Great Tribulation:

And I saw three unclean spirits like frogs come out of the mouth of the dragon, and out of the mouth of the beast, and out of the mouth of the false prophet (Revelation 16:13).

This is why it takes a prophet to handle another prophet (1 Corinthians 14:32), and also why a true prophet of God has been given divine authority and power to handle a false prophet. We are biblically instructed that this is the major reason for God's current manifestation of his true prophets.

The prophet must never be found guilty of the sins of omission and commission for this portion of their prophetic assignment. Neither should a novel prophet attempt to engage the presence of a false prophet. For the novel prophet must learn and grow before he attempts to handle demonic forces, for the presence of the false prophet is very cunning and skillful in the art of camouflage and illusion:

Beware of false prophets, which come to you in sheep's clothing, but inwardly they are ravening wolves (Matthew 7:15).

Not only will a false prophet's messages be misleading, but his messages will be highly intoxicating. His demonstrations will be also convincing and captivating. This strategy will make his ministry seem more credible and will even try to disdain the true prophets during the time of the false prophet's manifestation. This is why it takes spiritual maturity, within a reasonable length of seasoning, before one is ready to handle this kind of warfare. The unknown writer of Hebrews further clarifies the differences between those seasoned and those who are still drinking milk:

"…The time ye out to be teachers, ye have need that one teach you again which be the first principles of the oracles of God; and are become such as have need of milk, and not of strong meat. For everyone that useth milk is unskillful in the word of righteousness: for he is a babe. But strong meat belongeth to them that are of full age, even those who by reason of use have their senses exercised to discern both good and evil" (Hebrews 5:12b-14).

The Doctrine of Prophecy

Outwardly, false prophets look rather harmless. They will look like your average person or church-going friend. But inwardly, they are very dangerous. Their true identity is like a wolf. This is why dressing the part, looking the part, and externally pretending to be the part, doesn't cut it any longer. This is also why the prophetic anointing must be more about the soundness of biblical content and not just about the image of what appears to seem "prophetic." This is what will separate the true prophets from the false ones. And what is coming in this season is an attitude of undesirable tolerance for the truth, meaning that the time of hearing anything and everything that sounds good will be preferred to sound doctrine and truth:

"Now the Spirit speaketh expressly, that in the latter times some shall depart from the faith, giving heed to seducing spirits, and doctrines of devils; speaking lies in hypocrisy..." (1 Timothy 4:1-2a).

So, a prophet of truth must have this primary understanding solidified within. When rebuking the presence of a false prophet, the only thing other than that prophet's faith that will stand is preaching and teaching the sound word of God. For the confirmation of the truth of Christ must be within every prophet. And that truth is this: Jesus is the Son of God (1 John 4:2-3)! And if Jesus lives in you, you will not become a target of false-prophetic infection and prostitution.

For the spirit of the false-prophet always seeks to recruit the erroneous ministry of another true prophet. And a false prophetic infection is that of contaminating a true prophet, thereby transforming him too into a wolf, hireling, or other satanic-like lion. This can happen especially when there is little embrace of Jesus Christ and his gospel. But the word of God says that we must make our election and salvation certain. And we must also walk in purity and honesty when dealing with the prophetic.

Handling the word like one who drinks milk, and with a false sense of spiritual maturity, is still a milk drinker at best. When you drink milk in the spirit, you are still a novelty word bearer. The novelty word bearer is likened unto the private in an army. The private is, therefore ill equipped to handle anything above his rank and entry-level position. But if you digest heavy scriptural understanding with proper intent and fullness of meaning, you have then become a meat eater within the spirit realm.

This reality makes you of full age within the word, elevating you to the level of seasoned elder who happens to also be a prophet. For it is the scripturally sound prophet that has the power and authority of God to engage, in a spiritual battle, the false prophets. So the differences between the two prophets and word bearers are certainly drastic. Simply stay in your lane. Do not do anything before it is time, and your time at that. Always consult God and another seasoned leader before you engage in demonic warfare.

But the goal here is to explain how one's prophetic is linked to eventual eldership, a strong word life and consistent spiritual growth, for there is much detriment in moving prematurely within your prophetic actions. This is not advisable, especially before true growth has occurred. Therefore, every true prophet must wait for his proper time of development. Premature ministry can yield horrible outcomes if one is not careful:

And the evil spirit answered and said, Jesus I know, and Paul I know; but who are ye? And the man in whom the evil spirit was leaped on them, and overcame them, and prevailed against them, so that they fled out of the house naked and wounded (Acts 19:15-16).

Please understand why it is very important for only seasoned prophets to solve the manifestation of false prophets. For the seasoned prophet is like an exterminator. When we discover rodents and bugs, we seek an exterminator, because he has the necessary tools to eradicate that type of infestation. Sure, we can go to the local store and get our own supplies. Oftentimes we do. But when we've noticed the rise of the larger influx of rodents, it is better to seek more skilled and knowledgeable help, rather than our method of getting the over-the-counter remedies. This is the same for handling the presence of a false prophet. The ministry of a seasoned prophet is the suitable prophetic exterminator, qualified to handle the rapid growth of a false-prophetic infestation.

The Termination Date for the Spirit of False Prophecy:

The enemy is so nervous! He has made many false prophets to attempt to conceal the presence of true prophets within every generation. But with the Holy Ghost, the exposure of such false prophets can be seen and thus evicted. If the church would prefer a true prophetic voice to an untrue one, this battle can quickly end. Thus, I prophesy that our victory surely will come to pass.

Zion, we must see how dangerous it is to allow a false voice to profane the presence of God. Beloved Church of God, we must also take on the high responsibility in the discernment of spirits. We must discern these professing prophets like never before. So, when a certain spirit of prophetic assertion comes in our midst, send forth the prophet to discern it at once:

Beloved, believe not every spirit, but try the spirit whether they are of God: because many false prophets are gone out into the world (1 John 4:1).

Soon will the spirit of false prophecy and the false prophet inevitably end dramatically – when and if the church will send in the big guns to battle them! For God will reckon greatly with the master of all false prophets (the Antichrist). And the final place for this type of demonic spirit and presence is surely within the Lake of Fire and Brimstone. Did you get it? Just as Jesus Christ is the master of true prophets, the Antichrist is the master of false prophets. But the Spirit and the master of all false prophets will find his final resting place in the Lake of Fire and Brimstone:

And the beast was taken, and with him the false prophet that wrought miracles before him, with which he deceived them that had received the mark of the beast, and them that worshipped his image. These both were cast alive into a lake of fire burning with brimstone (Revelation 19:20).

And the devil that deceived them was cast into the lake of fire and brimstone, where the beast and the false prophet are, and shall be tormented day and night for ever and ever (Revelation 20:10).

Until such time, God's unleashing of hell on earth for false prophets is surely wrapped in the ministry of the true prophet of God. The greatest rebuking and casting of calamity is not to the church. Neither is it to backsliders. Instead, the true prophet's greatest rebuke is to the false prophetic workers sent by the enemy. For these false prophetic workers seek to potentially convert others away from Christ. And they seek to distract others from coming to Christ.

This strategic battle is the beginning premise for the prevalence of a true prophet. Yet, it also reminds us that even if the true prophets hit and miss this responsibility, God will eventually destroy all false prophets. He will stop their demonic infection before Jesus returns with the eternal dominion that is predestined among the redeemed of mankind. Until then, every true prophet must be on duty and in their proper training and positioning so that we can collectively fight the spirit of false prophets and their false prophecies.

Apostle Sherman D. Farmer

CONCLUSION OF LESSON 3:

Conflict Resolutions Concerning Christian Socialism versus Christian Prophetism

THE IDENTIFICATION OF COMMON PROBLEMS:

Problem #1 – Excessive Denominationalism

Another reason God says that the prophetic is needed is because of the great disconnect between the different expressions of the Christian faith. The aggressive interjections of denominationalism affect the very presence of Christian socialism and Christian prophetism. This means that some people cannot readily accept the presence of prophets because of what they have been taught. Most have been taught that prophets do not exist anymore. But, as the Apostle Paul teaches, if one is operative in the five-fold, then that they are not on a denominational agenda. In fact they are on a kingdom agenda. More specifically, they are assigned to the true mission and ministry of Jesus Christ:

And He gave some prophets, For the perfecting of the saints, for the work of the ministry, for the edifying of the body of Christ: Till we all come in the unity of the faith, and of the knowledge of the Son of God, unto a perfect man, unto the measure of the stature of the fullness of Christ (Ephesians 4:11a, 12-13, KJV).

People are so on guard against false prophets that they cannot receive a true prophet when he comes. This is sometimes because of Denominationalism. Denominationalism has its good and bad points. In respect to its bad points its dysfunction usually cripples the agendas associated within kingdom realities. When people become too dogmatic, they too can create a church that prefers civil war from the doctrinal differences of Continuationism and Cessationism.

Continuationism is the belief that all spiritual gifts are presently active in the Lord's church and kingdom. It further believes that the gifts will not discontinue until the end of the church age. And the opposite of this teaching is the doctrine of Cessationism. This doctrine teaches that many of the gifts of signs, such as prophesying, speaking in tongues, miracles, and various healings, were discontinued shortly after the early church. Those under this teaching believe that those operating in such practices do so under a false spirit! They further believe that they are inordinate in their behavior and in their convictions as Christians.

This conflict is what feeds the presence of our problems with Christian socialism. Denomination fights denomination. Please do not think that the prophetic subject matter takes a back seat. In fact, its bashing becomes the church's headliner. But God's agenda is much bigger than denominationalism! Even though I am a firm believer that God moves any true ministry that is historically and accurately reflecting the spirit of Jesus Christ, all ministries need to check their motives and their ambassadorial skills! For an ambassador never seeks to offend, but instead always seeks to promote his leader, his country, and his overall agenda. We, too, have to start promoting our leader (Jesus Christ), his country (the kingdom of heaven), and the overall agenda (preaching the Gospel).

Problem #2 – Prophetic Misdiagnosis Which Causes Prophetic Murders

Unfortunately, this is not the only problem with Christian socialism and prophetism. Our conflict, however, is so much deeper than doctrinal differences and denominational traditions. We can summarize this type of concern and fear factor with respect to belief systems, especially when Jesus is on his way to the cross. First, the people respected him as a prophet. At that time, he was well liked. This, of course, was when Jesus healed the sick, performed miracles, and raised the dead:

And the multitude said, this is Jesus the prophet of Nazareth of Galilee (Matthew 21:11).

But the tables immediately turned. And this turning only took seven days. For seven days later, Jesus was considered a false prophet. Seven days later, Jesus became a sign of contempt. He was then violently abused and labeled as one who was not truly sent by God. But some of those very same people, seven days prior, were praising Jesus and his prophetic ministry. Then they turned against him. And the truth behind this is because Jesus did not
continue to produce in the manner they desired:

What think ye? They answered and said, He is guilty of death. Then did they spit in his face, and buffeted him; and others smote him with the palms of their hands. Saying, prophesy unto us, thou Christ, who is he that smote thee? (Matthew 26:66-68).

What this teaches is another important lesson. That lesson contains this truth: history certainly repeats itself. Just as the people of the New Testament had a love-hate relationship with Jesus, so did Israel do the very same thing among their former prophets. So a prophetic killer does not care about Testaments or generations. No, in every generation there is always a spirit attempting to create prophetic genocide. The Apostle Paul refers to such a spirit when he educates the church of Thessalonica:

"...Killed...their own Prophets" (1 Thessalonians 2:15).

This is why we must be careful that we don't label true prophets as false prophets. This again is another issue. People do not readily receive most true prophets, because they lack true biblical understanding and real discernment. Some people honestly do not know how to navigate and discern the presence of a true prophet. And the ministry of the Apostles provides clear examples of what we should and should not do when we subjectively face an assumed prophetic voice. The key is **love**!

Love is the only remedy to handle the case of demonic infection and any wicked spirit. **Agape** love is the key to overriding any satanic operation within the fold of God. For the false prophet cannot show **agape** love, and neither can the Holy Spirit misuse a prophet who desires **agape-love's abiding**. This is the major factor between the differences of a true and false prophet, and even a true Christian and false Christian. For love is the secret of any type of discernment. When love is absent, so is the truth. For truth and love are the same:

And because iniquity shall abound, the love of many shall wax cold (Matthew 24:12, KJV).

Jesus said that many will lose the love of God because of sin. Thus, a false prophet will be one of many operating without true agape love because their main purpose is to be sinful under the guise of being "prophetic." This alone is the deciding factor of proper Christian socialism discern of Christian prophetism.

It is also the means of providing true integration of Christian prophetism with a community or society of various expressions within the Christian faith. This is why *agape*-love is so necessary in the reception of any voice that comes into the body of Christ. We must not despise the office and gift even though we have seen it on so many occasions experience failure. Simply put, let love expose the falseness. For a false prophet cannot hide inside the love of God. And time will tell if love is truly abiding within any spirit. Herein is the very motive behind the spirit of murder that's afflicting the family of God. This is causing family to slay family, and people to destroy the wrong prophets. It also causes a dysfunctional mentality in the prophet. Like Job's three overly critical friends, we, too, must pray that the church stops randomly slaying the true prophet. While exalting the presence of a false prophet!

Problem #3 – The Prophet's Mentality Applied to the Wrong Testament

When a prophet stands aloof from Christian society, pretending to be like an Old Testament prophet, or John the Baptist even, he is in fact demonstrating the problematic and unresolved issues that Christian socialism has with Christian prophetism. None of these practices edify God. So it is imperative that we resist the urge to operate in any of them.

Now, we must not misconstrue prophetic understanding. With the exception of Old Testament prophetic companies, guilds, and families (1 Samuel 10:5; 2 Kings 2:3, 5; Micah 6:4), prophets use to walk alone. And there are exceptional times when one's prophetic assistants or apprentices did worked with him (2 Kings 4:12). But, for the most part, the former prophet's integration into society was not a welcomed standard. Neither was it typical.

The cohabitation of Israelite prophetism and Israelite socialism was a chronic issue. And currently it is the same in today's expression of Christian prophetism with Christian denominationalism. This issue never seems to resolve. The reason being is that the effects of yesterday are still felt today. But yesterday's errors in Israelite socialism are not an excuse for the misuse and mishandling of the Lord's prophets in Christian prophetism. Neither is it an excuse for a current prophet to be antisocial.

Yes, the prophet should guard his heart. And it is readily understood that this type of mentality becomes a means of protecting the heart and life belonging to the prophet. And, yes, it is also true that God makes each prophet conditioned with the necessary fortification. It is God himself that insulates the prophet's thoughts by creating a divine resistance against society's feedback and the opinions of a demonic or dogmatic people (that may rise against him).

But the message appears to be more important than the messenger. Sure, the message and messenger are united in a sense. But the strengthening of the prophet's character implies that the prophet's discomforts of people will never be more important than the relevant prophetic message to which he is sent to minister. Simply put, prophets need to get over themselves. If the old prophets had to minister in the face of interpersonal conflicts, so will the current prophets!

In short, the very people a prophet is sent to speak to will most likely attempt to silence him. And because of this reality, most prophets walk a lifetime of isolation and discomfort within their prophetic ministry. But prophets must come to understand that they were not made to become social outcasts among their immediate church family, even though at times they are treated as such.

And the truth behind this conflict is not the personality of the prophet alone. Instead, it is the conflict of personality against personality. It is a true prophet's unique manifestation usually dictating his eccentric behavior. And the creation of the underlying issue of prophetic rejection and the lack of spiritual receptivity make matters worse when it comes to a prophet's normalcy in socialism. But regardless of people's facial expressions, undertones of disrespect, and energetic disdains, a prophet's assignment is to release the word of the Lord! Whether people accept or reject it!

Problem #4 – The Chronic Presence of Disobedience

There is another major reason for the chronic conflict between those involved with Christian socialism and Christian prophetism. For at the core of such issues is usually disobedience before God. And this is why people often refuse to accept the ministry of a prophet. Even in today's church, there are residual effects of this chronic disrespect. Some portions of the body of Christ hate the prophetic ministry with a passion, and some of this hatred is inherited. In fact, this conflict gets its genesis from biblical history. We clearly see its resemblance in today's prophetic administration.

For it is amazing how people forget the beauty and dynamics they experienced under a true prophet's anointing. This is hard to accept, especially when a prophet's words have continuously come to pass. Nevertheless, no matter how accurate or anointed, the prophet is surely unwelcomed and truly hated. This usually takes place in modern times when the prophet's message switches from sweet to sour, just as Jesus' ministry shifted from working miracles to presenting a greater message that he was God! This is when prophets are rejected the most!

But the deeper issue here is that when you are chronically disobedient, you will always be irreverent towards the things of God. Thus, every true prophet must remember the words God gave to Samuel. God said to the prophet, when the people wanted a king, "they have not rejected you, but they have rejected me" (1 Samuel 8:7). In like manner, when people forget God, they will certainly forget the prophet, who represents God.

The funny thing is that the people are the very reason the prophet came into existence! Lest we forget, prophets are the very representatives nominated into existence, which was especially true in the days of Mt. Sinai. In fact, Moses did not even want the position in the first place. But the people were reluctant to approach God at the mountain, so they decided that Moses would remain their representative. And thus the continual ministry of the prophet was born:

And all the people saw the thunderings, and the lightnings, and the noise of the trumpet, and the mountain smoking: and when the people saw it, they removed, and stood afar off. And they said unto Moses, Speak thou with us, and we will hear: but let not God speak with us, lest we die. And Moses said unto the people, Fear not: for God is come to prove you, and that his fear may be before your faces, that ye sin not. And the people stood afar off, and Moses drew near unto the thick darkness where God was (Exodus 20:18-21, KJV).

This is how Moses became the continual prophetic representative responsible for the interfacing between God and the people. Vice versa, the people would communicate with God through Moses. Yes, the people asked for the presence of the prophet, just like the people asked for the king because they wanted to mimic foreign nations and not be original, as God had intended. So the essence of the problem is this: you asked for it, so now deal with it! And just as Israel had to cope with this so does the church!

Whether they like it or not, the prophetic office is here to stay! It is not finished until the Lord Jesus returns to the earth in his millennial reign! For as long as there are cycles of blood moons, and episodes of sun reaching eclipses, God promises that the prophetic anointing is here to stay (Acts 2:20). And if you create a due diligence of research, you will discover how blood moons truly exist. In fact, NASA charts every blood moon and every total eclipse of the sun. There is a record for not only the past years, but also the current and future moments of this phenomenon. And during 2015, there will be two episodes of blood moons as well as two solar eclipses.

The next dates for the blood moons are March 4th, 2015 and September 28th, 2015. Oddly enough, the date in March is the same date of the Feast of Passover. And the date in September is the same date for the Feast of Tabernacles. The two solar eclipses will take place in March and again in September. The September eclipse will be on the Feast of Trumpets, also known as Rosh Hashanah. This date is the civil New Year among the Jewish people. And this is why prophesying is no joke. It is something that must be adhered to and respected. For when Paul wrote to the church of Thessalonica, there was similar disrespect. But the Apostle's resolve was in this exhortation:

Despise not prophesyings (1 Thessalonians 5:20).

If disobedience is the core of errors in Christian socialism, then wicked manipulation is the hull that infects the core of prophetic expression. Prophets are constantly being maneuvered into a prophetic work similar to divination, all because people manipulate to gain insight, but never truly commit to Christ.

For Jesus was accepted as a prophet as long as he prophesied what the people wanted. The moment his prophetic messages became harder, the more the people rejected them. This is why if we are not careful, the prophetic can be damaged among the motives of men. Yes, the gift of prophecy and the office of the prophet have almost become totally polluted by immature people.

And seemingly, people are never interested in the heart of the prophet who carries the heart of God. This, however, should be a common interest between people and God's prophet. Simply put, God is the only reason the prophet exists! And the main reason God creates prophets is for a stronger connection with his very people. But it is the people who reject the prophet. And in such, they reject God.

Simply put, people have become accustomed to using the prophet's ministry like one uses a beverage for consumption. We all know that once the consumption of the beverage has been used, the container is then tossed. And prophets of today are seemingly used only for a people's personal manipulation, entertainment, and gain. Again, the root of this is their chronic disobedience! Just as Cain slew his brother, Abel, so does the very society birthing the prophet decide to kill the prophet:

"O Jerusalem, Jerusalem, which killest the prophets, and stonest them that are sent unto thee; how often would I have gathered my children together, as a hen doth gather her brood under her wings, and ye would not!" (Luke 13:34).

This has been known to be true ever since the first church of the wilderness (Acts 7:38). And even now it has never been truer within the current church of the Lord Jesus Christ. So it is the family of God that destroys the messenger of God. It is a harsh but true reality. We can recall how Jesus was celebrated and tolerated. But then again, he was also rejected and crucified. Thus, prophets are only needed for seasonal fleshly gratifications among a sinful people.

This is why the spirit of a prophet needs the relational connection of other prophets. In my other book, "The New Prophetic Generation," I showed that the Lord has given clear insight as to why prophets are in need of prophetic families for the continuation of their literal survival. For it is true: a prophet is best understood, appreciated, and accepted by one's own kind. And this sense of community, even now within the New Testament, is a means of ensuring the continuation of God's holy prophets.

Just like a modern day Obadiah, who was the servant of Ahab and Jezebel, the contemporary prophets are emerging to protect the prophetic gift and personality. In the storyline, the relevance of this revelation is found when Jezebel attempted to dissolve all the true prophets of God. It was Obadiah who took 100 prophets and hid them in a cave. And he fed them bread and water for their survival. This act of kindness demonstrates how some in the world will see the importance of the prophetic gifting:

"...Obadiah, which was the governor of his house, (Now Obadiah feared the Lord greatly: For it was so, when Jezebel cut off the prophets of the Lord, that Obadiah took an hundred prophets, and hid them by fifty in a cave, and fed them with bread and water.)" (1 Kings 18:3b-4, KJV).

This is why prophetic community is so important. It is the presence of prophetic community that will bring necessary healing to those who are scorned for being prophetic. This explains why Moses would have not made it without Aaron and Miriam, and why Samuel would have not made it without David, and David without Nathan. It also explains why Elijah and Elisha would have not made it without the sons of prophets.

And Jesus also needed John's ministry just as much as John needed Jesus' ministry. For there is no wonder why John the Baptist's mentality was socially awkward and disengaging from the very people he was sent to prophesy. For John remained in the wilderness, alone, eating wild locusts and honey. He dressed with an avant-garde flare to repel possible candidates of contamination, disruption, and pending demise (Matthew 3:4; Mark 1:6). But this still did not excuse him from needing a prophetic connection and confirmation, which only Jesus could provide.

But the fact still remains that John mimicked the lifestyle and clothing of the Old Testament prophet Elijah (2 Kings 1:8). And John deliberately wanted to remain aloof from society so he could prevail long enough to disseminate the messages of God. But we cannot function like John in this present age. God has established that the church functions like a family. And so this calls and commands all prophets to be delivered from social awkwardness.

Because when God originally created the prophet, it was never for the purpose of attacking people. Never was the prophet designed to stand before a people and make them hate the very presence and purpose in which they were called to serve. The ultimate purpose was to show them God!

However, because of people's sinfulness and unwillingness to progress spiritually, the prophet perpetually struggled with acceptance, respect, and proper recognition. This is evident when he said, "thus saith the Lord" to the people of God. For the power of those words can either cause a people to cheer or to shout, "crucify him," a prime example of the disconcertion that comes with prophets being disconnected from their people. And the people's disconnect from prophets occurred when Jesus visited his hometown, Nazareth:

And it came to pass, that when Jesus had finished these parables, he departed thence. And when he was come into his own country, he taught them in their synagogue, insomuch that they were astonished, and said, Whence hath this man this wisdom, and these mighty works? Is not this the carpenter's son? Is not his mother called Mary? And his brethren, James, and Joses, and Simon and Judas? And his sisters, are they not all with us? Whence then hath this man all these things? And they were offended in him. But Jesus said unto them, a prophet is not without honor, save in his own country, and in his own house. And he did not many mighty works there because of their unbelief (Matthew 13:53-58).

Simply put, being a prophet is not an easy job! For one must master emotions while simultaneously honing one's gift. The first lesson is to overcome feelings and contrary thoughts about those closely assigned to walk with you. And even those who will oppose you! For prophets particularly learn this lesson when dealing with family. If a prophet cannot fortify his feelings, then his emotions will overtake his ministry. This will cause his ministry to function with unfruitfulness. And the biggest test is always whether your immediate family will believe or truly recognize the prophetic gift in you. Even Jesus went through this same ordeal:

After these things Jesus walked in Galilee: for he would not walk in Jewry, because the Jews sought to kill him. Now the Jews' feast of tabernacles was at hand. His brethren therefore said unto him, depart hence, and go into Judaea, that thy disciples also may see the works that thou doest. For there is no man that doeth any thing in secret, and he himself seeketh to be known openly. If thou do these things, shew thyself to the world. For neither did his brethren believe in him (John 7:1-5).

Thus, it is imperative that the prophet never become confused about societal depravities. Neither can he allow a lack of intimacy with both his natural and spiritual family's socialism to impair his assignment. For the prophet must remain vigilant and strong while mastering his ministry. For this is more important than comfort. And the chronic issues with Christian prophetism and Christian socialism will prevail onward. And so must you! For you are called to reach those you can reach and leave the rest to God.

THE IDENTIFICATION OF UNIVERSAL SOLUTIONS

Solution #1 – The True Context of Ephesians 4:11-16

Concerning the chronic issues of Christian socialism and Christian prophetism, this closing will be meaty. So brace yourself! #1 - Ephesians 4:11-16 precisely explains why God sends prophets. They are sent to bring the people together under the banner of Jesus Christ (Ephesians 4:13). This is also why they are still needed. For a prophet is a director for the people under God. And whether past or present, God uses the *prophet* to sometimes speak strong words of correction unto a people. But even when this was the case, God prepares the prophet for the worse reactions possible:

Be not afraid of their faces: for I am with thee to deliver thee, saith the Lord (Jeremiah 1:8, KJV).

Thou therefore gird up thy loins, and arise, and speak unto them all that I command thee: be not dismayed at their faces, lest I confound thee before them. For, behold, I have made thee this day a defenced city, and an iron pillar, and brazen walls against the whole land, against the kings of Judah, against the princes thereof, against the priest thereof, and against the people of the land. And they shall fight against thee; but they shall not prevail against thee; for I am with thee, saith the Lord, to deliver thee (Jeremiah 1:17-19).

As an adamant harder than flint have I made thy forehead: fear them not, neither be dismayed at their looks, though they be a rebellious house (Ezekiel 3:9).

David's and Saul's classic storylines serve as an example of this. For their relationship directly speaks to the potent ills that come from the emergence of any true prophetic anointing. For instance, Saul became deranged and displaced from the will of God. As a result of continuous disobedience, God took the anointing and position of king from Saul. God then decided to elevate David to Saul's place. In Saul's jealousy, he sought to kill his young armor bearer and chief musician.

Despite these trifles, David constantly honored the anointing of God once placed upon him. This is the secret, right here! We must fight to get along instead of fight to fall apart! Even if other people do not change, it is the responsibility of the prophetic leader to change. We must change our hearts towards people, even when people's hearts towards us have not changed, or will not change, because they are limited in their thinking and understanding.

As in the case with Saul and David, we know that Saul relentlessly continued to chase David around many regions of southern Israel. Through many caves and many corners, David ran for his life. When Saul eventually died in battle and the report came to David, he showed great respect for the position of the formerly anointed king. And David's anger towards the young Amalekite, who reported the taking and ending of Saul's life, further expresses how God has a protocol for consistent respect of his anointed vessels and chosen leaders. It further displays David's disdain towards anyone who deliberately mishandled a fellow leader in the anointing (2 Samuel 1:13-16). It is David who created a famous mantra with respect to anointing and ministry. For the word of God declares:

"Touch not my anointed and do my prophets no harm" (1 Chronicles 16:22; Psalm 105:15).

Like Saul and David, there is continual conflict between those without the anointing and the anointed, or, as it is best described, between the spiritually relevant and those lacking spiritual relevance. The same is the case with those who believe in prophetism and those who do not. So, when the church handles false prophets, we must also realize that some false prophets are unknowingly and possibly true prophets. And they, too, need a chance at salvation. This is why the Gospel is preached by all who are called and chosen. Furthermore, when a true prophet encounters a false prophet, we must realize that there is a soul planted within him, and that there is an opportunity for deliverance, but only if we administer the **agape-love of God**.

Yet this doesn't negate the fact that not all false prophets and unsaved prophets of error will accept Jesus Christ. It does, however, help to deescalate the conflict between Christian socialism and Christian prophetism. Simply put, judge no man. And leave all judgment of a man's soul to God. For a false prophet is, by definition, one who prophesies in error and from a wrong spirit. Technically speaking, this includes anyone who can be tricked or tempted into the spirit of a false prophet if not careful. This is why righteous judgment must be applied to every case when encountering the prophetic.

We are not to judge outward appearances. But we are to judge the results of the prophet's purpose and how that purpose affects the local church and kingdom at large. No matter how large the demonic-infection of false prophecy becomes, God promises a remnant of true prophetic proportions:

Lord, they have killed your prophets; they have demolished your altars, and I alone am left, and they seek my life. But what is God's reply to him? I have kept for myself seven thousand men who have not bowed the knee to Baal. So too at the present time there is a

remnant (a small believing minority), selected (chosen) by grace (by God's unmerited favor and graciousness) (Romans 11:3-5, Amplified Version).

Simply put, within every sphere of Christian socialism, there are some who will be consistently genuine with the things of God. The Apostle Paul used this historical fact about Elijah, the 100 prophets, and the remaining 7,000 true worshippers, to explain how God always preserves a remnant. This is applicable to prophets, apostles, pastors, ministers, and believers in general. There will be those who are diligent with authenticity and sincerity. Of course there will some who are not. But a primary assignment of the true prophet is to remain true. It is the responsibility of the prophet to remain in the righteous remnant and never be found on the wrong side of God.

Additionally, the hardest thing to learn about a remnant is that no one knows for whom the true remnant consists. For many proclaim their allegiance, but not everyone professing is truthfully connected. The resolve is in a personal connection and relationship with Jesus Christ. The general trends of society reveal and teach how the majority of those in society do not truly have adequate measures of biblical knowledge.

This is why they are likened to sheep that are easily led astray. When Jesus arrived in Jerusalem, he performed many miracles, and the people were very confused because they lacked spiritual understanding. It wasn't entirely their fault. Some of it was due to the mentality and evil motives of the religious leaders of their day, while other matters pertained to the lack of scriptural knowledge and understanding. But even in those days there were some who truly kept the faith, even if you can't count them among the crowds that followed Jesus. You can surely find them among his apostles. So in essence Paul's thoughts are true. Never is a true prophet alone. There are more of us out there! We just have to trust that even if we do not see them, they are there. God says it is so!

But in the interim we must return to the fight at hand. That fight is against the religiosity of those who falsely carry the title of leader. For even during the days of Jesus this problem persisted. And even now it is the same issue. Because the self-righteous leaders' major concern was preeminence and pomp and circumstance rather than compassion and concern for deliverance. This is why we must work hard at getting along. And every leader who is connected to the truth about the five-fold is seeking to bring the church together, not dismantle it!

This, again, is why the prophet of God is so greatly needed. You are not in this alone prophet of God! Stand up and recognize that you represent a minority of people who believe.

And even though the number is smaller than the majority, it does not take much to accomplish God's business. Truly, faith of a mustard seed can move mountains.

This is why the message of the prophet must still be integrated with the perils of the Christian community. This prophetic revolution is a means and opportunity to provide a clear portal for the people to find their true deliverance. What we cannot see is the heart of a soul on the microscopic level. Yes, the erring soul devoid of honesty may in fact want a change and deeper commitment with God. But it is hard to determine when that soul is muddied with the heaviness of sin and a lack of understanding.

But the Bible is clear: Jesus' mission is to see that no man perishes! And thus the prophet has the same objective! No longer can we have this denominational and highly judgmental immaturity parading among the body of Christ. We have countless examples of misinformed prophets vomiting excessive zealousness and denominational fanfare. But again, it is important to realize that there is a surviving remnant of righteous prophets sent in every age to assist one another with this assignment.

Solution #2 – The Constant Review of the Plan of Salvation

This is why it is imperative that all who say they are prophets or prophetic start with the first principle of prophecy, which is accepting the Lord Jesus Christ as their personal savior, for the gifts and callings of God are without repentance (Romans 11:29). And a spiritual gift does not confirm one's salvation. Therefore, a prophet can have much demonstration and yet still find himself on the way to hell.

One must also realize that anointing of the prophet does in fact start in the womb. Again this is not a strange concept. For some psychics are merely unsaved prophets. And the unsaved prophet is a reality and phenomenon that truly exists within the body of Christ. But there is still hope even for the false prophet. That hope, however, will only be fulfilled if he desires to truly repent of his wicked ways. Take for example the young girl who had a spirit of divination. Once the spirit was evicted from her, she became a candidate for salvation (Acts 16:16-18). Any person practicing prophecy must come to this understanding. Everything starts with Jesus!

Solution #3 – The Goal is to Keep It Always About Jesus

Yes, the gift of the prophet is perfect and from above (James 1:17). Yet the character and disposition of the individual using such gifting is another matter altogether. The entire purpose of the five-fold was to bring alignment into the work of Jesus Christ. Subsequently, after Jesus' resurrection, every prophetic voice stands within the halls of faith. Every voice is here to present its prophetic message in the name of Jesus. For it is that name that we are assigned to prophesy in. And it is that name that we have accepted for our prophetic purpose. This purpose is exclusive.

And those who are prophetic and a prophet must never fret. Let it be resolved that you are a true prophet in motive and deed because you believe in the words, work, and witness of Jesus Christ. Let it be resolved that your prophetic ministry is solely established by God through his spirit because God wants to use you as part of the five-fold team. And please be resolved that it is this team's responsibility to help develop the saints into greater works of God.

Whether a person remembers a prophetic word or not, whether a prophetic word is partially true or false, and whether a prophetic word is done in judgment or with wrong intent, nothing goes unnoticed in the eyes of God. We must remember that every true prophet's ministry is recorded in the Lamb's book of life.

Similarly, every false prophet's ministry is recorded and will be reviewed at the white throne of judgment. In the case of the true prophet, however, God will review the works of that prophet before the Bema Seat of Christ. And when the prophet stands, and if he has ever been out of order, God will repay. Thus, we must trust in God and never worry about a prophet's presence and true or false attempts at ministry. Jesus tells us in his word that nothing will stop the true church from progressing:

"...Upon this rock I will build my church; and the gates of hell shall not prevail against it" (Matthew 16:18b).

Therefore, we are all called to love one another as Christ has loved us. We must provide progression and reassurance that we are not like the former churches of the wilderness and early church, for they were not always receptive of the prophetic conduits of God. And we must resolve to become gladly receptive of the prophet's ministry. Subsequently, the prophet should not be made to feel reluctant to prophetically perform among a people.

As Paul told Timothy, we must stir up the gifts that God has given. The prophet is also without excuse in the expression of such gift because they are walking in false humility and apprehension, which is another function of disobedience and pride. We cannot be like the wicked and slothful servant, who hid his talent and pound, with an outdated excuse of his lord being hard and intimidating (Matthew 25:24; Luke 19:20-21). No, now the prophet walks in heavy grace to perform such. For what is being done by the prophet is exclusively about Jesus Christ!

Solution #4 – The Greatest Solution is God's *Agape*-Love

Thankfully, this ministry is more powerful than the frailty of a prophet, and even the mistakes that a prophet will make. But it also behooves a people to show the same grace to the prophet, just as the prophet is required to show grace to a people. For Paul taught that the best way to minister is always in love:

"But speaking the truth in love, may grow up into Him in all things, which is the head, even Christ" (Ephesians 4:15).

Love is the key ingredient missing for improving the prophetic. Love will help prophets become better socialists and make the people more receptive. Love is also the remedy for prophetic abuse of the people, as well as the people towards the prophet. It is a sad reality when you cannot find a church or a prophet that will not engage each other in the expression of God's *agape*. This alone will bring solution to the proper usage of the said gift. This, too, will break the cycle of the chronic issues with prophetism and spiritual socialism within any community of God.

Jesus instructs us to love God and each other. Therefore, if we love our neighbor as ourselves, we will not speak irreverent and harsh words under the guise of prophetic anointing. If we love our neighbor as ourselves, we will not reject ourselves, because the prophet is each of us as much as we are of the prophet. If we love our neighbor as ourselves, we can see how to properly minister to one another so that social harmony among the body of Christ can grow to a greater manifestation of the presence of Jesus Christ:

Though I speak with the tongues of men and of angels, and have not charity, I am become as sounding brass, or a tinkling cymbal. And though I have the gift of prophecy...and have not charity, I am nothing (1 Corinthians 13:1, 2b).

When Paul finished teaching the protocols of prophetic anointing, like speaking in tongues and interpreting tongues, he said something very powerful and prolific. He stated that it is a subjective reality that any man is asserting that he is indeed a prophet. And if he is indeed a prophet, he will come into immediate compliance concerning the scriptural protocols of the doctrine of prophecy:

If any man think himself to be a prophet, or spiritual, let him acknowledge that the things that I write unto you are the commandments of the Lord (1 Corinthians 14:37).

For in this, every prophet must understand that the mentality of walking as an Old Testament prophet is certainly over. The contemporary prophet is challenged to live among a society of saints that he or she is responsible. It is going to take love to properly hear God's voice for that particular fold on a consistent basis.

And never will that prophet be greater than the pastor or senior prophet of his household. But a prophet will always have a specific place among a specific people. A prophet is not only judged for every word that he has spoken; he is also judged for every word he neglects to say!

Solution #5 - Leave the Consequences to God

The final good news is this: God will take care of all the words of false prophets. And God will also severely judge the originator of all false prophets. For the originator is the Antichrist, and the Antichrist is the devil himself, except in another form. Furthermore, prophets are assigned to properly represent the Lord Jesus and his mission within his Holy Church. We must stop making the prophetic seem too mystical and filled with too much emotion. Though it is an ecstatic gift, the prophet must execute rational proportions within the practice of this office, not only for the sake of calming the concerns of the people, but also for a greater care of God's namesake.

If a prophet views these requirements, it is quite possible for prophetic acceptance and inclusion to grow. The prophet and the people must allow prophetic integration, growth, and purpose to live vibrantly within him. For it is well overdue, and it is surely the time for eradicating prophetic awkwardness in the context of socialism.

Whether you are strange or not, you still owe your life to God and to his people. Whether you are currently active or not, you still owe your anointing to the accountability of a governing community of other prophets. Regardless of how many false prophets, novelty prophets, and erroneous prophets there are. We are called to live harmoniously under the same banner of Jesus Christ. For no one truly under the banner of Jesus Christ will try to turn against Jesus' mission and ministry:

If Satan also be divided against himself, how shall his kingdom stand? Because ye say that I cast out devils through Beelzebub. And if I by Beelzebub cast out devils, by whom do your sons cast them out? Therefore shall they be your judges. But if I with the finger of God cast out devils, no doubt the kingdom of God is come upon you (Luke 11:18-20).

Jesus clearly explained how a person trying to destroy God's plan would not build at the same time. Neither of them was on the same side. Here is the proper way to handle someone who is working with the will of God. A perfect example of this confirmation is during the days of the Book of Acts. The famous Pharisee and master teacher Gamaliel instructed the Jewish leaders about how to handle various personalities emerging with the assumed position of servants of God:

Then stood there up one in the council, a Pharisee, named Gamaliel, a doctor of the law, had in reputation among all the people, and commanded to put the apostles forth a little space; and said unto them, Ye men of Israel, take heed to yourselves what ye intend to do as touching these men. For before these days rose up Theudas, boasting himself to be somebody; to whom a number of men, about four hundred, joined themselves: who was slain; and all, as many as obeyed him, were scattered, and brought to nought. After this man rose up Judas of Galilee in the days of the taxing, and drew away much people after him: he also perished; and all, even as many as obeyed him, were dispersed. And now I say unto you, refrain from these men, and let them alone: for if this counsel or this work be of men, it will come to nought. But if it be of God, ye cannot overthrow it; lest haply ye be found even to fight against God (Acts 5:34-39, KJV).

The wisdom of Gamaliel teaches us that time will illuminate all matters, and that history has a way of repeating itself. It is not a marvel that men can build a following. We have countless biblical and historical examples of great cultish leaders throughout the ages. But what Gamaliel also teaches is the maturity of knowing that God is in control, even when men seem out of control. This lesson is designed to reveal the importance of staying with God and not worrying about the wiles of men or the enemy's plans. For the power of God is greater than any satanic plot.

Finally, let it be resolved that your entire purpose for embracing the prophetic is not for personal gain, gratification, or greed. For there are hearts filled with filthy lucre and evil gain, as they strive for demonic goals. This is why I present you with this truth. We are still in an age with the same desires. For the pleasures of sin over the sacrifice of dying in the flesh to please God is still a prevailing conflict. But the true prophet will overcome such tendencies.

Because you are accepting your assignment within the prophetic, you are fully aware that God still uses prophets in today's time. For God will judge every prophet's work, whether true or false, accurate or inaccurate. The words that are spoken by a prophet are important and should never be taken lightly. Neither should a prophet haphazardly prophesy anything unto any man. Jesus explains how all words hold special significance in the eyes of God. It is with great significance that every word be weighed during each man's moment of final judgment. This includes the ministry life of the prophet and every prophetic word formerly uttered.

Therefore, the problems in Christian socialism as opposed to Christian prophetism are no excuse for the prophetic ministry to come forth. After all, our greatest fight is not our brother or our sister. It is the fight against the enemy! Once we focus our fight in the right direction, we can obtain the sure victory! This is why the prophetic is certainly necessary. The prophet must work with the other four governmental gifts to prevent doctrinal errors and sensationalisms:

Then we will no longer be infants, tossed back and forth by waves, and blown here and there by every wind of teaching and by the cunning craftiness of men in their deceitful scheming (Ephesians 4:14, NIV).

Please do not let the scars of dealing with people deflect you from your overall assignment. Integrate fellowship with the body of Christ. Fight to get along. And stand for the cause of your spiritual family. For in it you will discover that a prophet has more in common with the people than we fail to admit! And we all carry the same blood within the Spirit of God. That blood is surely the blood of Jesus. And if blood is thicker than water, then it's time to become a better family member and not an antisocial one. Maybe your ministry can call a prophetic family reunion! The choice is up to you!

CHAPTER 4

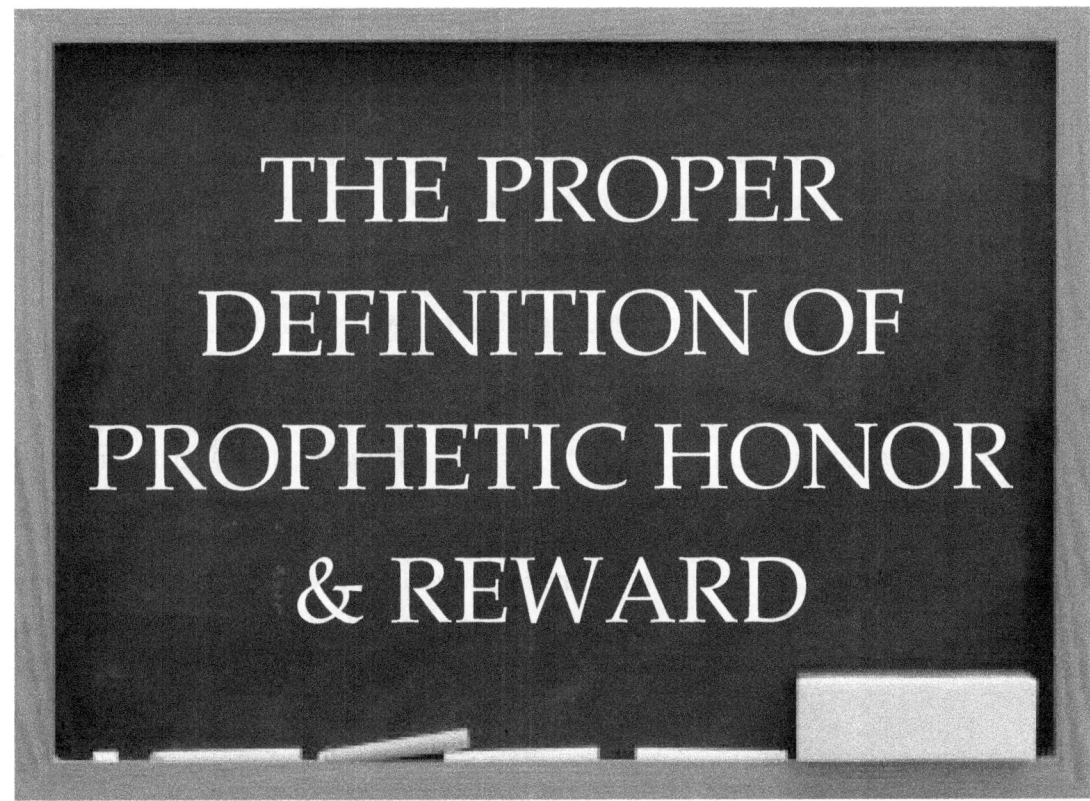

Where is a Prophet Most Prevalent?

"He that receiveth a prophet in the name of a prophet shall receive a prophet's reward..." (Matthew 10:41a).

The Overview

There is a popular trend these days in making the prophetic more about a marketplace paradigm than a ministry's purpose. But the true functionality of a prophet is to primarily remain a sanctuary gift for the Lord's church. In the Old Testament, there are secular injections regarding the prophetic anointing used outside of the chosen people of God. The most widely known are two prophets by the names of Joseph and Daniel. Each prophet served foreign kings with a unique ability to interpret odd things while they administered with a divine strategy of wisdom. Again, the prophetic is most prevalent within the church and God's kingdom. In this age, prophesying is not for the unbeliever as much as it is for the believer:

Wherefore tongues are for a sign, not to them that believe, but to them that believe not: but prophesying serveth not for them that believe not, but for them which believe (1 Corinthians 14:22, KJV).

Thus, it is the prophet's primary responsibility to rely on God and not the world. The spiritual arena is the primary jurisdiction of the prophet. Even if the prophet may be called to marketplace or non-spiritual purposes, they must not reside there for long, for we are reminded that the chief assignment is not to become entangled by the world. The Apostle John preached clear admonitions concerning our connections with this sinful world:

Love not the world, neither the things that are in the world. If any man love the world, the love of the Father is not in him. For all that is in the world, the lust of the flesh, and the lust of the eyes, and the pride of life, is not of the Father, but is of the world (1 John 2:15-16, KJV).

Ye are of God, little children, and have overcome them: because greater is He that is in you, than he that is in the world. They are of the world: therefore speak they of the world, and the world heareth them. We are of God: he that knoweth God heareth us; he that is not of God heareth not us. Hereby know we the spirit of truth, and the spirit of error (1 John 4:4-6, KJV).

This does not mean that a prophet cannot be a witness to the world. Rather, it means that the responsibility of opening the world's door is more for the anointing of an evangelist rather than the anointing of a prophet. Therefore, it is very important that the true prophet of God does not become confused. The prophetic gift is for the Lord's church and kingdom. And the prophetic gift is about building up God's people and not the children of the world:

For the perfecting of the saints for the work of the ministry, for the edifying of the body of Christ: Till we all come in the unity of the faith, and of the knowledge of the Son of God, unto a perfect man, unto the measure of the stature of the fullness of Christ (Ephesians 4:12-13, KJV).

In a time when ministry has become more business minded, we must make sure that we do not favor the dollar over the deliverance of souls. A prophet is not here to be a money-maker. Therefore, money is not where the prophet is most prevalent. Instead, ministry is the important feature of prophesying. For the spirit of this world will tell you that most of what the world cares about is how to make more money. Sure, the word does say that money answers all things (Ecclesiastes 10:19). But this scripture must be placed within its proper perspective. Money will never replace ethical and integral responsibilities that our God requires among his holy prophets. If you love money more than you love ministry, you are truly missing the point:

But the love of money is still the root of all evil (1 Timothy 6:10).

This supports the idea how the prophet must make their prevalence about Christ's kingdom compared to the world. The Apostle Paul said to be not conformed to this world, but to be transformed by the renewing of your minds (Romans 12:2). For it is important that we never overly spiritualize this admonition. It does not negate the fact that oftentimes money must be used in the ministry of the prophet. But it does mean that we are not here to make money as much as we are here to serve.

This is why the marketplace prophet of today's time is not any greater than the ministry-minded apostles and prophets of the Lord's church. Some refute that the Christian prophet, who only focuses on the things of God and his church is outdated. They further assert that that type of prophet makes them appear too "holier than thou," thereby implying that they are inaccessible or not relatable. But Paul taught about the power of adaptability within ministry (1 Corinthians 9:18-23). He also taught against the power of compromise, for this is the motive behind most ministries' adaptability and conformity. But heed this exhortation:

"...We have received, not the spirit of the world, but the Spirit which is of God..." (1 Corinthians 2:12a, KJV).

Thus, temptation from the world will attempt to entice the prophet with a mindset of capitalism, especially when there has been a chronic disrespect and rejection by the church. This is how true prophets are lured into taking their gift out of the church and into the world. This form of prophetic trafficking is being overlooked and widely accepted. And if they are not

The Doctrine of Prophecy

marketplace minded for the world, they will bring this spirit of prophetic prostitution back into the church, whereby they make it seem that the epitome of prophesying must have a dollar sign attached to it. But never is this behavior acceptable, advisable, or justifiable.

A classic example of this type of compromise is found in the storyline of the book of Nehemiah. Shemaiah, a true prophet of Israel and God, was persuaded to deceive and utter false prophecy to entrap Nehemiah (Nehemiah 6). The five-man confederacy of Sanballat, Tobiah, Geshem, the false prophetess Noadiah, and the compromised prophet Shemaiah, worked as a team, attempting to stop the plans of God:

One day I went to the house of Shemaiah son of Delaiah, the son of Mehetabel, who was shut in at his home. He said, "Let us meet in the house of God, inside the temple, and let us close the temple doors, because men are coming to kill you—by night they are coming to kill you." But I said, "Should a man like me run away? Or should one like me go into the temple to save his life? I will not go!" I realized that God had not sent him, but that he prophesied against me because Tobiah and Sanballat had hired him (Nehemiah 6:10-12, NIV).

Another example is the prophet Balaam. Numbers, Chapter 22:7, refers to the way Balak hires Balaam to speak a curse of prophecy over Israel. But instead, God transformed the prophet's awareness and brings Balaam to another word instead (Numbers 22:8-14). Balak persisted to request Balaam's services in producing a curse instead of a blessing. He sent back more men with a higher level of honor. He attempted to appease Balaam with honor, wealth, and prestige. But Balaam rightly declined:

And Balak sent yet again princes more, and more honorable than they. And they came to Balaam, and said to him, Thus saith Balak the son of Zippor, Let nothing, I pray thee, hinder thee from coming unto me: For I will promote thee unto very great honor, and I will do whatsoever thou sayest unto me: come thefore, I pray thee, curse me this people. And Balaam answered and said unto the servants of Balak, If Balak would give me his house full of silver and gold, I cannot go beyond the word of the Lord my God, to do less or more (Numbers 22:15-18, KJV).

This is why the prophet must never play with the power of prophecy or the benefits of being prophetic. The prophetic is what provides financial wealth and prosperity to the prophet. I have a slogan: I have never met a prophet who will not be cared for and whose pockets will be empty. The Lord always causes men to give from the bosom to the prophet. But it is the prophet's responsibility to stay prevalent in God and not in distractions like success, money, fame, or fortune.

The Prevailing Conflict of Honoring a Prophet

The power of a prophet is so great that it can shift an entire jurisdiction when that prophet enters a place. This is why people would give the prophet automatic honor. But this honor is not always generated from a sincere place. Back then it was given out of duty or fear. And in most cases it was not given because the people operated maturely, the reason why ancient Israel had a common question that it would ask the prophet when he entered their city:

And Samuel did that which the Lord spake, and came to Bethlehem. And the elders of the town trembled at his coming, and said, Comest thou peaceably? (1 Samuel 16:4).

But a prophet would only be asked this question because of the spiritual condition of the people within that city. Remember that disobedience is the recurring conflict of socialism and prophetism. In other words, the prophet has too much to do in the church. There are people who still cannot fathom the possibilities of the prophetic. And here again is why the prophet's prevalence must not be in the world, but rather among God's people.

Primary Point: It is a People's Disobedience That Attacks a Prophet's Honor

As discussed earlier, the prophetic voice was often slighted and disrespected, not because the people did not know any better, but because the only morsel of respect would be draped with fear. When people experienced the presence of a prophet, they did not see the prophet as a likeable person. Rather they saw the prophet as someone that brought dread and terror. This was not because the prophet wanted to come across as being super spiritual or intimidating. Instead, it was because the people were sinful. For sin, which is personified as disobedience, is a killer of all prophets:

And it came to pass, when Ahab saw Elijah, that Ahab said unto him, Art thou he that troubeleth Israel? (1 Kings 18:17).

The best way to explain this is to compare it to a parent who gets a certain look and tone in his voice before disciplining a child. The child instinctively knows that the parent has not come to hug them. Nor will the child be greeted with peaceful words. In fact, the child knows that something serious is about to happen that involves a correction, a beating, or some other form of punishment. It was in the same manner when the Old Testament prophet came to town.

The Doctrine of Prophecy

The people saw the prophet as a sign that something was wrong, or that someone was in big trouble. Even though the people feared the Lord, the people did not stop disrespecting the prophet. However, prophets remained prevalent among God's people.

This lack of honor towards the Old Testament prophet was solely attributed to the fullness of disobedience to God. So, in essence, the people didn't want to truly hear from God's prophet. For the prophet of God and the voice of God are synonymous with God, and the prophet's position as God's proxy made the people feel as if they were before the presence of God. So then dishonor associated with this behavior is to God alone and never the prophet. And certainly this is hard to decipher, especially when the prophet is challenged to not take it personal. A people's religiosity is another prevalent attack towards a prophet's honor:

They answered and said unto him, art thou also of Galilee? Search, and look: for out of Galilee ariseth no prophet. (John 7:52).

In this scripture, it is apparent that a spirit of error was trying to bring confusion within the prophetic work of God. This erroneous argument was based upon the forefathers' rigidity towards prophets since the beginning of the prophetic ministry. Even though it speaks specifically to one particular facet, we must keep in mind that the prophetic is always attacked in the area of religious disagreements. This is why the religious leaders of Jesus' day stated that the antithesis of Galilee was not where prophetic families lived and came from.

On the contrary, even they were sadly mistaken. Within the recorded annals of former prophecy and genealogy there was a misunderstanding about prophetic trends and emergence. As the word declares, it was prophesied that a greater work would be accomplished in the land of Galilee among the Gentiles. It was the prophet Isaiah who assists with this revelation:

Here is the original prophecy given by the Prophet Isaiah:

Nevertheless the dimness shall not be such as was in her vexation, when at the first he lightly afflicted the land of Zebulun and the land of Naphtali, and afterward did more grievously afflict her by the way of the sea, beyond Jordan, in Galilee of the nations. The people that walked in darkness have seen a great light: they that dwell in the land of the shadow of death, upon them hath the light shined. (Isaiah 9:1-2).

Here is the Apostle Matthew's interpretation of Isaiah's prophetic words:

Now when Jesus had heard that John was cast into prison, he departed into Galilee; and leaving Nazareth, he came and dwelt in Capernaum, which is upon the sea coast, in the

borders of Zebulun and Naphtali: that it might be fulfilled which was spoken by Isaiah the prophet, saying. The land of Zebulun, and the land of Naphtali, by the way of the sea, beyond the Jordan, Galilee of the Gentiles; the people which sat in darkness saw great light; and to them which sat in the region and shadow of death light sprung up. (Matthew 4:12-16).

The main premise of this argument is how the Pharisees told Nicodemus to search the scriptures. Simply put, there would be a prophet capable of handling even the worst area of Palestine. But instead of their true sight with Isaiah's text, the Pharisees negated Nicodemus with blinding jealousy.

This is why his scriptural accuracy and aptitude was challenged by a sound and seasoned prophet. Although Nicodemus was not a prophet, he was sound in his theology. But the religious leaders insinuated that Nicodemus was the one who was inaccurate. But Nicodemus did not have the problem concerning the qualifications of the geographic origins of the true Messiah (John 7:52). It was the Pharisees who did.

So, in essence, they were rebuking him for believing in a man claiming to be the Messiah who was associated with the wrong hometown. After all, the crowds considered Jesus Galilean. But, technically speaking, Jesus was only a citizen from Nazareth of Galilee. However, Jesus' lineage was from Judea. This was clarified when Joseph took Mary and Jesus to be counted in the census (Luke 2:1-7).

It is also true that the Old Testament says Christ would originate from Judea and not Galilee (Genesis 49:8-12; Isaiah 11:1). But the religious leaders took it a step further to say that no prophet would ever come from this region! Here again they were wrong! And herein is why Jesus apparently began the crux of his ministry there. This, then, is the danger or religiosity. For their religiousness brought them to the spirit of error instead of the spirit of truth. Thus, religiosity is always used to cripple the honor due to the prophet.

These men of God were arrogantly expressive about the idea that the Messiah's origins could only be that of Judean descent. In all actuality, this was true. For the Messiah came from Judean descent, and his heritage would be from the House of David. But the arrogant assumption of making Christ a Galilean prophet was because the people briefly assessed how his followers were primarily Galilean.

Never did they do further research by simply asking Jesus if he could prove his ancestry. And never did they tell the truth about Joseph's lineage, which by natural law was of Judean descent. This again confirms that God often takes a prophet from his own country and places him within another region so that he might be accepted and received as a true prophet. For people have a hard time receiving someone they are most familiar with. Regardless of their religiosity and their contempt for an assumed familiarity, the Bible does clarify that Jesus was Judean but raised in the districts of Galilee (instead of Judah, which is his actual birthplace and family's hometown):

And it came to pass in those days, that there went out a decree from Caesar Augustus, that all the world should be taxed. (And this taxing was first made when Cyrenius was governor of Syria.) And all went to be taxed, every one into his own city. And Joseph also went up from Galilee, out of the city of Nazareth, into Judea, unto the city of David, which is called Bethlehem; (because he was of the house and lineage of David:) to be taxed with Mary his espoused wife, being great with child. And so it was, that, while they were there, the days were accomplished that she should be delivered. And she brought forth her firstborn son, and wrapped him in swaddling clothes, and laid him in a manger; because there was no room for them in the inn (Luke 2:1-7).

Ironically, there is another prophet who comes from this same region of Galilee, named Jonah. The prophet Jonah, famous for living three days in the belly of the fish, was born near this very city in which Jesus would be raised and thus start his ministry. Jonah was sent to a foreign city named Nineveh, but demographically speaking, Jonah's hometown was two miles northeast of Nazareth. So this makes the prophet Jonah a Galilean prophet, which also rebukes the spirit of error upon the wickedness exhibited by the Pharisees! For a pericope within the Old Testament clarifies this rebuke:

Jeroboam restored Israel's border from the entrance of Hamath to the [Dead] Sea of the Arabah, according to the word of the Lord, the God of Israel, which He spoke through His servant Jonah, the son of Amittai, the prophet from Gath-hepher (2 Kings 14:25, Amplified Version).

Jesus' prophetic testimony also correlates with Jonah's storyline in the belly of the whale. And the greater irony here is that Jesus would later use Jonah as the chief and principle sign in speaking when referencing the condition of the present generation. Jesus understood that the Jews wanted a sign. And as a rebuke, he gave them a message that the only sign would be Jonah. This parallelism speaks to the period when Jesus was slated to die, be buried in a grave, and experience the first fruits of resurrection on the third day:

Then certain of the scribes and of the Pharisees answered, saying, Master, we would see a sign from thee. But he answered and said unto them, an evil and adulterous generation seeketh after a sign; and there shall no sign be given to it, but the sign of the prophet Jonas: for as Jonas was three days and three nights in the whale's belly; so shall the Son of man be three days and three nights in the heart of the earth. The men of Nineveh shall rise in judgment with this generation, and shall condemn it: because they repented at the preaching of Jonas; and, behold, a greater than Jonas is here (Matthew 12:38-41).

So, the mistake of the Pharisees, who attacked Nicodemus, also proves the omnipotence and omniscience of God. For Jesus was legitimately the Messiah. But their religiosity was overshadowing their sensibility and scriptural training. Here is an important observation that, with slight exhorting, must be applied: **when your religion or denominationalism is imbalanced, you, too, will fall victim to this same proportion of prophetic disdain.**

The truth about their argument is this: the prophet's natural orientation does not matter. When the prophet is called of God, all matters can never outweigh the prophet's primary prevalence. And that primary prevalence is to minister to God's people despite whether they can receive him or not!

A People's Disbelief is Another Prevalent Attack on a Prophet's Honor:

Many people are, by nature, cynics, skeptics, and pessimists. And faith is not as easy as people make it out to be, especially when referring to the faith given by men. This is why the man at the bottom of the mountain, who desperately wanted his son's deliverance, said, **"Lord, I believe, but help my unbelief" (Mark 9:24)**. For many people need to flat out admit it: they, too, cannot believe in a man or woman being used of God in the capacity of a "so-called prophet!"

Here is another area of dishonor: faith. Faith is the primary place in which the prophet is dishonored. This is certainly true when men don't fit the description of what society may think is "prophetic-worthy." But only what God says is truly prophetic is what truly matters! We see this in Saul's elevation as he prophesied among the prophets of Gibeah. One prophetic moment in a prophetic atmosphere, and the people of the town of Gibeah dramatically shun Saul:

And it came to pass, when all that knew him beforetime saw that, behold, he prophesied among the prophets, then the people said one to another, what is this that is come unto the son of Kish? ***Is Saul also among the prophets? (1 Samuel 10:11).***

We can vividly see this, too, when Jesus engaged Nathanael:

The Doctrine of Prophecy

"And Nathanael said unto him, can there any good thing come out of Nazareth?" (John 1:46a).

A man's demographic and socio-economic status is brought up every time a particular conversation about the prophetic occurs. True, it is good to know where a person comes from. But it is not appropriate to overly judge their prophetic potential just because a person may not come from a religious background and upbringing or previous prophetic confirmation of one's office. Thus, the spirit and infection of skepticism, cynicism, and pessimism lead to the doorway of disbelief. But for the record, disbelief will not stop the power of that called prophet. But fellowship and socialism play vital roles in the fluidity of this spiritual gift. When doubt is heavy in an atmosphere or environment of the prophetic work, gifts of healing and miracles usually diminish. The word of God declares that on some occasions Jesus did not supernaturally perform because of the disrespect within that city:

And he did not many mighty works there because of their unbelief (Matthew 13:58).

However, in other regions and communities, a prophet is gladly received. This here is why I believe the marketplace and the world are more favorable to the ministry of the prophets. For at times the prophet is accepted by the world more than the church. And the echoes of Christian socialism as opposed to Christian prophetism provide credence to these statements! The prophet Abraham here is our prime example. God removed Abraham from his very own people. This was because God needed Abraham to move into a greater dimension of his life and destiny, so God relocated him in a foreign land away from his native terrain:

Now the Lord had said unto Abram, Get thee out of thy country, and from thy kindred, and from thy father's house, unto a land that I will show thee (Genesis 12:1).

This teaches us that the prophet's conflict is solely because of familiarity, which continuously breeds contempt, especially with regards to siblings, cousins, friends, or even a next-door neighbor! Joseph's brothers would not believe in his dreams (Genesis 37). Many of Jesus' family members did not believe in him until he died and was resurrected. These examples surely teach that people can be quite ruthless, as well as how people will demonstrate their inability of showing mercy and respect unto God, who is absolute in his transformational power! As the word declares, ***if any man is in Christ, he is a new creature. Old things pass away. And all things become new (2 Corinthians 5:17).***

For it is God that favors a man to be a prophet. But the prophet is at the mercy of the favor of men too. This is why Jesus received favor with God as well as with man (Luke 2:52).

However, God alone has the power to determine if one will be prophetic or not, even if he doesn't fit the prophetic parts or criteria that is deemed subjectively acceptable by that given Christian community. So the bottom line is this: people cannot live without the prophetic. And the prophet cannot live without the people. Here, again, is the place of the prophet's prevalence! For every prophet has been called to accept this uncomfortable truth.

And among the children of Israel, a prophetic voice was more honored in death than in life. This means that the people of God would respect a prophetic voice years later. Never was that prophetic voice respected during its lifetime. But, as Jesus basically states, what good is this type of delayed honor?

Woe unto you, scribes and Pharisees, hypocrites! Because ye build the tombs of the prophets, and garnish sepulchers of the righteous, and say, if we had been in the days of our fathers, we would not have been partakers with them in the blood of the prophets. Wherefore ye be witnesses unto yourselves, that ye are the children of them which killed the prophets (Matthew 23:29-31).

Shortly before Jesus' passion and death, he addressed this truism with the religious leaders. Their displaced loyalty and delayed respect was ultimately hypocritical. They honored the deceased prophets of long ago, but they did not truthfully follow the words they have left to be obeyed. And even now, we do the very same thing. Martin Luther King, Malcolm X, and people of this caliber were honored only when they were martyred!

Another damaging effect of religiosity occurs with this type of delayed spiritual realization. A religious person is always behind the time instead of on time. A religious person is never connected to the revelatory work of God. For his connection is sadly in the pretense of being connected, when truthfully they are disconnected. These collective disparages are the primary reasons for such a high disregard of God's divine gift and why many who are called to this office are afraid to accept and appropriate their assignment. For the hardest task doesn't seem to be the ministry of prophesying. No, the hardest task is the disconnection a prophet feels from the very people they are assigned to.

Disdaining and disrespecting a prophet is indirect disrespect of God. And this practice and behavior is quite real. It is also not new and it will never go away. At least, not until the end of the last age, which is the Great Tribulation! This is why it has been a recurring theme in scripture and history. Not only does the prophet emotionally and psychological become affected. But oftentimes, despite the encouragement of God, the prophet literally takes this disconnect very personal.

However, this is a life lesson. Without a shadow of doubt, the prophet must learn to overcome the alienation and disrespect of those who do not agree with what they are doing.

When God asked prophets to sacrifice their personal lives, the response was to feel pain. This was not because they did not want to give up sin, but because they did not want to endure the negative reactions of the people.

We see how Jeremiah became greatly distressed when God told him he could not marry because of Israel's sinfulness (Jeremiah 16:2). Jeremiah grew angry with God, telling God he would never speak again! As a result of this heavy assignment, Jeremiah wanted to live his life on earth as a regular man. He was willing to be AWOL before the Lord. And in his season of fiery trials, Jeremiah spoke the following words because of the chronic abuse and struggles attached with the prophetic office and gift:

O Lord, thou hast deceived me, and I was deceived: thou art stronger than I, and hast prevailed: I am in derision daily, every one mocketh me. For since I spake, I cried out, I cried violence and spoil; because the word of the Lord was made a reproach unto me, and a derision daily. Then I said, I will not make mention of him, nor speak any more in his name. But His word was in mine heart as a burning fire shut up in my bones, and I was weary with forbearing, and I could not stay (Jeremiah 20:7-9).

Jeremiah helps us understand that the prophet's job is very hard. But people's hearts are even harder. Some people become enraged when the prophets confront them with truth. And when a prophet comes in their midst, they automatically create a wall and put their guards up. And skepticism towards a prophet is rooted in faithlessness, not to mention the fact that most people choose never to spiritually grow! They also desire to remain unchallenged, and they do not want to change! Take the Deacon Stephen for example. Before his death, he rebuked the people sharply concerning previous afflictions done unto the prophets of the past:

Ye stiff-necked and uncircumcised in heart and ears, ye do always resist the Holy Ghost: as your father's did, so do ye. Which of the prophets have not your fathers persecuted? And they have slain them which showed before of the coming of the Just One; of whom ye have been now the betrayers and murderers: (Acts 7:51-52).

The seasoned prophet, within accountability of his office, had come to clearly understand this dilemma (Hosea 4:6). So we, too, must understand that regardless of age and dispensation, people's reactions usually remain the same. The lack of knowledge and truth perpetuates the spirit of skepticism, cynicism, and pessimism, and the continual dishonoring of the prophet will continue. This will not change until people change their hearts, and most hearts will not change because they have the freewill to do so. But my prayer is that the kingdom and church will choose more wisely!

The Intoxication of Prophetic Persecution:

The people of God were informed never to put their hands on a prophet. Never abruptly or violently should the prophet be mishandled! For the scriptures teach that we are instructed to respect and show reverence to the gifts of God. But oftentimes, this commandment is ignored and perpetually disobeyed, and not just among the body of believers, but also among non-believers.

Take Daniel, for example, who was cast into a lion's den (Daniel 6:16), or Jeremiah who was thrown into a ditch-like prison at the request of the people and king (Jeremiah 37:15). And we cannot forget John the Baptist, who was cast into prison and eventually beheaded because of the lustful wickedness of a king (Mark 6:21-28). The persecution of prophets has always been at the hands of their very own people. And very rarely is it at the hands of a stranger. And even if a stranger does arrive somewhere behind the scenes, the culprit can always be traced back to the family of the prophet:

"...I will send them prophets and apostles, and some of them they shall slay and persecute" (Luke 11:49b).

Wherefore, behold, I send unto you prophets, and wise men, and scribes: and some of them ye shall kill and crucify; and some of them shall ye scourge in your synagogues, and persecute them from city to city (Matthew 23:34).

This is why prophets are so anti-social and socially awkward. They realize that the very same people they are called to serve may demand their crucifixion (sooner rather than later)! And adding injury to insult, the children of Israel's ancestors are the premiere prophetic assassins. We see this when Jesus was active in his earthly ministry. He confronted them about this very issue. Below are a few scriptural examples of Jesus placing Israel into contempt for the former desolations made of the lives of God's prophets:

Ye are the children of the prophets, and of the covenant which God made with our fathers, saying unto Abraham, And in thy seed shall all the kindreds of the earth be blessed (Acts 3:25).

Woe unto you, scribes and Pharisees, hypocrites! Because ye build the tombs of the prophets, and garnish the sepulchers of the righteous (Matthew 23:29).

And say, If we had been in the days of our fathers, we would not have been partakers with them in the blood of the prophets (Matthew 23:30).

Wherefore ye be witnesses unto yourselves, that ye are the children of them which killed the prophets (Matthew 23:31).

Let's not forget, too, the story of Joseph and his brothers (Genesis 37), or Isaiah, who was rumored to be sawed in half (Hebrews 11:37a). Unfortunately, it is the same with the Christian people against the Christian prophet. We have seen this in the more current examples of Dr. Martin Luther King, who was surely a prophet of God, murdered on a balcony in Memphis at the hands of another professing Christian and brother! Even though his murderer was of a different kind, the fact remains that he was a brother in Christ nonetheless.

And within the Muslim world, Malcolm X was murdered by a fellow Muslim while speaking at a religious service. These examples teach that prophets die by the hand of their very own people. And a death of a prophet, by the hands of his fellow brother, surely demonstrates that a prophet is without honor among his very own people. It further teaches how far people will go to exercise prophetic dishonor. In fact, they will take dishonor to high levels of ridicule, abuse, slander, and even physical death if need be.

And when there is no prophetic honor, persecution, disbelief, disrespect, and disdain are realities. In some cases, even death might occur. But God always honors his prophet! And in that divine honor there is certainly more than enough inspiration to sustain the prophet's ministry. But it is truly unfortunate that we are not our brother's keeper. It is equally unfortunate that we keep doing harm to the prophet. This is why I believe that persecution and prophetic attacks are more enthralling than reverence and respect, which are so deserved.

But God says that he is not mocked. What a man sows that he shall also reap. The prophet who faithfully serves will reap an undeniable great reward. The prophet slayer that relentlessly severer a prophetic voice from the intended target of a people, will certainly reap the darkest dungeon in the depths of hell. There they will reside until the Lake of Fire and Brimstone has reached its highest boiling point, joining all wicked men who find themselves eternally therein!

The Conclusion of the Conflict Concerning Prophetic Honor:

Yes, God is still sending prophets (Ephesians 4:11). But fellow men are still persecuting and attempting to kill them: Matthew 23:34. For Jerusalem is personified as the prophet's murderer (Matthew 23:37a; Luke 13:34a). Thus, it was the Jewish people that persecuted the Jewish prophets (Matthew 5:12; Matthew 23:31b; Acts 7:52 and cr. Amos 7:12). So it would be Christians that kill Christian prophets.

Jesus testified continuously of this until his final days of ministry. He explained that even he would be offered as a living sacrifice on the behalf of the sins of the world. He further explained that this sacrifice (execution style) would come at the request of his very own people. And the very people Jesus ministered, a week before, later yelled out, "crucify him!" (Mark 15:13-14, Luke 23:21, John 19:6).

Please realize that if they will kill Jesus, they can certainly try to kill you too! So every prophet must become conditioned with this understanding. Each prophet is sent to live by the church, and certainly each one will die because of, or at the hands of the church. Jesus knew that he had to die inside the gates of Jerusalem and not in the hands of the outside world:

Nevertheless I must walk today, and tomorrow, and the day following: for it cannot be that a prophet perish out of Jerusalem (Luke 13:33).

See other translations for additional confirmation:

"...Surely no prophet can die outside Jerusalem!" (NIV)

"Besides, it's not proper for a prophet to come to a bad end outside Jerusalem" (Message)

But there is vindication promised for every persecution, attack, slander, and even murder of any true prophet. God will require every drop of blood extracted out of a prophet's life by the hands of every man who has ever hurt him. And God will cause this retribution to be paid in full. And each generation that is a prophet-slayer must become accountable for every prophet's suffering and murder: Luke 11:50-51. This is why prophetic persecution is mentioned in the word. But it is also how prophetic persecution will be resolved by God's word.

I tell you, people will not get away with anything! If God is tough on prophets, then he is going to be equally tough on those who have to receive prophets. The church is without excuse. And the church will be held accountable. This is why the church must overcome this inherited behavior. In addition, the church has been called to progress within the necessity of building better fellowships and relationships with God and one another. And it is my strong belief that a prophetic community is birthed for this very reason. The prophetic community was established to cover and care for the prophetic voice and gift. And the purpose and revelations about prophetic community are discussed further in the book *The New Prophetic Generation*.

Despite the various prophetic communities, general socialism must be activated even more, and the prophet must be able to integrate among his own type of people. By bridging the gap between the prophet and his people, there will grow a healthier prospective of functionality among the prophets who minister, as well as among the people who are assigned to receive their ministry. Hopefully, the church will awaken to her proper consciousness. The more honors God's prophets receive, the more the church glorifies God. For this honor is retroactively due to all prophets – past, present, and future!

The Proper Honor Due to the Prophet:

The Primary Point to a Prophet's Prevalence is Honor

Just as there are ways to dishonor the prophet, there are certainly ways to honor the prophetic anointing. The presence of obedience, belief, and mature spirituality establishes prophetic honor! For we must realize that the prophetic anointing, the voice of God, and the authority of God's word are all synonymous. Thus, the believer is advised to learn to trust and obey the Lord through the ministry of the prophets.

"...Believe in the Lord your God, so shall ye be established; believe His prophets, so shall ye prosper" (2 Chronicles 20:20b).

This teaches that believing in the prophet of God, because you believe in God, is what produces legitimate and authentic prophetic honor. We understand there is certainly a love-hate relationship between the people of God and God's true prophets. But the prophet is uniquely designed for the promotion of belief. And the goal of the people is to make sure they do not miss God's move by missing the move of God's prophet. Usually, the lack of spirituality and supernatural awareness become the major means of unclear discernment for any true prophetic voice:

Also, thou son of man, the children of thy people still are talking against thee by the walls and in the doors of the houses, and speak one to another, every one to his brother, saying, come, I pray, and hear what is the word that cometh forth from the Lord. And they come unto thee as the people cometh, and they sit before thee as my people, and they hear thy words, but they will not do them; for with their mouth they show much love, but their

heart goeth after their covetousness. And, lo, thou art unto them as a very lovely son of one that hath a pleasant voice, and can play well on an instrument: for they hear thy words, but they do them not. And when this cometh to pass, (lo, it will come,) then shall they know that a prophet hath been among them. (Ezekiel 33:30-33).

This scripture teaches how the encountering of the prophetic, for most people, is often delayed. In the abovementioned excerpt, the people were mesmerized by the existence and ability of the prophet. Yet at the same time, they were intrigued that the prophet was sent as a literal spokesman of God. For the people of God knew that if they needed any additional help with basic or advanced matters concerning the natural and supernatural realms – all they needed to do was find the prophet of God. But their lack of obedience, faith, and reception caused enduring hesitancy.

For the prophet of God was designed to help them solve any dilemma. But they also understood that if they would seek the presence of the prophet, then honor would have to coincide with their approach. And the first level of honor is true recognition of the prophet's ability. This again is the subjective matter of faith in God, and faith in God's prophet. For when there is true faith, there emerges the beginning of true honor towards the prophet:

Then said Saul to his servant, but, behold, if we go, what shall we bring the man? For the bread is spent in our vessels, and there is not a present to bring to the man of God: what have we? And the servant answered Saul again, and said, behold I have here at hand the fourth part of a shekel of silver: that will I give to the Man of God, to tell us our way. (1 Samuel 9:7-8).

The proper reception of prophetic words from any prophet, both past, present, and even future, is to provide true honor to the prophetic presence within a given kingdom. And this same respect is now required even within his Holy Church. The Apostle Paul taught the importance of giving honor to those considered worthy of being called honorable:

Render therefore to all their dues: tribute to whom tribute is due; custom to whom custom; fear to whom fear; honor to whom honor. (Romans 13:7).

Even though the prophet does not have honor within his own country, it is still the job of all believers to restore honor to the name and presence of the prophet. We are to respect the prophet's gift, and we are to recognize this gift is established among the body of Christ. Just as the nation of Israel was called to respect the prophetic presence, we, too, within his Holy Church, are called to do the same. And it first starts with faith. For it is the presence of the prophet and the name of the prophet that God greatly considers. And if we don't have faith, we cannot please God (Hebrews 11:6). But if we do have the faith, we not only please God, but we can also honor the prophet of God more properly.

For we also realize that in the presence of a true prophet, a better faith is procured. We don't have to worry about losing faith, but we do have to prepare for gaining more faith. The word declares: faith comes by hearing and hearing by the word of God (Romans 10:17). It is in the hearing of the prophetic word that another dimension of faith is gleaned. And since this revelation is made clear, honoring the prophet only establishes the opportunity to please God, gain more faith, and receive the greater answers that only a prophet can provide.

Even when Paul taught Timothy about the system of honoring that exists among the ecclesia, Paul told Timothy that certain leaders will labor in both word and doctrine. Paul said that if a prophet were a true prophet of God, he, too, would become an elder of word and doctrines. For even Apostles were first made elders (1 Peter 5:1).

But a rouge and renegade prophet will have not finalize his first works or principal steps of eldership, which are certainly based on the doctrine of ecclesiology. This is not something that should be done through the Internet and shady online acquisitions, or by unqualified reformations. Instead, it should be done in a solidified body of a local church under one's current pastor or spiritual parent. If not through this means, then it should be done through a formal university of Christian studies and theological development.

If the first works associated with the doctrine of ecclesiology are not completed, prophetic authority will certainly diminish along with the potential to procure honor within the body of Christ. For only those who are ordained elders elevated into the office of prophet are given double honor (1 Timothy 5:17). In this New Testament era, apostolically speaking, we are to ordain elders first, in every church, before we focus on confirming of asserting to the five-fold gifting:

For this cause left I thee in Crete, that thou shouldest set in order the things that are wanting, and ordain elders in every city, as I had appointed thee (Titus 1:5).

What the doctrine of ecclesiology teaches us with the doctrine of prophetism is this: there is a criterion for conferment of honor unto the prophet just as there is a criterion for the prophetic recipient to show honor to the prophet. And if the prophet is not confirmed in the Lord's church, that prophet is not worthy of the honor of which we speak. But if that prophet has been confirmed in the Lord's church, we are to give that prophet honor as the word of God informs:

- One, because they are God's man of God
- Two, because he is properly ordained as an elder in the Lord's church
- Three, because he is known for laboring in the word and doctrines of God
- Four, because he is a true preacher of the Gospel of Jesus Christ
- Five, because his prophetic works and messages are sound and with a proven track record of coming to pass

So, when we honor the prophet and properly receive him, we are merely setting ourselves up to prosper. One cannot obey the words of the prophet if one does not also respect the messenger. The obedience we give to true prophetic voices establishes a door opening in heaven. God releases manifold blessings as the result of such honoring. When this honoring comes forth – and this proper recognition will come forth – the prophet's reward is not too far behind.

And in the eyes of God, Christian socialism and prophetism are required to become more operative and less dysfunctional. Sure, we are to try a spirit by the Spirit, and we are to allow the spirit of the prophet to be subject to the prophet. For in the prophet's ministry, there reside possible ventures of victory, blessings, and divine benefits. And the only way to respect someone is to learn from him. It is time for the congregation of God to learn the personality, purpose, and presence of the prophet:

We ask you, brothers, to respect those who labor among you and are over you in the Lord and admonish you, and to esteem them very highly in love because of their work. Be at peace among yourselves - 1 Thessalonians 5:17-20 (ESV).

Prophets who are properly integrated into each local congregation can have a positive impact on the congregation. And they do not have to always have a negative reputation as many would like to give them. As in the case of Israel when they were under attack by the tri-fold threat of Ammon, Moab, and Mt. Seir, it was the voice of the prophetic that directed the king and the nation. It was Jehoshaphat who had the highest respect and regard for any true prophetic voice, being a man well acquainted with prophets and prophecy. So, when the Levitical-prophet stood and prophesied within the camp, no one rejected the words of the Lord that flowed from God's mouth:

The Doctrine of Prophecy

Then upon Jahaziel the son of Zechariah, the son of Benaiah, the son of Jiel, the son of Mattaniah, a Levite of the sons of Asaph, came the Spirit of the Lord in the midst of the congregation (2 Chronicles 20:14).

You cannot go wrong when you deliberately and intricately follow the instructions of the prophet. In the instructions, you are exemplifying your faith in God. And the prophet who gives such instructions must also have confidence in a prophet's prophetic office and the source of his prophetic work. God will never let a true prophet's words fall to the ground, because that prophet is ordained to speak in the name and power of God.

What society and the church have to learn is that the protocol of the prophetic is virtually the same, even in today's time. And God requires sacrifices and gifts whenever a person is in the presence of a true prophet. Again, honoring the prophet first starts with the right mentality. You must come with faith when you are allowed to be in a prophet's presence. A great example of this is when the woman encountered Elijah on her way to prepare her last meal for her son, before accepting their moment of death. When she met him, she was very skeptical about giving up the last bit of oil and meal. But she had to first feed the prophet. And in those instructions, it was clear that not only a challenge had arrived, but also an opportunity for a breakthrough:

So he arose and went to Zarephath. And when he came to the gate of the city, behold, the widow woman was there gathering of sticks: and he called to her, and said, Fetch me, I pray thee , a little water in a vessel, that I may drink. And as she was going to feth it, he called ot her, and said, bring me, I pray thee, a morsel of bread in thine hand. And she said, as the Lord thy God liveth, I have not a cake, but a handful of meal in a barrel, and a little oil in a cruse: and, behold, I am gathering two sticks, that I may go in an dress it for me and my son, that we may eat it, and die. And Elijah said unto her, fear not: go and do as thou hast said: but make me thereof a little cake first, and bring it unto me, and after make for thee and for thy son. For thus saith the Lord God of Israel, the barrel of meal shall not waste, neither shall the cruse of oil fail, until the day that the Lord sendeth rain upon the earth (1 Kings 17:10-14).

The Apostle Paul has given further clarity that God made the prophet one of the chief governmental gifts within the five-fold and His the church (Ephesians 4:11; 1 Corinthians 12:28). This teaches that the prophet is called, in some respects, to have greater rule over you than a pastor or a bishop. And when you submit to the ruling and ministry of a prophet, you are thus properly honoring the prophetic gift and anointing. More importantly, you are now honoring God! Never is the prophet God! But God is the source of the prophetic anointing! And in that prophetic anointing may reside you next blessing and or breakthrough!

Apostle Sherman D. Farmer

The True Definition and Application of a Prophet's Reward: *"He that receiveth a prophet in the name of a prophet shall receive a prophet's reward..." (Matthew 10:41a, KJV).*

Systematic giving unto a prophet demonstrates high prophetic honoring! And an Israelite's typical approach towards an Old Testament prophet was to bring a love offering or gift as a form of respect. This respect was always for God as well as for the prophet's position and purpose. Usually, the person could offer whatever means of accommodation of honor. This usually ranged from money, livestock, food, or other resources:

And it fell on a day, that Elisha passed to Shunem, where was a great woman; and she constrained him to eat bread. And so it was, that as oft as he passed by, he turned in thither to eat bread. And she said unto her husband, behold now, I perceive that this is a holy man of god, which passeth by us continually. Let us make a little chamber, I pray thee, on the wall; and let us set for him there a bed, and a table, and a stool, and a candlestick: and it shall be, when he cometh to us, that he shall turn in thither. (2 Kings 4:8-10).

Whether the prophet is liked or disliked, God creates a special way to provide for the prophet. We see this clearly with Elijah at the brook Cherith during a famine. In that scene, God miraculously sent provisions to the man of God so that he could be sustained. This teaches that no true man of God will ever lack. God will always allow the life of his prophet to prosper. Even in the midst of recession and famine, God will ensure survival through the use of miracles, as well as through requiring people to honor the prophet by giving from their bosom, especially in their time of need:

And the word of the Lord came unto him, saying, get thee hence, and turn thee eastward, and hide thyself by the brook Cherith, that is before Jordan. And it shall be, that thou shalt drink of the brook; and I have commanded the ravens to feed thee there. So he went and did according unto the word of the Lord; for he went and dwelt by the brook Cherith, that is before Jordan. And the ravens brought him bread and flesh in the morning, and bread and flesh in the evening; and he drank of the brook. (1 Kings 17:2-6).

The survival of the prophet in any condition, reality, or experience is what we can call the prophet's favor. This favor is also called "a prophet's reward." It is also important to note that the prophet who understands God has established a unique bartering system between the prophet and a prophetic recipient. God makes miraculous merchandise by way of the prophetic gift. He will cause miracles to flow from the hands of the prophet because the prophet is connected to the source of miracles – God. The prophetic recipient is thus required to make the sacrifice to assist the prophet by following his instruction, as they also enters into a greater act of worship unto God. Even Jesus uses this system! Jesus demonstrated that giving will open certain portals in heaven by way of the Spirit:

Then cometh He to a city of Samaria, which is called Sychar, near to the parcel of ground that Jacob gave to his son Joseph. Now Jacob's well was there. Jesus therefore, being wearied with His journey, sat thus on the well: and it was about the sixth hour. There cometh a woman of Samaria to draw water: Jesus saith unto her, give me to drink. (For His disciples were gone away unto the city to buy meat.) Then saith the woman of Samaria unto Him, how is it that thou, being a Jew, askest drink of me, which am a woman of Samaria? For the Jews have no dealing with the Samaritans. Jesus answered and said unto her, if thou knowest the gift of God, and who it is that saith to thee, give me to drink; thou wouldest have asked of him, and he would have given thee living water. (John 4:5-10).

Thus, giving is a sacred part of worship. Giving teaches one to be selfless before God. In biblical times, whether Levitical, priestly, or prophetic, the system of giving to spiritual leaders was not as much for leaders as it is for worshippers. Today, the prophet's reward remains that of effective operation within the body of Christ. In fact, Jesus Christ mentions this during the writings of the New Testament era. For a Prophet's reward isn't merely having supernatural and spiritual favor from God. A prophet's reward is also a dual favor among the natural and human realms:

"And he said to Gehazi his servant, call this Shunammite. And when he had called her, she stood before him. And he said unto him, say now unto her, behold, thou hast been careful for us with all this care; what is to be done for thee? Wouldest thou be spoken for to the kin, or to the captain of the hosts?" (2 Kings 4:13a).

However, the reward is not one that the prophet should conjure or compel men to give to them. Instead, it is a special act of giving that is done from one's heart. It is through divine compulsion that the worshipper gives to God. And those who are prophetic, and clearly operate under the New Testament dispensation of grace, must understand that this system is solely because Jesus has released it.

Apostolically, it is my job to share with you that this principle is to remain (i.e. it is considered a binding section within the word of God). Therefore I exhort to you that God is continuously allowing this. So it will not be dissolved or become loosed by rabbinical standard (see Matthew 16:19). And Paul, the Apostle, further assists with this understanding:

As we have therefore opportunity, let us do good unto all men, especially unto them who are of the household of faith. (Galatians 6:10).

Who goeth a warfare any time as his own charges? Who planteth a vineyard, and eateth not of the fruit thereof? Or who feedeth the flock, and eateth not of the milk of the flock? Say I these things as a man? Or saith not the law at the same also? For it is written in the law of Moses, thou shalt not muzzle the mouth of the ox that treadeth out the corn. Doth God take care for oxen? Or saith he it altogether for our sakes? For our sakes, no doubt, this is written: that he that ploweth should plow in hope; and that he that thresheth in hope should be partaker of his hope...Do ye know that they which minister about holy things live of the things of temple? And they which wait at the altar are partakers of the altar? Even so hath the Lord ordained that they which preach the gospel should live of the gospel. (1 Corinthians 9:7-10, 13-14).

What this means is this: it pays to take care of the people of God, and even more, the man of God This is not a private interpretation, as the Bible declares about all teachings on prophecy (2 Peter 1:20). Thus, giving to the prophet is both reasonable and sound. This principle of the past is certainly applicable for the present and future. This, then, is still an act of worship, not to the prophet, but always to God. Because God is the maker of prophets. And this type of worship is God's alone.

Nevertheless, the modern New Testament Prophet is a preacher of the Gospel first and foremost. For the prophetic mantle is intricately wrapped into his gospel ministry. He, too, lives by the work of the Gospel. And it is still safe to say that the prophet should continually live by means of the prophetic, never making money his prevalence and instead making people – the true essence of ministry – the primary source of his prevalence. Even Paul teaches that he who preaches the gospel must live off the Gospel (1 Corinthians 9:14). In like manner, so should the prophet naturally survive from their prophetic anointing!

Here, the prophet is charged and challenged to remain ethically and biblically sound. This is imperative. The prophet's reward should not be marred by greed or controversy, and it should instead bring more glory to God. It should not be a cause of hindrance to the power of the prophetic or the proclamation of the Gospel! And when the church restores such harmonies, the prophet's prevalence can fully return to the body of Christ. For it is in honoring and respecting the prophet that the prophet can highly function. Yet the word of God declares that:

"...The laborer is worthy of his reward" (1 Timothy 5:18b).

In Jesus' ministry, for example, when the lack of faith was present, Jesus still preached. However, he did not prophesy and produce miracles in certain regions that were devoid of the essentials of faith and friendliness towards the prophet. Neither did he perform on demand just because people wanted proof or performance like Jesus was a side-show or spectacle. Take the example of Herod:

And when Herod saw Jesus, he was exceeding glad; for he was desirous to see him of a long season, because he had heard many things of him; and he hoped to have seen some miracle done by him. Then he questioned with him in many words; but he answered him nothing (Luke 23:8-9, KJV).

CONCLUSION OF LESSON 4:

The prophet's prevalence should not come in the form of entertainment, mockery, or worldliness. Furthermore, the prophet is most prevalent in the realm of faith. And the combined actions of faith, obedience, and abstinence from sin must always be found within the body of Christ. For without faith there is no pleasing of God (Hebrews 11:6). And without these three virtues, there is no true prophetic performance.

Subsequently, money is a byproduct of God's service. It is never the original intention to accept the assignment for service. However, it will come along whether one does proper prophetic service or not. For a man that does not work does not eat (2 Thessalonians 3:10). And it is true though that all men will be judged for the type of work they built on the foundation of Jesus Christ (1 Corinthians 3:11-15).

When prophets walk in more integrity, the conflicts of socialism and the misdiagnosis of true prophets will dissolve. Until then, the prophet has to endure hardships caused by those familiar and unfamiliar to him. Realizing that one's ministry is ultimately about hearing God saying, "well done thy good and faithful servant" (Matthew 25:23). The prophet is to remain always vigilant. For the prevalence of ministry is about people, and the gift of God profits men more than it should the prophet (1 Corinthians 12:7)!

CHAPTER 5

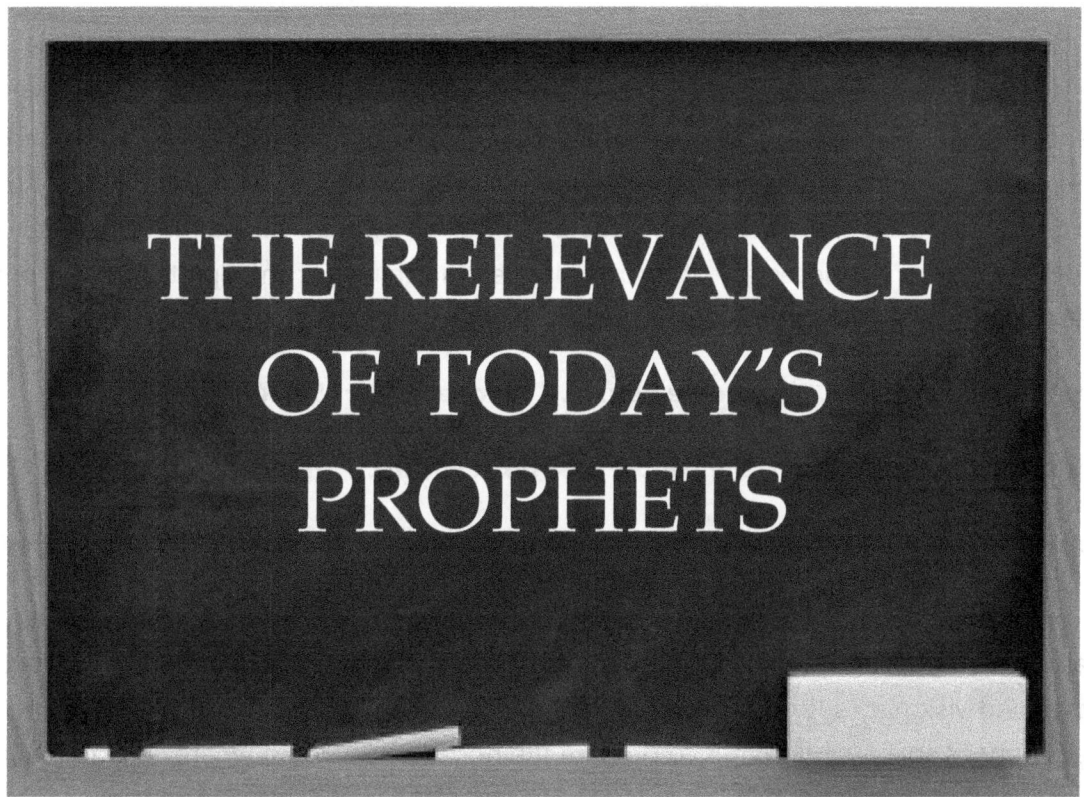

Why is the Prophet Still Necessary?

And I fell at his feet to worship him. And he said unto me, see thou do it not: I am thy fellow servant, and of thy brethren that have the testimony of Jesus: worship God: for the testimony of Jesus is the spirit of prophecy (Revelation 19:10).

Overview - Visions and Visionaries:

I will stand upon my watch, and set me upon the tower, and will watch to see what He will say unto me, and what I shall answer when I am reproved. And the Lord answered me, and said, write the vision, and make it plain upon tables, that he may run that readeth it. For the vision is yet for an appointed time, but at the end it shall speak, and not lie: though it tarry, wait for it; because it will surely come, it will not tarry (Habakkuk 2:1-3, KJV).

This biblical declaration demonstrates how vision is vital like air and water are natural needs. Without vision, people have a tendency to become spiritually paralyzed and in some cases endure a spiritual death. This is why the prophet of God must seek vision. Habakkuk, then, acts as a classic example of this. He sought God to clarify the situations of his day. As a prophet and priest he stood on the watchtower. Like a faithful watchman, he waited for clarity. This is why the prophetic is still necessary. It further clarifies the things of the Spirit. And the power of prophetic vision will prevent spiritual destruction:

"Where there is no vision, the people perish..." (Proverbs 29:18a, KJV)

"Where there is no revelation, the people cast off restraint..." (NIV)

"If people can't see what God is doing they stumble all over themselves..." (Message Bible)

We need visions as much as we need prophets. And visions typically occur when man's spiritual eyesight becomes dim. This is the sole purpose of a visionary. The prophet is a watchman and visionary set on the wall of two worlds: the spirit world and this decaying world. But the prophet's sole assignment is to prepare the house of God with whatever God reveals:

Son of man, I have made thee a watchman unto the house of Israel: therefore hear the word at thy mouth, and give them warning from me (Ezekiel 3:17, KJV).

This is why the presence of a legitimate prophet is still necessary. Now, in fact, we need a prophet more than ever before! We need a prophet who accurately voices the truth of God through the ministry of Jesus Christ; one who speaks clearly and accurately the mysterious ways of God through Jesus Christ; one who clearly interprets the wisdom found within the spirit realm that is accessible by faith in Jesus Christ; one who can discern the times, seasons, and world events as well as their relevance to the testimony of Jesus Christ; and one who can consistently break the cycle of the lack of understanding, discretion, and divine direction. If you find one who can do most of that, then he is your prophet!

Again, notice the reference to Proverbs 29:18 and its various translations (see page 130). For the consequences are grave when the prophetic voice is absent. Simply put, it is very important to have vision and a visionary! If there is no vision, chaos will ensure. There will be stumbling, followed by casting off restraint, which unfortunately ends with great fatality, spiritually and physically. In the spirit realm things always happen first spiritually, but they are always followed by the natural.

Surely these are the consequences for a place and a people lacking prophetic voice and vision. If the prophet is absent, silenced, or forced out, then catastrophic events are sure to come. Because the prophet's purpose is to protect a people by prophetic intercession, which is the means whereby God prevents anything from removing people from God's presence and plan.

And as a mouthpiece of God, the prophet can only transmit what God wants and says. For the prophet of God is a revealer of God's secrets, as well as of the people's errors, which lead to a decline in their faith in God. When the prophet releases the divine word of God, his words authenticate a prophet's ministry. Only a true prophet has spent time with the Lord. This is how true prophets are exclusively entrusted with great mysteries:

And he said unto him, behold now, there is in this city a man of God, and he is an honorable man; all that he saith cometh surely to pass: now let us go thither; peradventure he can show us our way that we should go (1 Samuel 9:6).

If a prophet never prophesies, he is still required to provide spiritual answers. A prophet provides both natural and spiritual direction. He is God's skilled agent for suitable articulation of the supernatural realms. He is also an equally skilled agent of knowledge, understanding and wisdom concerning the natural. This is why people went to the prophet to inquire about major and minor life events. Even if a person loses an object or a person, the prophet's ability to talk with God provides true clarity and undeniable resolution. The status of the misplaced thing or person would eventually change after speaking with a true prophet. Not only do prophets provide general counseling, but they are also used as geographical compasses:

And Jehoshaphat said, is there not here a prophet of the Lord, that we may inquire of the Lord by him? And one of the king of Israel's servants answered and said, here is Elisha the son of Shaphat, which poured water on the hands of Elijah (2 Kings 3:11).

Thus, the true prophet's ministry will always advertise itself. And the reputation of the win-win scenarios a prophet provides is impeccable. You will know a true prophet by the fluidity of his gift. You will also hear of the consistent, rock solid testimonies of a prophet's ability. This, then, is the only way to confirm a prophet. After the prophet is called and released, he has to build a consistent track record. Only time and maturity can solidify such claims, and every prophet mentioned in scripture has this same testimony.

Thus, Jesus gave this gift to the church by giving various men and women this assignment. We who are of such assignment were strategically placed in our mother's womb and with our parents DNA and God's divine directive upon our lives. We are responsible now for remaining true to our Christian heritage and faith. Thus, God has given prophets of the New Testament because we are still within the New Testament period. He has given them and those of us this assignment to assume the same responsibility for the current manifestation of God, which is none other than Jesus Christ.

This is why we are still in need of later-day New Testament prophets of God. For the later-day New Testament prophets of Jesus Christ are still relevant in modern times and this spiritual dispensation. For somewhere in this world, right now, there is wrong insight, vision, and perspective of God. And God has released the resolution in the current manifestation of the prophetic ministry. Both vision and visionaries are yet alive and are here to reveal the vision of Jesus Christ, through his glorious Gospel. They are here to stand as representatives of Jesus Christ, the truest visionary of all visionaries!

How Should the Contemporary Prophet Begin?

Jesus Christ

And I fell at his feet to worship him. And he said unto me, see thou do it not: I am thy fellow servant, and of thy brethren that have the testimony of Jesus: worship God: for the testimony of Jesus is the spirit of prophecy (Revelation 19:10).

The last clause of this very scripture should become the mantra of every current prophet's ministry. For without the manifestation of such revelation, the purpose of the later-day New Testament prophet literally will be obsolete. This revelation has the power to dissolve the conflict between the doctrines of Continuationism and Cessationism. If Jesus' testimony is the premise to the prophetic anointing, then the prophetic anointing cannot dissolve until the testimony of Jesus is fully completed. Therefore, we who are fully aware of the theology of Christ know that Jesus' work is still being accomplished:

Then cometh the end, when he shall have delivered up the kingdom to God, even the Father: when he shall have put down all rule and all authority and power. For he must

reign till he hath put all enemies under his feet. The last enemy that shall be destroyed is death. For he hath put all things under his feet. But when he saith all things are put under him, it is manifest that he is excepted, which did put all things under him. And when all things shall be subdued unto him, then shall the Son also himself be subject unto him that put all things under him, that God may be all in all (1 Corinthians 15:24-28).

Say this with me:

The Spirit of Prophecy is the Testimony of Jesus Christ

Note: the testimony of Jesus is why the prophetic anointing still exists!

It is true that the Bible says that when we see Jesus, we shall be like him (1 John 3:2). It is also quite obvious that the church is not finalized in this regard. Jesus is still coming for a church without spot or wrinkle (Ephesians 5:26). Until then, the church must continue to reach its highest and fullest measure of maturity. And we who are of the five-fold are entrusted agents of this gradual type of change.

The purpose of creating such a divine complement in the formation of the Bride of Christ speaks to the depths of the combined prophetic and Gospel message. Most are taught that the Gospel surely resides only in the death, burial, and resurrection of our Lord. Unfortunately, we are sadly mistaken. If we keep ourselves from the totality of our Lord's testimony, we will continuously miss the very premise of the prophetic anointing. Simply put, Jesus has been resurrected, but his work is being finished in us. And the Bible says that Jesus will finalize his work at the appointed time. Until such time, the prophet of God is called to release greater works within each distinct anointing that God has given each prophet:

Verily, verily, I say unto you, He that believeth on me, the works that I do shall he do also; and greater works than these shall he do; because I go unto my Father (John 14:12).

The prophet is birthed into a New Testament church to produce greater prophetic works. These prophetic works are greater than the ones that even Jesus and the prophets of old performed. The Greek word for testimony is *martyria* (mar-too-ree-ah), which simply means, "testifying." We are to testify of him through our distinct ministries. But we all come together when we testify. Therefore, we all should know the full scope of Christ's testimony:

- ➤ Jesus Christ was born and he literally lived upon the face of this earth for 33 years.

- ➤ Jesus Christ died and was buried, but he rose again on the 3rd day after his death.

- Jesus delivered the Old Testament saints from the depths of Hell during the periods of his ascending and descending between the world and heaven.

- Jesus sojourned on the earth for 40 days before his final ascension.

- Jesus is coming back for his church through the rapture.

- Jesus will then release the Great Tribulation (7 years – 3 ½ years of peace and 3 ½ years of war).

- Jesus shall return for a millennial reign (1,000 years as a symbolic act of restoring dominion to mankind).

- Jesus will create the great culmination and consummation after the millennial reign. This is the period when all things will be returned back into the hands of God the Father. This is the end of the Testimony according to scripture.

Thus, Jesus' testimony is more than his life, death, burial, and resurrection. It surely extends into the other aspects just mentioned. Thus, we who are of Christ must believe in the totality of his testimony, which is still prophetic in nature. His testimony is still about a prediction that has not fully been completed! The Apostle Paul explained some of this fact very eloquently and concisely, as he wrote to his beloved son Timothy:

And without controversy great is the mystery of godliness: God was manifest in the flesh, justified in the Spirit, seen of angels, preached unto the Gentiles, believed on in the world, received up into glory (1 Timothy 3:1).

So we must thoroughly learn his testimony in order to become a better prophet of God. For the Gospel and prophetic work are undeniably interconnected. Truly there is no possible avoidance of this truth. Again, this is the very reason why the prophetic is still necessary. Jesus' life, death, burial, and resurrection, as well as the rapturing of the church, the second coming, and the millennial reign, all must be seen. They are not just parts of the puzzle. Neither can the portions of Jesus deemed worthy of emphasis be done by a church's subjective taste. But every single aspect of the scriptures must come to pass!

And even every prophet must be just as passionate about Jesus' testimony as he is about his own distinct prophetic mantle. This is very necessary for any Gospel-preaching prophet and not just a prophet who prophesies. For every five-fold gift is a representative of Jesus Christ, and therefore, each gift should uphold the same regard for the blood-stained banner. This is why the New Testament prophet's ministry truly begins with the testimony of Jesus Christ:

"Christ has generously divided out his gifts to us." As the Scriptures say, 'when he went up to the highest place, he led away many prisoners and gave gifts to people.' When it says, 'he went up,' it means that Christ has been deep in the earth. This also means that the one who went deep into the earth is the same one who went into the highest heaven, so that he would fill the whole universe. Christ chose some of us to be apostles, prophets, missionaries, pastors, and teachers, so that his people would learn to serve and his body would grow strong.

This will continue until we are united by our faith and by our understanding of the Son of God. Then we will be mature, just as Christ did, and we will be completely like him. We must stop acting like children. We must not let deceitful people trick us by their false teachings, which are like winds that toss us around from place to place" Ephesians 4:7-14 (Contemporary English Version).

Thus, regions, operations, administrations, mantles, mediums, messages, dispensations, time dimensions, development of prophetic productivity, sensitivity, and vocality all lead us directly to Jesus Christ. Yes, we will discuss all of these matters later on in the book. But the point is this: nothing a prophet does is without the mission and ministry of the Lord Jesus Christ! If we have Christ, we have our relevance.

Prophesying is a Christian work! Never should prophesying be performed under the guise of an Old Testament spirit and mentality. The current prophetic expression is drenched in the great grace and mercies of God. Again, this work is done solely under the auspices of Jesus Christ. Whether past, present, or future the prophetic office has maintained this functionality.

Thus, everything we read in the Holy Bible, whether we understand it or not, points to Jesus Christ. It is the safest resolve for any five-fold ministry. Simply put, if you walk with Jesus, you'll never mess up your prophetic ministry! Let's break it down even further: apostles should be about Christ! Prophets should be about Christ! Evangelists should be about Christ! Pastors should be about Christ! Teachers should be about Christ! Bishops should be about Christ! Elders should be about Christ! Deacons should be about Christ! And ministers should be about Christ! All these are Christian positions within the Lord's church. So they should have a Christian agenda.

This is the strongest answer to all conflicts and difficulties that arise when anyone reads or hears the word of God. Simply put, Jesus is the answer for everything in scripture. Take for example when the Ethiopian Eunuch was reading a passage of Isaiah's prophetic collections. In this story, the Bible says that the Lord sent a witness in his direction named Philip.

The Doctrine of Prophecy

Philip was an appointed deacon in the Lord's church. And Philip was also called to be an Evangelist by way of the five-fold ministry. For God had ordained Philip to the position of Evangelist even before the people appointed him as a Deacon (Acts 6:1-7). And, as the Lord's evangelist, Philip readily and easily explained scripture to the Eunuch, essentially stating that all roads point in the direction of Jesus Christ:

And the angel of the Lord spake unto Philip, saying, arise, and go toward the south unto the way that goeth down from Jerusalem unto Gaza, which is desert. And he arose and went: and, behold, a man of Ethiopia, an eunuch of great authority under Candace queen of the Ethiopians, who had the charge of all her treasure, and had come to Jerusalem for to worship. Was returning, and sitting in his chariot read Esaias the prophet. Then the Spirit said unto Philip, go near, and join thyself to this chariot. And Philip ran thither to him, and heard him read the prophet Esaias, and said, understandest thou what thou readest?

And he said, How can I, except some man should guide me? And he desired Philip that he would come up and sit with him. The place of the scripture which he read was this, He was led as a sheep to the slaughter; and like a lamb dumb before his shearer, so opened not his mouth: In his humiliation his judgment was taken away: and who shall declare his generation? For his life is taken from the earth. And the eunuch answered Philip, and said, I pray thee, of whom speaketh the prophet of this? Of himself, or of some other man? Then Philip opened his mouth, and began at the same scripture, and preached unto him Jesus (Acts 8:26-35).

This passage further explains the definition of not only the true prophet, but also a false one. For a false prophet will not preach the name of Jesus or his testimony! And a false prophet will not evangelize the cause of Christ. This is how the people and a true prophet can discern a true prophet from a false one. For a false prophet does the work of Satan and never of Christ. This is how we are told to judge every spirit that comes into a congregation making such claims. And if their testimony isn't solidified in Jesus, then their ministry is ultimately invalid.

Hereby know ye the Spirit of God: Every spirit that confesseth that Jesus Christ is come in the flesh is of God: and every spirit that confesseth not that Jesus Christ is come in the flesh is not of God: and this is that spirit of antichrist, whereof ye have heard that it should come; and even now is it in the world (1 John 4:2-3).

What this unfortunately means in prophetism is that there will unfortunately be many around the prophetic who are not truly prophetic. There will be many who imitate such ability. This is why prophets must be designated by God exclusively and not by men. And what a prophet knows about Jesus will certainly determine how effective one's prophetic ministry shall be. There is no alternative or deviation from this truth.

We must be about the work of Christ so we can remain connected to an authentic and prophetic ministry. For there must be an initial confession that confirms one's true connection to the Holy Ghost as well as to the validity of such ministry (1 Corinthians 12:3). Remember: we must be born again, as Jesus told Nicodemus. The prophet's true ministry does not start until he has become a born-again believer who now prophesies for the Lord Jesus Christ. Below is the plan of Salvation, which God has easily mapped out for you:

But what saith it? The word is night thee, even in thy mouth, and in thy heart: that is, the word of faith, which we preach; that if thou shalt confess with thy mouth the Lord Jesus, and shalt believe in thine heart that God hath raised him from the dead, thou shalt be saved. For with the heart man believeth unto righteousness; and with the mouth confession is made unto salvation. For the scripture saith, whosoever believeth on him shall not be ashamed. For there is no difference between the Jew and the Greek: for the same Lord over all is rich unto all that call upon him. For whosoever shall call upon the name of the Lord shall be saved (Romans 10:8-13).

Then Peter said unto them, Repent, and be baptized ever one of you in the name of Jesus Christ for the remission of sins; and ye shall receive the gift of the Holy Ghost (Acts 2:38).

It is quite obvious that the primary infancy of our prophetic voice must start with the articulation of the Gospel of Jesus Christ! This is the very first prophetic word that we must put into practice! If your salvation is not clarified, then it is likely your prophetic ministry will remain obscure and diminished form its fullest capacity. Afterwards, a continual confessional should become the proper lifestyle of any prophetic mantle. Simply put, the prophet should even preach Jesus on a consistent basis!

The following questions now come to mind. What do you believe? Do you believe in Jesus Christ? If so, how strong is your belief in his testimony? For all complexities and roads within the depths of God trace its point of origin to this unforgettable truth: it's all about Jesus! Prophecy is all about Jesus! *Prophesying* is all about Jesus. And prophetic words, given in today's church, must always align with the testimony of Jesus.

We are either prophesying about his birth, death, resurrection, second coming, millennial reign, or final consummation before the heavenly Father. It doesn't matter if the prophetic message is about marriage, ministry, money, or mystery – somewhere within the essence of the prophetic word, Christ must be the center! The more we realize this, the more sound our prophetic expression and responsibility will become. This is why denominationalism or church reformation is not as important when learning the foundational doctrines of prophecy! For our religion should be that of Christianity, and our activity within our religion should be that of true discipleship:

And whatsoever ye do in word or deed, do all in the name of the Lord Jesus, giving thanks to God and the Father by him (Colossians 3:17).

This quote is very important. Many prophets today prophesy under the wrong influences and other spirits. And many prophesy under the guise of other hybrid of religious understandings. But it does not matter if you are Baptist, Holiness, Charismatic, or any other denomination, one thing remains chiefly universal: the Gospel of Jesus Christ is the password for all believers alike! And the doctrine of prophecy is one of many doctrinal byproducts that join the collective of our overall religion – Christianity!

A Lifetime Commitment and Study of Both Testaments

Study to shew thyself approved unto God, a workman that needeth not to be ashamed, rightly dividing the word of truth (2 Timothy 2:15).

Everything starts with a frame of reference. The airplane, for example, is modeled after a bird. A submarine is modeled after a fish. So it is with the prophetic gift. A prophet is modeled after the word of God. And the primary frame of reference found within the word of God is that of the angels. Angels and prophets share the same commonality. They both have orders. They both have divisions. And they both have unique purposes. But they all have the same fundamental objective: They are sent to reveal a message from God.

The more a prophet learns the whole counsel of scripture, the more prolific the prophet will become. The point is this: you cannot build anything without a proper blueprint. It is quite clear, too, that Jesus is the blueprint of every true prophet. And so the first portion of his blueprint begins with the Old and ends with the New Testament.

Even jobs of every industry come with a distinct jargon, meaning that certain words become sub-culture and the bedrock of communication within a particular group. For example, the language of healthcare practitioners (nurses and doctors) is different from the language of musicians. In the same vein, the language of the prophet is different from the language of the apostle and other five-fold gifting. Therefore, it is imperative that one learns the language of the prophet. Again, the prophet's finalization of its language, believe it or not, is the Gospel!

Unfortunately, many people mistakenly create a language apart from the word of God when functioning within prophetic ministry. This reason alone is why many prophets are confused about what true Christian prophetism entails. Therefore, each prophet must learn from his destined prophetic community. Only that particular community has the proper voice and anointing to give birth to them. And it is God who has predetermined which community they are actually assigned. For in that prophetic community resides the universal and personal prophetic language applicable to that prophet's gifting.

Just as one must learn the alphabet before writing sentences, the first voice of prophetic language that one must learn is one's own personal journey is through the word of God. We discover this by researching the prophets of old. The Bible is clear that the spirit of Christ was in every Judean and early Christian prophet as well as every Hebrew prophet. Therefore, we must study all of them. We must also analyze their words and understand their methods by confirming scripture with scripture. If we follow this blueprint, then a better building of prophetic ministry will happen.

And the first strategy is to pray before any method of study. As we pray, we must understand that our spirit is indeed willing but our flesh is weak. Paul taught that the war between the flesh and the spirit is the cause of all spiritual inertia. The place of spiritual inertia always finds its resting spot in the soul of man. Spiritual inertia causes the mind not to focus. It also causes a lack of achievement. Spiritual inertia will kill all goals, especially the important ones that you set out with the intention to fulfill in Christ (Galatians 5:17). Even studying the word of God will cause sluggishness. In fact, one of the wisest men, King Solomon, taught the ramifications of much study:

"...Much study is a weariness of the flesh" (Ecclesiastes 12:12b).

But after prayer, we must take our time and dissect the common phraseologies of the biblical prophets. Again, not only is this our means of language. But this is also our Christological legacy. I wanted you to be prepared for what I have discovered after many years of seeking truths through the word of God. And sometimes when people study, they instantly lose focus because of the written information. So, when all else fails, trust the God in you to teach you how to be a better prophet. For most people think spirituality is in the offering of another's lengthiness of expository or explanation. But the best teacher will always be God:

But the anointing which ye have received of him abideth in you, and ye need not that any man teach you: but as the same anointing teacheth you of all things, and is truth, and is no lie, and even as it hath taught you, ye shall abide in him (1 John 2:27).

For the ultimate goal is to present more of Christ from you into the world. Even while you're demonstrating prophetic ministry! And if this is your goal, then reading will have to become a routine part of your life. In fact, I now charge you to accept the reality of a lifetime of study. For there is much success when we study the word of God with the intention of using the word to edify others. And that world starts with the prophets of the Holy Bible. Because the truth is this: combining your anointing with the word of God will make a better prophet out of you!

Embrace the Collective Witnesses of the Evangelistic and Prophetic Anointing

The scriptures reveal that prophets and evangelists are constantly used as a synergy to promote more of Jesus' testimony within the world. The story of the Samaritan woman shows how prophets push the emergence of evangelists. The Samaritan woman first had to perceive that Jesus was indeed a prophet. After doing so, the ministry of the evangelist was born in her, and she became the greatest evangelist within her region:

The woman saith unto him, Sir, I perceive that thou art a prophet (John 4:19).

After the woman's divine conversion, she became the first evangelist of Samaria. And the Samaritan woman's zeal for Christ made her destiny emerge. She evangelized through the entire city with rapid energy and a diehard passion. Unfortunately, though, because of her former reputation, the people of Samaria did not want to receive her. But their doubts and discrepancies did not prevent her destiny. See the illustration clearly. Jesus the prophet helped the Samaritan woman, who then became an evangelist:

The woman then left her water-pot, and went her way into the city, and saith to the men, Come, see a man, which told me all things that ever I did: is not this the Christ? Then they went out of the city, and came unto him...and many Samaritans of that city believed on him for the saying of the woman, which testified, He told me all that ever I did (John 4:28-30, 39).

As you can see the socialism and prophetism issues are not that far removed even from those who operate as evangelists. When people learn your past, they will try to block you from your future. But it is God who qualifies. It is also God who calls. But the importance of this lesson is not just about validation, but also about vacillation. For the evangelist and the prophet's ministries both bring a people to the location of Jesus Christ.

The evangelist does it through the Gospel. The prophet does it through the prophetic word and the Gospel. And these sister gifts are in the same vein and complement one another. For the prophet does not disrespect the purpose and functionality of the evangelist. They are both harmoniously synchronized for the sole purpose of broadcasting the presence and power of God. In fact, both offices can shift between each other's function if they so desire. And what this also teaches is that the prophet of God must learn the work of evangelism. Also, the evangelist should venture to learn the work of prophetism. Yes, both are required to understand each other's purpose. For in each other's purpose is mutual fortification.

Another example is the evangelistic father, who has four prophetic daughters. During one of Paul's missionary journeys, he sojourned with the deacon and evangelist Philip. And it was at Philip's house that we learn that Philip's daughters were all prophetic:

And the next day we that were of Paul's company departed, and came unto Caesarea: and we entered into the house of Philip, the evangelist, which was one of the seven; and abode with him. And the same man had four daughters, virgins, which did prophesy (Acts 21:8-9).

Prophetic and evangelistic works can be coupled together as a sign of the evolution of the prophetic and evangelistic ministries. I like to call this hybrid of apostolic reality either "the prophetic-evangelist" or "the evangelistic prophet." And the revelation of these two gifts merging speaks to a greater purpose. If the prophet becomes a Gospel preacher, he will steer clear from doing wrong within his prophetic office. If the prophet is a messenger of the good news of God, his social status within the community and kingdom will change.

For the former functionality of the prophet's disposition brought the feeling of gloom and doom. But those who are prophets under the cause of Christ are inspiring praise and worship, greater fellowship, and stronger relationships by the goodness of God that leads men to repentance (Romans 2:4). Yes, we are still to rebuke sin. And we must continue to advocate for true conversion. But we must also trust the power of God's word. The Bible says that God's gospel has divine effectiveness (Romans 1:16)!

Simply put, there is good news, people – good news! Come on, prophet, become a great preacher as well as a great prophet! For the current prophet is here to represent the good news of Christ! Not the glooms of times past! We certainly do not have time for that! In all honesty, people need to hear the reason of the hope that resides beyond the grave. And people need encouragement, not execution!

Even the Apostles of the Bible were Gospel preachers as well. A great example is when the day of Pentecost occurred. The Scripture says that the Holy Ghost made his sudden entrance into the house with a great display. It was then that the Apostle Peter quoted the prophet Joel:

The Doctrine of Prophecy

Acts 2:16-18. And the Apostle Peter began his sermon with the doctrine of prophecy. But he ended his sermon with the methodology of evangelism. The combination of these two offices not only read the hearts of men. But it brought those same hearts to Christ:

Now when they heard this, they were pricked in their heart, and said unto Peter and to the rest of the apostles, Men and brethren, what shall we do? Then Peter said unto them, Repent, and be baptized every one of you in the name of Jesus Christ for the remission of sins and ye shall receive the gift of the Holy Ghost. For the promise is unto you, and to your children, and to all that are afar off, even as many as the Lord our God shall call (Acts 2:37-39).

Now, the only difference between the prophetic and evangelistic is their target audience. For the prophet's sole responsibility is to reach those who do believe (1 Corinthians 14:22). And the evangelist is solely responsible in speaking to those who do not yet believe. The evangelist is the office required to speak to all men so that they might be saved (1 Corinthians 9:16-22). But it is the office of the prophet that speaks to men so they might fully know the one who has saved them (1 Corinthians 14:24-25). Nevertheless, each is a messenger of Christ, and their messages works side by side.

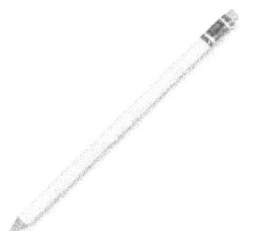

CONCLUSION OF LESSON 5:

The true prophetic network has always been about Jesus Christ. Whether it is about the annals of the past or the works of the present, the truth concerning prophets of God is sewn into this glorious connection. However, there are many modern prophets who fail to realize that their primary assignment is to become a minister of the Gospel, and an elder of the Lord's church. And within these structural guidelines are the purposes of governance and respectability for all five-fold gifting.

If one does not make his mission and ministry about Jesus Christ's mission and ministry, he will run the risk of creating another cultish frenzy. All ministries should get their basis of understanding from the will of the Lord. But the will of the Lord must be properly extracted based upon the principles of proper biblical interpretation. Thus, the prophet who has grown to love the Gospel will come to discover the Gospel gives clues about greater prophetic destiny.

And whether you are prophetic or a prophet of God, it is very important that you advocate for such prophetic protocols and privileges to be returned to the Lord's church. We are in desperate need of the Gospel to provide more grace to God's current and future prophets. For the elder's position is to instruct the people in the ways of righteousness. Therefore, my emerging prophet, and soon to be elder prophet in the Lord, you must realize this.

Please make sure you take this entire section to heart. For God requires that we preach these truths so the church can excel with the aforementioned gift. And as long as Jesus' destiny is still relevant, all who rest in the five-fold are relevant. Here is a final warning: When a practicing prophet loses the relevance of Jesus, he also loses the relevance of his ministry, so the prophet is only as relevant as he is willing to preach the gospel within his prophetic ministry. This is truly in the heart of that professing prophet. And this is the means to the beginning of every emerging prophet's ministry. Contemporary prophet, there is nothing outdated about God's Gospel of his son, Jesus Christ!

PART 2

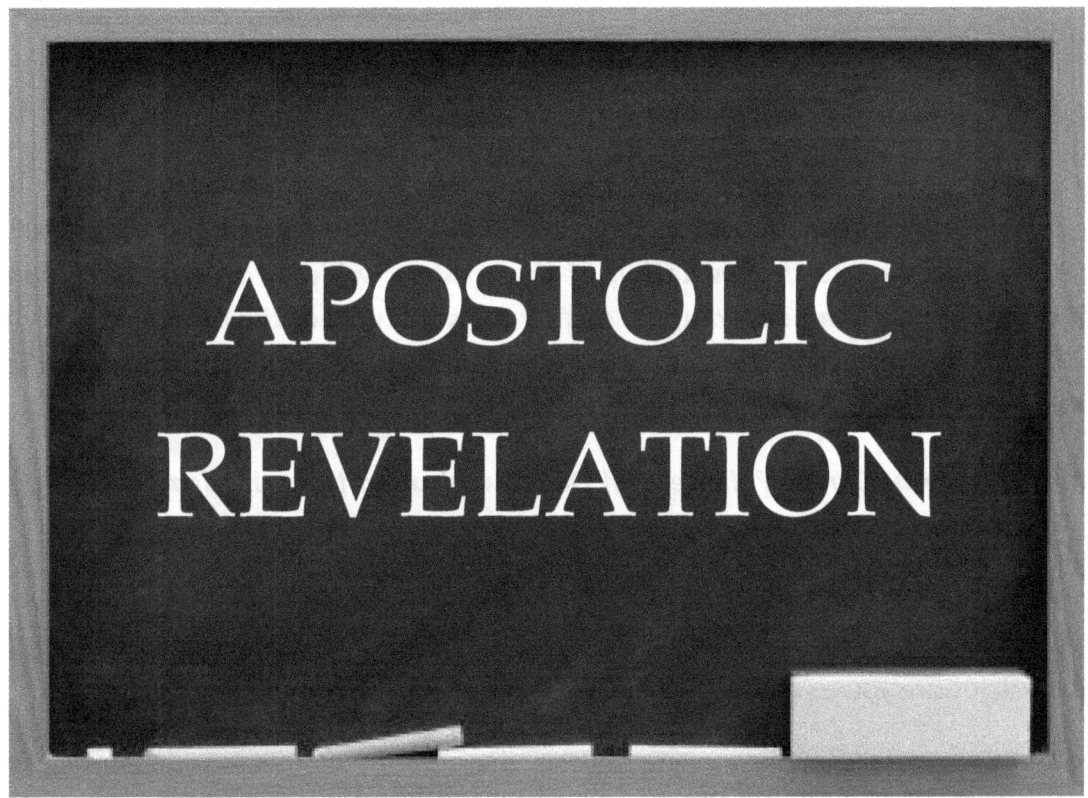

And He taught them many things by parables, and said unto them in his doctrine (Mark 4:2).

"...The Gospel of Uncircumcision was committed unto me, as the Gospel of Circumcision was unto Peter" (Galatians 1:7b).

THE SECOND INTRODUCTION

An Apostolic Revelation About Prophecy 101

Before there is revelation, there must be a solid foundation. Section 1 establishes a great deal of biblical foundation. The first five chapters confirm a general and comprehensive understanding of factual information concerning prophecy. These next seven chapters will provide a brief portion of the revelatory teachings used at the New Kohath Prophetic Institute.

This curriculum is globally accepted among all the churches within our reformation. In fact, it is our prophetic Gospel, just as Paul declared that 'his gospel" was the only gospel that his churches were instructed to follow:

Now to him that is of power to establish you according to my gospel, and the preaching of Jesus Christ, according to the revelation of the mystery; which was kept secret since the world began, but now is made manifest, and by the scriptures of the prophets, according to the commandment of the everlasting God, made known to all nations for the obedience of faith (Romans 16:25-26, KJV).

Remember that Jesus Christ of the seed of David was raised from the dead according to my gospel (2 Timothy 2:8, KJV).

Apostolic Disclaimer: Remember to eat the meat and spit out the bones. What is for you is for you. And what is for your prophetic ministry is for your prophetic ministry. Hopefully, this revelation will inspire you to enhance what God is prophetically doing in you!

For this apostolic understanding reveals that every apostolic assignment is different (Galatians 2:7-8). I publically declare that my primary apostolic assignment is designed to provide more prophetic guidelines unto the body of Christ. I am only here to assist the modern day prophet with his prophetic identity. So, as a prophetic-apostle, I now share God's revelation given to me. For now it is released and destined for you.

CHAPTER 6

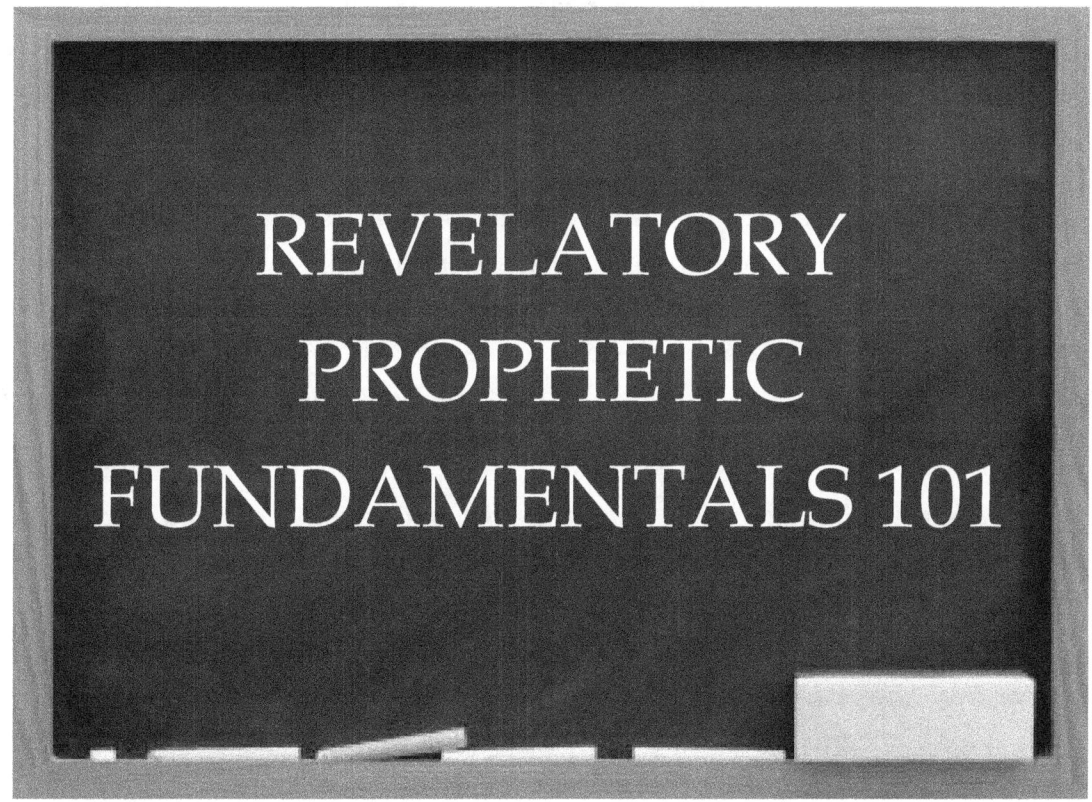

How Does the Prophetic Operate? – Part 1

"...If there be a prophet among you, I the Lord will make myself known unto him in a vision, and will speak unto him in a dream" (Numbers 12:6b).

"...And the similitude of the Lord shall he behold..." (Numbers 12:8a).

The Conventional Prophetic Mediums

Overview: The Supreme Medium is Always God

There are many types of labor within the prophetic office, and in these next two chapters we will discuss the fundamentals of each one. The first labor is the labor of mediums, and the first responsibility for this labor is to understand that the chief medium of the prophetic is always God. For the Holy Spirit is the highest means of connection for any prophet. Regardless of mode, mantle, message, etc., we cannot negate the fact that the Spirit of God nominates and navigates a prophet's ministry.

The Apostle Paul teaches the inability of the natural as it relates to the spiritual (1 Corinthians 2:14). He also explains that God's ultimate pursuit comes from the spirit in man, by way of man's heart. For the spirit is where God places the deeper things of himself within man. And the process of spirituality is a Spirit-to-spirit connection within the life of every believer. This experience is true even for today's prophet. Without the Holy Spirit, there is no true source of spirituality or divine inspiration:

But as it is written, eye hath not seen, nor ear heard, neither have entered into the heart of man, the things which God hath prepared for them that love Him. But God hath revealed them unto us by His Spirit: for the Spirit searcheth all things, yea, the deep things of God. For what man knoweth the things of a man, save the spirit of man which is in him? Even so the things of God knoweth no man, but the Spirit of God. Now we have received, not the spirit of the world, but the Spirit which is of God; that we might know the things that are freely given to us of God. Which things also we speak, not in the words which man's wisdom teacheth, but which the Holy Ghost teacheth; comparing spiritual things with spiritual. But the natural man receiveth not the things of the Spirit of God: for they are foolishness unto him: neither can he know them, because they are spiritually discerned. (1 Corinthians 2:9-14).

Whether prophets of old or new, each prophet has the same inward filling and outward anointing. There is a difference between the ways the Holy Spirit abides in the New Testament compared to the Old Testament. In the old experiences, there was a temporal abiding; and in the new experiences there is a continual and permanent abiding. Though we may become disconnected from the spirit from time to time because of disobedience, the Holy Spirit never leaves us. Nor does he ever forsake us. And the prophet must understand the direction of this new wind of God in order to understand how to prophetically flow.

And regardless of Testament, every prophet prophesies from the position of his inner spirit (1 Corinthians 6:17). A normal flow for any prophet is from the Spirit of God unto the spirit of that prophet. Then this flow transitions from the prophet's spirit into his heart (Proverbs 20:27). Finally, the flow manifests from within the prophet by exiting the heart and entering into the prophet's mouth (or whatever extremity God chooses). This is why God deals heavily with the heart of a people. However, we are cautioned sometimes that even the spirit of man can become infected and need spiritual cleaning (2 Corinthians 7:1).

But it is the heart's channel that experiences the greatest transition and need for cleansing and renewal. Before the prophetic word is uttered from a prophet's mouth, the prophet's heart must become conditioned to such speaking. This is because one's heart is desperately wicked (Jeremiah 17:9). And it also because out of the heart come evil things (Matthew 15:17-20). So the prophet has to have a consistent prayer life and allow God to check such content so that he may prophesy with honesty and sincerity and with a good heart, for God is still the seeker of hearts, even the prophetic ones:

"...The Lord seeth not as man seeth: for man looketh on the outward appearance, but the Lord looketh on the heart" (1 Samuel 16:7b).

Through the Spirit and from the heart, Isaiah prophesies that all flesh will see the move of the Spirit together (Isaiah 40:5). Joel prophesizes that God will pour out his Spirit on all men (Joel 2:28). Jesus, too, explains that the Holy Ghost has come to be a comforter and to help finish the work that he has started (John 16:7). And the dispensations of God never discriminate when it comes to the impartation of God's Holy Spirit. So it is the same with the contemporary prophet's job and his responsibility to first learn the true navigation within the Spirit of God. For such prophetic flow is the means of a sound prophetic voice. True prophetic flow is when a man's heart is aligned with the heart of God! And this starts with learning how to listen attentively to the voice of God.

Subsequently, there is more to the prophetic ministry than an expression of one's prophetic voice under the unction of the Holy Spirit. We must be clear: all prophets of God flow through the Holy Ghost to convey the messages of God. But God wraps each message distinctly within sub-mediums or different modes. We can call these mediums "avenues" or "doors." And the avenues of the prophetic are uniquely given to each prophet's ministry.

As we know, the voice of the prophet is conveyed through his own unique mantle. But each mantle also has a chief method of transmission. The following analogy might help you to better understand. There are several types of cars. Each car also has a different name. However, each car functions the same regardless of its name. Each car is also designed differently to drive at different speeds. Plus, there are expensive cars and there are inexpensive cars. Some cars require more gas than others. And so it is with the prophetic. There are many types of prophets, but they all function under the same spirit. They all have different names, but they are all for the same purpose. Each name determines the method of its functionality. Whether it is fast or slow, or more durable than others, God has provided these sub-mediums as a means to uniquely convey his messages. And God has predetermined the model each prophet shall be.

The Three Conventional Prophetic Mediums

"…If there be a prophet among you, I the Lord will make myself known unto him in a vision, and will speak unto him in a dream" (Numbers 12:6b).

"…And the similitude of the Lord shall he behold…" (Numbers 12:8a).

Whether done externally through angels or internally through other means, there has to be suitable mode of transportation for the prophetic word to leave heaven and enter the earth's realm. Regarding internal means, there are three known conventional prophetic mediums:

The three conventional and biblical prophetic mediums are:

- Visions
- Dreams
- Similitudes

The mediums of dreams, visions, and similitudes are supernatural downloads subjectively given by God to his prophet. Whether we use the word "vehicle," "conduit," or "stream," these words are all synonymous with the word "medium." The prophetic word never leaves heaven naked. It is always properly packaged so the enemy cannot intercept or decipher the contents of its message. And regardless of medium, all prophetic words are usually escorted from heaven by God's angels:

"…The promise was made; and it was ordained by angels in the hand of a mediator" (Galatians 3:19b, KJV).

It is the excitement of angelic activity that wants to look into what is being prophesied. The Apostle Peter refers to this in his Epistle (1 Peter 1:12b). And the Apostle Paul echoes these same sentiments when he reveals that, like a student in a classroom, angels watch the actions of the church. This means that angels come and spectate the interactions of Christ and his church (Ephesians 3:10). And since we understand that angels are interested, then certainly demons are as well. The archangel Gabriel clarifies that it was the princely demons of Persia and Greece that prevented Daniel's prophetic word from being answered. In fact, this word takes three weeks before it finally arrives. But the archangel Gabriel shares that the answer was released from heaven the first day Daniel prayed (Daniel 10:11-14, 20).

The purpose of mediums is to provide the skin that covers the bones of the body of the prophetic word. It is the proper means of sending God's message within a divinely sealed package, just like UPS, FedEx, and other mail carriers, mediums ensure suitable success when God's message is officially uttered into the earth's realm. This is why a prophet's service must be faithful. And in this assignment of being a sensitive student under the means of each common medium, God desires to use each prophet distinctively:

"The prophet that hath a dream let him tell a dream; and he that hath my word, let him speak my word faithfully..." (Jeremiah 23:28a).

Now, we can never exhaust the teachings about prophecy. So the goal is not to assume that all answers to the prophetic anointing are in this book. But the goal is to give you some foundational teaching with a touch of revelatory insight. So, based on each senior prophet's leadership, or your prophetic father's revelation and teaching, all mediums vary based on that teacher's listing of the name, and as he subjectively chooses to use.

But never do such names outweigh functionality, for there is universality even in the differentiation of name designations for each medium. This reveals how things can eventually become subjective as opposed to objective. And this is especially true regarding what is and what is not prophetic. But to avoid an argument, I would like to mention the most common biblical references of the conventional types of prophetic mediums are usually consistent with the aforementioned three terms (vision, dreams, and similitudes). And an inference in scripture also supports the notion that even other mediums may exist:

God who at sundry times and in divers manners spake in time past unto the fathers by the prophets (Hebrews 1:1).

The preceding scripture explains how God does not move the same way upon each prophetic worker and minister. This revelation should help validate the uniqueness of each prophetic expression. Again, a prophet's experience within the prophetic realms is solely subjective and individually received. It is also true that each prophet is not limited to one operation or function within a given medium.

One may experience many vacillations between mediums. Meaning the prophet may sometimes dream while other times see visions and sometimes experience divine occurrences in similitude. Never is there a monopoly on mediums. And never is any prophet confined to a singular function. But just as a believer can have predominant gifts operating within them, so does each prophet tend to favor one specified medium. Again, they are never limited. For we serve an unlimited God and we operate in this same vein.

Again, the purpose of a medium can best be explained by comparing it to the way we use our tongue, teeth, lips, and mouth to form suitable words. Without these means, we cannot communicate to one another. Likewise, it is the same regarding the usage of these three conventional prophetic mediums. And without mediums, our prophetic voice becomes mute and inexpressible. Thus the purpose of a prophetic medium is to help facilitate the voice of God from heaven into the earth's realm. It is the prophet's job, then, to receive such words within such manners. And every medium is required to be properly discerned and distinguished. So it is very important to define the differences of the mediums in order for each prophet to know which medium he is receiving the word of God, at any given time.

The Prophetic Medium of Similitudes

"...And the similitude of the Lord shall he behold..." (Numbers 12:8a).

I have also spoken by the prophets, and I have multiplied visions, and used similitudes, by the ministry of the prophets (Hosea 12:10).

The simplest definition of the word "similitude" is the word "image." And an even better word to use is "picture." Sometimes the prophet only receives figures, shapes, flashing, and fleeting objects during prophetic demonstration. Regardless, the main purpose of a similitude is to reflect the images that God best deems suitable for the prophet in order to properly interpret God's will. In fact, a great example of a chief similitude is how man is made in the similitude (or image) of God:

"And God said, Let us make man in our image, after our likeness..." (Genesis 1:26a).

Therewith we bless God, even the Father; and therewith curse we men, which are made after the similitude of God (James 3:9).

And the first time a prophetic similitude was expressed was during the ministry of Moses. Moses was the great prophet of God who saw the highest manifestation of God. The phrase "face-to-face" is used to describe the context of the highest transmission and encounter with God. Of course, we know, too, that no man can see God in the flesh and yet live (Exodus 33:20; Deuteronomy 4:12; John 1:18). But the purpose of the prophetic medium of similitudes is to depict God with a highest description and urgency. The reason we can emphatically state that the prophetic medium of similitudes is such a special practice is because it was only done with prophets and never with God's people:

And ye came near and stood under the mountain; and the mountain burned with fire unto the midst of heaven, with darkness, clouds and thick darkness. And the Lord spake unto you out of the midst of the fire: ye heard the voice of the words, but saw no similitude; only ye heard a voice…Take ye therefore good heed unto yourselves; for ye saw no manner of similitude on the day that the Lord spake unto you in Horeb out of the midst of the fire (Deuteronomy 4:11-12, 15).

The similitude of God is a chief vision that God gives to certain prophets. But the similitude of God is not the only form of pictures and images God may send to a prophet's ministry. Sometimes these shapes would be men or animals. Other times the images may even be hybrids of birds and men, or various colors, jewels, metals, and other bizarre images. And prophetic seers were usually the recipients of these types of prophetic occurrences.

This is why most of these moments of prophetic similitude need the assistance of other spiritual abilities. For these visions can have other spiritual gifts attached to their demonstrations. Examples of these gifts include the gifts of the word of knowledge and the gifts of wisdom that provide the prophet with a methodology for proper interpretation. The prophet can then divinely understand the relevance of the images that would come to them in various forms. And yet sometimes there are no interpretations at all. When moments like these occur, the prophet can immediately gather that it is for them to *utter* and not for them to *interpret*.

And the best interpreters of similitudes are observant prophets who are also highly analytical. Meaning that the trends of such usage revolve around those to whom God gives a certain level of vocational skill. Joseph, for example, was excellent at math (Genesis 39:1-6, Genesis 39:20-23). And Daniel was excellent at science. This is why it was Joseph and Daniel's destiny to serve in the courts of foreign kings. The King James Version of the accounts of Daniel's prophecies specifically say that Daniel was a scientific genius:

The Doctrine of Prophecy

"Children in whom was no blemish, but well favored, and skillful in all wisdom, and cunning in knowledge, and understanding science..." (Daniel 1:4b).

The understanding of science simply means the observations of things. Daniel had a natural and supernatural ability to look at things and automatically and organically know how such things work, and as well as what they should mean. A prime example of this ability is when the King of Babylon took the vessels of the temple of God that his father had confiscated during the deportation of Israel into Babylon.

He then used these vessels mockingly for a dinner party (Daniel 5:1-5). As a result, God grew angry with the king. Because of this anger, the Bible says that a finger appeared in the banquet hall of the king's palace and wrote words on the wall. From this came the famous expression, "the handwriting is on the wall." No one in the land could interpret this image or these words, except for the prophet Daniel:

Then was the part of the hand sent from him; and this writing was written. And this is the writing that was written, MENE, MENE, TEKEL, UPHARSIN. This is the interpretation of the thing: MENE; God hath numbered thy kingdom, and finished it. TEKEL; thou art weighed in the balances, and art founding wanting. PERES; Thy kingdom is divided, and given to the Medes and Persians (Daniel 5:24-28).

On many occasions, Daniel would simultaneously experience both a vision and a similitude during his prophetic ministry (Daniel 10:16). In this moment, with the handwriting literally on the wall, he interprets the similitude to actually be the son of man, which is essentially the manifestation of Jesus Christ. Though Daniel did not literally call him Jesus, Daniel was signifying and interpreting the similitude as such. It was Jesus whose hand had come to pronounce judgment on the king for mocking the things and people of God.

The main perspective of similitude, as a prophetic medium, is to speak to the presence of Jesus Christ both yesterday and today. Again, all prophetic words and interpretations link themselves to the ministry of Jesus Christ, who is the source of all prophecy: Revelation 19:10b. Now that we are under the dispensation of grace and the era of the New Testament, we must understand that the increase of similitudes among prophetic people and the prophet's ministry is relevant not for the prophet, but also for evangelistic means. For a similitude is another way of saying "sign and wonders." We know that signs and wonders are not for believers, but are used as a "tailgate" for the roadmap of unbelievers. And God continues similitudes as a means of helping unbelievers ascertain Christ through such divine navigation (Mark 16:17).

We do not even realize it, but we are in the prophetic medium of similitudes during the most simplistic of supernatural encounters. For example, when you wake from sleep and view the clock at the same time each night. That experience is a prophetic medium of similitude. This is because numbers are images and they are used to clarify general principles, not just within scripture, but also within the prophetic!

In spiritual numerology, we know that among the Israelite people, each number from 1-12 has a divine significance. Other higher numbers such as 40 and 50 are included in such interpretive methods as well. And another example is the significance of colors within similitudes. We know that colors also hold credence within scripture. The moment we experience such colors during a prophetic medium of similitude, we will uniquely see the creative particles of the prophetic conveying those colors with a specific voice.

Sometimes, the prophet will receive a word through vivid colors of red, green, yellow, or pink. But the most common are black and white. And in those flashing moments of colors, not only must we discern the energy of the color's presence in the context of the prophetic moment. But we must also be able to decipher the voice God has manifested within the color.

Unfortunately, this lesson is part of a series of classes on prophetic symbolism. And we must table this subject for now. For the goal here is to explain the generalization of how similitudes may operate within the prophetic. The ministry of the prophet, through the medium of similitudes, is heavily translated into the mantles known as the visionary prophet and the general-seeing prophet. Do not worry. We will discuss the names of mantles later. A great place to conclude is this: when one is experiencing a prophetic mantle, one should expect the possibility of God using prophetic similitudes.

The Prophetic Medium of Visions

"I was in the city of Joppa praying: and in a trance I saw a vision..." (Acts 11:5a).

The power of the prophetic medium of visions helps the people of God maintain true connection with God. The ministry of the prophet who operates with such anointing is gifted with revolutionary sight and the ability to hear and describe God. This, then, is the major difference between a dream and a vision: a vision is a prophetic occurrence that usually happens when one is fully awake and active. Being in a trance is similar to being in a blink-free stare or daydream. A trance happens when the mind and eyes no longer view what's before them, and the current consciousness is then grasped by the Spirit of God. Then the medium of prophetic vision comes and takes over the human heart and natural sight by propelling the prophetic host into another dimension. When a trance produces a prophetic vision, we must note that it is not easy to distinguish. And every supernatural exploit cannot always be classified as a prophetic vision. Take the case of the Apostle Peter when he was freed from jail. He, too, thought he was in the prophetic. When in actuality he was in the moment of deliverance, while at the same time existing in natural time (Acts 12:9).

God's gift of the medium of prophetic vision is to assist his kingdom with order and direction. The necessity of prophetic vision is vital because it provides a clear roadmap to him. For all prophetic means is the pursuit of true spiritual direction from God. And if there is no prophetic voice, especially through the prophetic medium of visions, then we will soon find ourselves in the midst of decay and destruction. For the Bible reveals the necessity of prophetic vision because it is the means of human preservation:

"Where there is no vision, the people perish..." (Proverbs 29:18a).

When understanding this statement, we must see that it is loaded with meaning. And researching this verse by other translations, we gain further meaning:

NIV: "Where there is no revelation, the people cast off restraint..."

Message: "If people can't see what God is doing, they stumble all over themselves..."

ESV: "Where there is no prophetic vision the people cast off restraint"

This confirms the warning to never hate or forsake prophesying (1 Thessalonians 5:20). It is imperative that we have prophetic visions. Not only must we have them, but we must also adhere to what they tell us. In fact, visions are so important within prophecy that God will use them beyond their normalcy.

This means that the power of prophetic visions does not exist only in the daytime. For example, one can experience a prophetic vision at night and yet not be asleep. The Apostle Paul experienced what I call a ripple-effect prophetic vision. And this experience was because of the prayer life of a Macedonian believer. God showed Paul this man's prayers in a vision. God also revealed to Paul, through a vision, the specifics of the Macedonian believer's prayer request. It was from this clear prophetic vision, which took place in the night, that Paul had his next set of instructions. For God was adamant about the direction of Paul's apostolic ministry and journey:

And a night vision appeared to Paul in the night; There stood a man of Macedonia, and prayed him, saying, come over into Macedonia, and help us. And after he had seen the

vision, immediately we endeavored to go into Macedonia, assuredly gathering that the Lord had called us for to preach the Gospel unto them (Acts 16:9-10).

When prophetic vision is open, God transmits an opportunity for preservation. The medium of prophetic vision is so serious that God opens and closes the heavens because of it. (In this context, Paul was given a vision from an open heaven.) God opens and closes portals in heaven for the sake of demonic activity as well, and other times because of the sinfulness of his people. And when prophetic vision is closed, God prohibits such preservations and allows mankind to voluntarily walk in their lack of restraint. Then the ending verdict of self-annihilation is surely inevitable.

This is why prophetic vision is so precious. When the word of the Lord is not delivered frequently, the people of God can become anxious over the start of the next prophetic shift. So, when prophetic vision comes forth, celebration should surely follow. Even now within the church, pastors should teach their congregations how to properly appreciate and receive the prophetic visions of God. For there are even occurrences in scripture that demonstrate how precious prophetic visions were to Israel:

"...the word of the Lord was precious in those days; there was no open vision' (1 Samuel 3:1b).

"...her prophets also find no vision from the Lord" (Lamentations 2:9b).

When there is prophetic depravity, we see mankind descend into proclivities such as unruliness. If man cannot find the prophetic means, he will certainly seek other means. We have seen this with the case of Saul. Saul was barred from the presence of God, but instead of accepting this judgment he sought an illegal opportunity to reach to the divine (1 Samuel 28:6, 15). This is when the competitive and wicked mediums of divination, witchcraft, sorcery, necromancy, mysticism, and psychic proportions come into play. And true believers of God, both past and present, have been surely warned not to partake or practice such means:

When thou art come into the land which the Lord thy God giveth thee, thou shalt not learn to do after the abominations of those nations. There shall not be found among you any one that maketh his son or his daughter to pass through the fire, or that useth divination, or an observer of times, or an enchanter, or a witch, or a charmer, or a consulter with familiar spirits, or a wizard, or a necromancer. For all that do these things are an abomination unto the Lord: and because of these abominations the Lord they God doth drive them out from before thee (Deuteronomy 18:9-12).

The Doctrine of Prophecy

This is why God differentiates the prophetic from the pathetic demonstrations of witchcraft and divination. When prophetic visions are uttered, they are also sealed within the earth until the appropriate time of release. A prophet must be able to discern the spiritual atmosphere when dealing with the prophetic ministry. And it is God who gives him this discernment through visions that seal such prophecy. This, too, implies that we must differentiate between even prophetic openings and closings. An example of prophetic sealing can be seen in the ministry of the prophet Daniel. Daniel witnessed such a sealing of prophetic vision when God finished the prophetic word's transmission into the earth through Daniel's ministry:

And the vision of the evening and the morning which was told is true: wherefore shut thou up the vision; for it shall be for many days (Daniel 8:26).

"...Seal up the vision and prophecy..." (Daniel 9:24b).

When prophecies are sealed, they are sealed for latter validation. A prophet must be sensitive to the transmission of vision. He must know the difference between God's opening or closing of the portal within the medium of prophetic vision. (Just for the record, the portal is surely opened! It does not close again until after the age of Great Tribulation!) For example, the Old Testament prophet Joel foretold a day and time when all believers would experience the medium of dreams and visions within the prophetic anointing of God:

And it will come to pass afterward, that I will pour out my spirit upon all flesh; and your sons and your daughters shall prophesy, your old men shall dream dreams, your young men shall see visions: and also upon the servants and upon the handmaids in those days will I pour out my spirit (Joel 2:27-28).

Joel envisioned a day when all men would walk in the prophetic anointing of God. One group of men would experience the prophetic in the means of the medium of visions, and the group responsible for this medium would be the young people of God.

Today, a recipient of this vision is one who is receptive to the Spirit of God's new move. This is why young men in particular are more destined to see visions. They are open to a new shift in God. They are opened to the changes that God is soon to make. For God does something new in every dispensation, age, and generations. This is why visions are experienced during moments of consciousness.

The Apostle Peter reiterated Joel's prophecy on the day of Pentecost (Acts 2:17-18). This is because the Apostle saw a new generation emerging that had no problem receiving God's new move. For Pentecost's outpouring of the spirit was indeed unusual and new. All flesh saw it together, just as the prophet Isaiah had foretold. Thus, the younger realm of mankind have the awesome task of receiving this medium within various prophetic mantles. So, young prophet of God, stay under the Holy Ghost's unction so that you, too, may be used in this capacity!

Three Greater Revelations About Prophetic Visions

The gravity of the medium of prophetic vision is so important that I must continue sharing a greater level of apostolic revelation! So we must further understand that even the medium of visions can become truly diverse. In fact, there are scripturally recorded incidents that exposed my spiritman into classifying three sub-diversities within the medium of prophetic vision. And they are:

➢ The general prophetic visionary experience

➢ The simultaneous prophetic visionary experience

➢ The ripple-effect prophetic visionary experience

The General Prophetic Visionary Experience

General prophetic visions clarify and direct the individual who has them. Meaning, God usually sends general visions to provide simple means of personal instruction. For example, when God spoke to Paul the Apostle about evangelistic endeavors, he used the prophetic medium of general envisioning to assist Paul with determining the proper way:

And a vision appeared to Paul in the night; there stood a man of Macedonia, and prayed him saying, come over into Macedonia, and help us. And after he had seen the vision, immediately we endeavored to go into Macedonia, assuredly gathering that the Lord had called us for to preach the gospel unto them (Acts 16:9-10, KJV).

Then spake the Lord to Paul in the night by a vision, Be not afraid, but speak, and hold not thy peace. For I am with thee, and no man shall set on thee to hurt thee: for I have much people in this city (Acts 18:9-10).

The results of a general vision guide a single individual unto the purposes of God. And in other cases it might assist even a great multitude of people in God. Usually, the vision of general envisioning is for the purpose of making clear the direction of a path and coming destination. The vision gives direction so that the prophet finds the right road to journey. But in Paul's case,

God wanted him to sometimes remain in a specific place in order to continue his apostolic work. This is when God used the medium of a general vision to encourage and to instruct him directly.

Application: We, too, as prophets of God, will experience the medium of general envisioning for this purpose. When it happens, we must understand that the vision is for the appointed time. After such experiences, it is important that we do not remain at the gate of the vision. Instead, we must progress towards fulfilling the instructions that were transmitted.

The Simultaneous Prophetic Visionary Experience

The presence of the medium of a corporately simultaneous prophetic vision experience occurs when two or more witnesses are of the same prophetic purpose and vision. It is like a family plan with a specific telephone carrier. Like multiple lines under a single plan, multiple prophets can exist on the same frequency. They can hear, see, or experience at the same time, or they may experience it nearly at the same time. A classic Old Testament example of this is when the sons of the prophets in Gilgal, Jericho, and Bethel all knew, along with Elisha, that Elijah was transitioning from the earth on that particular day: 2 Kings 2:1-5.

So simultaneous corporate vision usually transmits with similarities of words and or messages. As we know, the Bible declares that every word is established in the mouth of two or three witnesses. And God sometimes has to provide confirmation not only to a central prophetic vessel, but also to supportive individuals as well. The purpose of such transaction is always about expanding ministry and kingdom.

I believe that this is the method God wants us to use to return back to his holy church. I make this apostolic assertion based upon the New Testament writings of Paul. For a major example of the simultaneous corporate vision experience is possibly implied when Paul governs the many prophets in the church of Corinth (1 Corinthians 14:29-32).

But sometimes the words will not be for a corporate prophetic body. Remember that not everyone is a prophet, even though everyone can be prophetic. So, in the case of two average human beings, this transaction is not based on prejudice. It may happen even among the most unlikely of individuals. This type of confirmation is particularly seen within the Book of Acts.

While Paul was praying moments after his conversion, a particular disciple of Jesus named Ananias was receiving similar instructions. Paul knew that Ananias was coming because God gave him clear vision concerning Ananias' pending arrival. And Ananias knew he was meeting Paul because he was simultaneously in the same dream sequence:

And there was a certain disciple at Damascus, named Ananias; and to him said the Lord in a vision, Ananias. And he said, Behold, I am here Lord (Acts 9:10).

And the Lord said unto him, Arise, and go into the street which is called Straight, and enquire in the house of Judas for one called Saul of Tarsus: for, behold, he prayeth. And hath seen in a vision a man named Ananias coming in, and putting his hand on him, that he might receive his sight (Acts 9:11-12).

This text explains how Paul was soon to be fully invested as the Lord's apostle. And also how the bible does not reveal details about Ananias' position within the Lord's church. However, God's decision to use Ananias to help with Paul's completion of his conversion in Christ stemmed from their same frequency they both used to tune into is a corporate vision. And the reason this is so important is that not everyone has to be a prophet to receive a prophetic word. In fact, a prophetic word maybe given to another, regardless of station, rank, or ministry privilege. Corporate prophetic envisioning is for every true believer of Jesus Christ.

And this type of prophetic envisioning appears to help remove skepticism and fear, especially when there is a major urgency of purpose. God ensures the success of such purposes by allowing the manifestation and operation of this realm of visioning within two or more witnesses. Paul and Ananias didn't have to spend time discerning each other because they already knew each other by way of the Spirit and by way of the corporately simultaneous envisioning they experienced. This same process happens when a prophet confirms someone's dreams, thoughts, and actions. This is also how the prophetic can work together simultaneously for the act of prophetic interpretation:

Let the prophets speak two or three, and let the other judge. If any thing be revealed to another that sitteth by, let the first hold his peace. For ye may all prophesy one by one, that all may learn, and all may be comforted (1 Corinthians 14:29-31, KJV).

Application: In an era of skepticism regarding the prophetic anointing, if we had more demonstration of this type of prophetic visioning, then there would leave little room for doubt.

The ability for simultaneous corporate prophetic envisioning is a process that only God can determine when he wants such things to occur. But I also believe that every current prophetic school should pray for this type of synergy and unity. More importantly, they should send a clarion call for each prophetic student to find their prophetic home so they can be connected, with the right prophetic stream is also emphasized. For one day, all prophets will have to become part of the same network. And experiencing the same corporate prophetic envisioning will again be accomplished.

As mentioned earlier, this ideal is seen among the sons of prophets on the day Elijah was taken from them (2 Kings 2:1-5). The Apostle Peter and Paul both confirmed a prophetic generation. And even the Prophet Isaiah explained that the prophetic network of watchman should be of one accord:

Thy watchman shall lift up the voice; with the voice together shall they sing: for they shall see eye to eye, when the Lord shall bring again Zion (Isaiah 52:8, KJV).

My questions to you are these: Are you connected? And to where are you called to be prophetically connected? Every prophet should experience this type of connection at least once in his life!

The Ripple-Effect Prophetic Visionary Experience

Ripple-effect prophetic visionary experiences are visions that usually start with one person, in one isolated event. However, prophetic connectivity can also carry over to another person during another isolated event. These events do not have to be within the same measurement of time or season. Usually, these visions are fragments that are dependent upon one another. Ultimately, they come together to create a whole. We can imagine such envisioning like a domino effect. When one domino is knocked down in front of a row of dominos, the others will follow. This is because of the first domino's initial reaction. Likewise, this type of prophetic envisioning has the same concept within the spirit realm.

When God touches one individual with the first vision, others also receive additional parts. The complete understanding of the overall vision is within the connection of all the pieces. This is why I call this type of prophetic vision the ripple-effect prophetic envisioning. A classic example of this type of experience is the case of the Apostle Peter and the faithful believer Cornelius. Cornelius was in prayer at 3:00 p.m. (the hour of prayer for the Jewish people – Acts 3:1). And even though Cornelius was not Jewish, he was God-fearing, which means he was a follower of the Jewish faith rather than a converted disciple. And as Cornelius prayed at the specified time, a vision of God came upon him in the midst of his prayer. The vision informed him of the Apostle Peter's whereabouts. And it also informed him how the Apostle was soon to come to his house:

He saw in a vision evidently about the ninth hour of the day an angel of God coming in to him, and saying unto him, Cornelius (Acts 10:3).

But, on the other hand, when God came to the Apostle Peter, his vision was combined with similitudes as well as prophetic vision, which ended with God's adamant instructions. Peter's prayer time started a few hours before Cornelius'. For Peter started his prayer at noon (compared to Cornelius who began his prayer around 3:00 p.m.):

On the morrow, as they went on their journey, and drew nigh unto the city, Peter went up upon the housetop to pray about the sixth hour: And he became very hungry, and would have eaten: but while they made ready, he fell into a trance, and saw heaven opened, and a certain vessel descending unto him, as it had been a great sheet knit at the four corners, and let down to the earth: wherein were all manner of four-footed beasts of the earth, and wild beasts, and creeping things, and fowls of the air (Acts 10:9-12).

The Bible says that Peter's portion of the vision occurs three times (Acts 10:16). And the occurrence of the number three is also a common theme in Peter's testimony as a Christian and the Lord's Apostle (Matthew 26:69-75, John 21:15-17). Simply put, Peter was known for being stubborn and very hard headed. But the threefold occurrence was mainly because of Peter's devoutness as a Jewish believer, who so happened to now be Christian. For the Jews at that time had strict eating regulations for entering a Gentile's home. And because of Peter's disposition, upbringing, and placement, his interpretation of the prophetic vision was hard to ascertain (Acts 10:17).

But while Peter was meditating on the meaning of the vision, the Holy Spirit spoke to him while contemplating, informing him of the arrival of three men from Cornelius' house. Peter overcame his reluctance, because he could clearly discern God's spirit from any other. Eventually, it was clearly told to him that he would go with them. So Peter complied without question:

While Peter thought on the vision, the Spirit said unto him, Behold three men seek thee. Arise therefore, and get thee down, and go with them, doubting nothing: for I have sent them. Then Peter went down to the men which were sent unto him from Cornelius; and said, behold, I am he whom ye seek..." (Acts 10:19-21a).

When Peter arrived at Cornelius' house, they both had to share their portions of the vision (Acts 10:30-33). This, then, is the true essence of the simultaneous prophetic ripple effect. And in verse 30, Cornelius explains how four days before God connected him with Peter, he had to share the specified time God in which revealed this unique plan. This moment was as if Peter and Cornelius were locked inside a time capsule of a three-hour interval. And during this three-hour interval, God dramatically changed the dynamic of the Gospel heard not only to Jews, but also to the Gentiles.

In fact, these hours are very significant in scripture. The 6th hour (noon) was the hour that the scene on earth and at the cross dramatically changed concerning the testimony of Jesus Christ. And the 9th hour, the hour of prayer (3:00 p.m.), was the very same hour Jesus gave up the ghost and voluntarily died for the sins of world: Matthew 27:45-50, Mark 15:33-37; Luke 23:44-46; John 19:14-30. This lesson teaches that when visions come, whether at day or night, or even during a specific time or time period, the envisioning has an even greater purpose. It always leads us back to Jesus Christ.

Of course, corporately simultaneous and ripple-effect prophetic visions are rarely heard of these days! We hear of general visioning more frequently than the other two. But we should pray for God to activate all the mentioned types of prophetic visions, back into the body of Christ. This would take away the tendencies of false prophecies and strange prophetic experiences.

Application: If prophetic words become more distinct and concise, we would have little room for discrepancy. The clear intention of visions for New Testament times is for the mission and ministry of Jesus Christ. The awareness made of such visionary experiences now hopefully prompts your prayer life for similar experiences.

The Prophetic Medium of Dreams

"...A dream comes when there are many cares..." (Ecclesiastes 5:3a, NIV).

The purpose of dreams in general is to provide instruction to those who are not receptive when conscious. The mind is the means to many cares. God uses the multitude of cares within the mind of man to convey those particular cares through dreams. And dreams, then, are the alternative and the sister of visions. Dreams have been sent by God to put direction, instruction, warning, and clarity within the deep recesses of the mind of a man:

God always answers, one way or another, even when people don't recognize his presence.

"In a dream, for instance, a vision at night, when men and women are deep in sleep, fast asleep in their beds—God opens their ears...." (Job 33:14-16a, Message Bible).

In this reference, Job explains how some nightmares are God's prophetic means of warning, especially when mankind refuses to listen. Out of all dreams, remember that a nightmare is easier to remember because of its effect on the human mind. A prime example is the foreign king Abimelech, who was warned in a dream about Abraham's wife. Abimelech desperately wanted to marry Sarah the moment he saw her. But the problem was that she was already Abraham's wife. So God put a stop to this by sending him a very disturbing dream. In fact, this dream would most certainly be considered a nightmare:

But God came to Abimelech in a dream by night, and said to him, Behold, thou art a dead man, for the woman which thou hast taken; for she is a man's wife (Genesis 20:3).

This is why a prophet must be careful even when receiving nightmares. For the power of prophetic nightmares within dreams holds great importance. Nightmares are the most traumatic because their trauma allows for greater memorization, even after the individual awakens. When a prophetic dream or nightmare is given, God is speaking urgently:

Even then you frighten me with dreams and terrify me with visions (Job 7:14, NIV).

I had a dream that made me afraid. As I was lying in my bed, the images and visions that passed through my mind terrified me (Daniel 4:5, NIV).

Another example of the power of dreams is when God prevented the deceptive Laban from causing any physical harm to his son-in-law Jacob. Jacob had faithfully worked for him for 14 years, but not without deception and attempts to prevent Jacob from leaving Laban's home. So Jacob left unannounced with his wives (Laban's daughters) in the middle of the might. And when Laban was resting in his bed the Lord placed a word of instruction in a dream:

And God came to Laban the Syrian in a dream by night, and said unto him, Take heed that thou speak not to Jacob either good or bad (Genesis 31:24).

We must understand that dreams are of greater importance than visions. When God gives a dream, it is usually transmitted very quickly into the individual's sub-conscience. This is why dreams are often hard to remember upon waking. If you are a dreamer, I strongly encourage you to keep a pen and paper near your bedside. For the swiftness of a dream may leave you in limbo if you miss the opportunity to write it down:

"They fly off like a dream that can't be remembered..." (Job 20:8a, Message Bible).

And the recipient of the dream must be ready to explain what the dream provided immediately upon waking from sleep. His time with that dream's memory will be often limited and fleeting. But it is the responsibility of the prophetic dreamer to be a good steward of God's divine interruption within his mind and spirit. The transmission of a dream or vision is not something to handle haphazardly or lightly. When a dream is given, we must avoid laziness and remain diligent in the appreciation and appropriation of the dream, for within the dreams lies hidden messages and clues that may bless you and better you:

"...Daniel had a dream and visions of his head upon his bed: then he wrote the dream and told the sum of the matters" (Daniel 7:1b).

And the Lord answered me, and said, write the vision, and make it plain upon tables, that he may run that readeth it. For the vision is yet for an appointed time, but at the end it shall speak, and not lie: though it tarry, wait for it; because it will surely come, it will not tarry (Habakkuk 2:2-3).

But when dreams are given multiple times, even from similar perspectives, it is surely because God has a mandate and agenda concerning a major shift that must take place inside the earth's realm. The dreamer is conflicted and afflicted with the reoccurrence of certain dreams because God does not want that particular dreamer to miss the importance of such an urgent matter and its pending arrival. Joseph was able to readily discern why Pharaoh experienced the same dream in two similar dreams that reoccurred successively:

The reason the dream was given to Pharaoh in two forms is that the matter has been firmly decided by God, and God will do it soon (Genesis 41:32, NIV).

Joseph personally experienced this when he dreamed about his family and himself twice (Genesis 37:5-11). Though Joseph's dream took place thirteen years after his initial receipt of his dream, the repetition, with images slightly altered, suggests the same word with an urgent delivery and destination of discernment. We, too, must have a spiritual sensitivity with dreams. Never should we avoid the manifestation of dreams. For it is possible that a dream could be a matter of life and death, success and failure, and peace and chaos. This is why even prophetic envisioning and dreamers are instructed to write certain dreams down for further clarity and future confirmation.

The Interpretation of Prophetic Dreams

"If there be a messenger with him, an interpreter, one among a thousand..." (Job 33:23a).

If dreams are the twin siblings of visions, then the gift of interpretation is their first cousin. Though this is not a prophetic medium, it is very important to discuss. And we must first start with this: not all visions and dreams are designed to be prophetic messages. There are times when visions and dreams are prophetic solely because they have been transmitted through prophetic people.

And not every prophet will be able to, or responsible for, interpreting his own dreams. Sometimes the gift of interpretation is not in the prophetic messenger. In the case of the Bible, there were two major interpreters we must mention from the hall of fame of prophetic workers. Their names are Joseph and the prophet Daniel:

"And Joseph said unto him, this is the interpretation of it..." (Genesis 40:12a).

"...Daniel had understanding in all visions and dreams" (Daniel 1:17b).

In Daniel's case, he was said to have been the best demonstrator of such gifting. When Nebuchadnezzar dreamt a dream, he lost the entire sequence of the dream. As a result of his frustration, the King of Babylon wanted all specialists and spiritualists within his kingdom to be executed. When word of the pending execution began to circulate, Daniel, who intervened and interceded on the behalf of his people and the countless others whose lives were at risk, prevailed with his interpretation of dreams. He had to interpret the king's dream again in Chapter 4 and in Daniel 5:12. The Bible says that on several occasions, God would release entire sequences of interpretations to Daniel, through Daniel's prayer time with God or during Daniel's prophetic experiences with God:

"Then was the secret revealed unto Daniel in a night vision..." (Daniel 2:10a).

Not only was Daniel gifted with this ability, but Joseph was as well. When Joseph was cast into prison for the false accusation of raping Potiphar's wife, he was joined with two inmates who had a simultaneous prophetic dream sequence experience (Genesis 40:5, 8-22). Joseph would not only accurately interpret their dreams, but because of his accuracy, Joseph would also interpret Pharaoh's dreams (Genesis 41:7b, 11, 15-24). The key verse of this account can be epitomized by verse twenty-five:

And Joseph said unto Pharaoh, the dream of Pharaoh is one: God hath showed Pharaoh what He is about to do (Genesis 41:25).

The gift of interpreting prophetic dreams is like an endangered species. In other words, it is rare. Job said that an interpreter is like one among a thousand. So prophetic dream interpreters are hard to find. And not everyone who is prophetic will have this gift. But this gift is a gift that is surely needed especially if there are episodes of prophetic dreaming occurring within the body of Christ.

This ability is just as valid as the prophetic anointing operative within the medium of similitudes, visions, and dreams. One must not disdain this ability. We must pray for the emergence of those who are truly gifted with this ability. For when the dreamer releases his true prophetic dream interpretation, the interpretation relieves him (Job 33:24-26).

Apostle Sherman D. Farmer

CONCLUSION OF LESSON 6:

However, in this I must emphasize a strong warning about the operation of any medium. And that warning is this: demonic deception within these mediums is still a threat! Especially even now, within the Lord's church. Because of this threat, we must be very careful about the medium of prophetic visions, dreams, and similitudes. And even the demonstration of the gift of interpreting prophetic dream, vision, and similitude!

God requires us to understand that many will come with false motives and teachings. This is nothing new. In fact, this has been the strategy of the enemy since God's acceptance of Israel as his first church:

If there arise among you a prophet, or a dreamer of dreams, and giveth thee a sign or a wonder, and the sign of the wonder come to pass, whereof he spake unto thee, saying, let us go after other gods, which thou hast not known, and let us serve them; thou shalt not hearken unto the words of that prophet, or that dreamer of dreams: for the Lord your God proveth you, to know whether ye love the Lord your God with all your heart, and with all your soul (Deuteronomy 13:1-3).

In conclusion, the expression of any medium within the prophetic is never about a people leaving their God. It should always end with a people drawing closer to God. This is why we must have a sober prayer life and study life to combat the forces of darkness. For they will try to deceive God's very elect. Therefore, this call requires that we remain accurate and sober in any perspective of the prophetic anointing. This is why the Holy Ghost must be the supreme conduit or medium that brings all other mediums as sub-methods when venturing into the true prophetic anointing.

CHAPTER 7

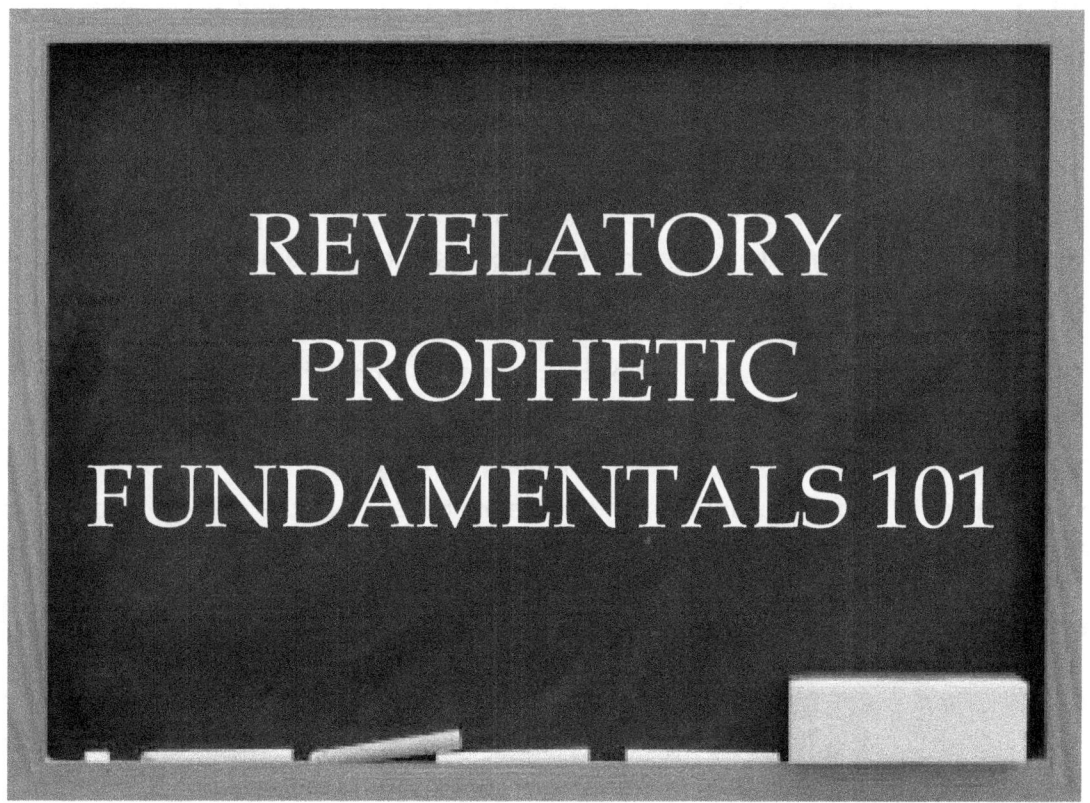

How Does the Prophetic Operate? – Part 2

But ye shall receive power, after that the Holy Ghost is come upon you: and ye shall be witnesses unto me both in Jerusalem, and in all Judaea, and in Samaria, and unto the uttermost part of the earth (Acts 1:8)

Prophetic Dispensations; Methodologies; Dimensions; Graces; & Diversities

The Dispensation of Grace versus the Dispensation of the Law

Under Jehovah God's administration, a series of different dispensations and covenants have transpired within the New Testament. As discussed in Chapter 2, the Old Testament experienced Edenic, Adamic, Noahic, Abrahamic, and Mosaic Covenants, which were coupled with the dispensations of environment, conscience, government, promise, and the law. Within each of these dispensations and covenants, God's mandates shifted based on the agreements he made with humanity. Thus, the prophetic voice had to be cognizant of each period and speak parallel with each covenant and dispensation.

If the prophetic voice is unaware of the present administration, covenant, dispensation, and testament, there will be a tendency to confuse such prophetic purposes. Usually, the confused prophetic voice will speak words irrelevant to the current prophetic flow and divine expression that God is currently speaking. All prophets should want to speak only what God wants him to. For all other words are failures and deviate from his true prophetic office.

But there is still good news even in this reality! God has created a new covenant that is surely able to handle all errors. And there is great virtue within this current dispensation that we can readily become excited about! For the unlimited supply of grace is able to handle the spirit of error and the spirit of false prophecy. This is mainly because of the current dispensation that we are in. And the name of this dispensation is grace:

"...The dispensation of grace..." (Ephesians 3:2b).

Therefore, it is our responsibility to speak, receive, and to judge prophetic messages of God with more grace and love. Rather than prophetically judging with a severity of law! For I strongly believe God will handle the lies of false prophets! And God will also handle the spirit of error of the misled prophets. Though we are under the dispensation of grace, this still requires sheer scrutiny when discerning current prophecy:

Beloved, believe not every spirit, but try the spirits whether they are of God: because many false prophets are gone out into the world (1 John 4:1).

With that being said, I would like to introduce what I believe are biblically sound, new and improved protocols to help us measure the prophetic presence and messages of today. First and foremost, because the mandate and assignment is slightly different, our operation for discernment and delivery should also be different. And here's the difference: the prophets of old spoke much judgment. It appears that it was without the fluidity of grace.

But now grace must meet the prophetic! Yes, the prophetic still receives judgment. But it should be one of righteous judgment (John 7:24). Furthermore, the New Testament later-day prophet's messages should be delivered with consistent prophetic passion. But this current prophetic demonstration must be tempered with more grace and compassion (or mercy).

Many will find their prophetic gifts and other gifts. For the scriptures teach that it is not a marvel to have a prophetic or spiritual gift. For the gifts and callings of God are without repentance (Romans 11:29). We are seriously warned. It is about relationship with God through fruitful character development in Christ that must come along with this gift. And if we are not careful, there is always the possibility of being eternally disqualified, especially when the first works of true repentance, salvation, and the Holy Spirit's baptism are not involved in any aspect of Christian ministry:

Many will say to me in that day, Lord, Lord, have we not prophesied in thy name? And in the name have cast out devils? And in thy name done many wonderful works? And then will I profess unto them, I never knew you: depart from me, ye that work iniquity (Matthew 7:22-23).

So the prophet, or exerciser of the prophetic, must possess a personal relationship with the Lord Jesus Christ. The prophet must receive Jesus as Lord, and from the pardon of their sins. The prophet must also truly believe in the life, death, burial, and resurrection of the Lord Jesus Christ. Finally, he must seek to live in obedience to the commandments of Christ for a fruitful conversion into the image of Christ's character (Romans 8:29).

You might wonder why we repeat this so much. Good question! If you have not received grace, how can you properly impart grace prophetically? Right now in prophetic ministry there are many whose salvation is not certain. Therefore, their prophetic ministry and Christianity alike are uncertain as well. So we all must have this well clarified before we can venture anywhere in God! Secondly, we must remind ourselves that many can prophesy without being saved! For we realize that every good work (including prophesying and being prophetic) was preordained to coincide with the response of our salvation through Jesus Christ:

For by grace are ye saved through faith; and that not of yourselves: it is the gift of God: not of works, lest any man should boast. For we are His workmanship, created in Christ Jesus

unto good works, which God hath ordained that we should walk in them (Ephesians 2:8-10).

But the gift is still without repentance! Therefore, the later-day New Testament prophet cannot become more intimate with the Spirit of God unless he has fully received the testimony of Jesus Christ, which is the spirit of prophecy (Revelation 19:10b). This process is unavoidable. Furthermore, the later-day New Testament prophet cannot receive a full commission in Christ to be a New Testament prophet, or exercise relevant prophecies under the dispensation of grace, unless they have received the true Holy Ghost:

"...No man can say that Jesus is the Lord, but by the Holy Ghost" (1 Corinthians 12:3b).

There is no other way around this. Once the spiritual perspective of the prophet or the prophetic exerciser is correct, then there will be a greater opportunity to expand prophetically and properly within this current age. Again, this current age is about the grace of God through Jesus Christ! And never can any man give grace unless they have first received it! For grace is the only way any of us, in spite of ourselves, can do what God has called us to do:

As every man hath received the gift, even so minister the same one to another, as good stewards of the manifold grace of God (1 Peter 4:10).

The Three New Testament Prophetic Messages of Grace

Let your speech be always with grace, seasoned with salt, that ye may know how ye ought to answer every man (Colossians 4:6).

The word of God exhorts all believers to use grace when speaking to every man. The Bible also teaches us that grace heard will edify those who hear it. This means that the church is responsible for creating momentum with grace, in grace, and through grace. But why is grace needed so much? The answer is this: spiritual inertia!

Spiritual inertia results in the immobilization of the mind, body, life, and yes, ministry. At the root cause of spiritual inertia are the destructive effects of sin. This is why the prophetic gift must not only be called a spiritual gift. But the prophetic must also be called a gift of grace! And when the prophetic speaks in grace, there are three major portals of activities that the prophetic should produce within the life of the believer:

But he that prophesieth speaketh unto men to edification, and exhortation, and comfort (1 Corinthians 14:3).

So, within the New Testament later-day prophet's ministry, three messages of grace are applicable for modern prophetic expression:

- ➤ Edification
- ➤ Exhortation
- ➤ Comfort

And regardless of its dimension of time or its mediums, prophecy as a gift should function under these three messages. When we prophesy in the gift domain, we should be cognizant of the context in which we are prophesying. All five-fold gifts are primary gifts of grace. These gifts are under the dispensation of grace, presented in their unique functions as messages of Grace for these primary purposes:

For the perfecting of the saints, for the work of the ministry, for the edifying of the body of Christ (Ephesians 4:12).

Let's break this down a bit more:

- ➤ "For the perfecting of the saints" = for the nurturing (spiritual development) of the saints
- ➤ "For the work of the ministry" = for the purpose of serving the saints
- ➤ "For the edifying of the body of Christ" = for the greater establishment of the Saints as bonafide parts (or members) of the Body of Christ

New Testament Prophetic Message #1 - The Message of Prophetic Edification

Let us therefore follow after the things which make for peace, and things wherewith one may edify another (Romans 14:19).

The word "edification" means "to build up." This is the process by which a messenger is sent to speak to a person or a people who are developing and need their confidence in order to advance. When the prophetic message of edification is uttered, the desire for harsh criticism or severe correction disappears. But the goal of this type of prophetic experience is to leave the person confident, clear minded, and confirmed in what God has called and assigned. In other words, this message promotes peace, and it promotes unity. Edification is not about self; instead, it is the selfless modality of speaking that develops a person's self-esteem in God and allows it to grow.

Building is another helpful context for understanding prophetic edifying. When we build natural things, we must first have every utensil and resource necessary for the building. Once utensils and resources are found, then we must find the blueprints. Step by step, and piece-by-piece, the accessories are connected together so that a foundation can first be built. Afterwards, the other portions of the buildings can be built. It is the same with the ministry of any form of edification. We are there to help put the pieces together. We are there to help assemble things that seem disassembled. And edification is needed when things are broken down and disheveled.

The ministry of edification speaks to build a better experience and reality. And the general understanding of edification is in the same vein of prophetic edification. We are called to help people retrieve the parts of God necessary for their destiny. We help clarify questions that have been unanswered or questions answered but not yet implemented. We provide more pieces to this puzzle called life. And we share confirmations and revelations from the mind of God, which provides people with the necessary tools for their continued journey with God. Prophetic edification is all about presenting positive facts about God's will to an individual or a given people.

When someone is using the prophetic to constantly disdain, demoralize, and humiliate, they act in opposition to God's intentions for edification. This comes out of the spirit of condemnation. And the spirit of condemnation is usually drenched in self-righteousness. We must state that this is a very bad learned behavior! And it should not be condoned in Christianity!

For prophetic edification seeks to build people up and not to tear them down! It seeks to provide more of God's plans for his people. And when this happens, we can see more clearly. Because the intended recipient of such prophetic demonstrations leaves him built up and more confident in the very assignment and purpose of his life in God, rather than the opposite, which is self-degradation and mutilation!

New Testament Prophetic Message #2 - The Message of Prophetic Exhortation

"Wherefore (as the Holy Ghost saith, To day if ye will hear his voice, Harden not your hearts as in the provocation, in the day of temptation in the wilderness...But exhort one another daily, while it is called To day; least any means of you be hardened through the deceitfulness of sin" (Hebrews 3:7-8, 13).

The word "exhorts" means "to strongly convince or urge." When one exhorts, he attempts to move a person from a moment of natural or spiritual inertia. When someone has spiritual inertia, he is, in simple terms, stuck. He may be stuck in a mental rut, an emotional rut, ministerial rut, or a spiritual rut (just to name a few). And whether this rut is due to sin or ignorance, the exhortation is to motivate and inspire spiritual movement. It is the means of helping a people or person achieve a specified movement from one place in God to the next. There is a simple application that must be adhered to in order for this exhortation to reach its objective. A slight change is expected when the exhortation is uttered, not at the will of the prophet, but hopefully through the will of the intended recipient. This happens only if the word is truly exhortative and not overbearing.

For exhortation is not permission to be rude. It has a gracious and gentle disposition within its aggressiveness, and there is a fine line between being obnoxious and overbearing. As an adversity partner, I say to the other person that I am willing to motivate and inspire them by any means necessary, but in a loving way, since God has instructed for us to love our neighbor as ourselves.

We must understand that we can only provide the means of motivation and inspiration through the aid of the spirit. There are some miracle-working gifts associated with such movement. It takes the gifts of healing to work alongside such ability because people are often afflicted and oppressed by sinful disposition or demonic presence. But again, because of freewill every individual has the right to choose, whether he responds to such exhortations or not. We use prophetic exhortation with the utmost scrutiny of personal discernment.

For when one is prophetically exhorting, he is speaking divinely to the heart of the believer, thereby causing that believer to desire change and to powerfully except that change, and hopefully on that given day. Whether the change is in the mind or body, the prophetic art of exhortation makes the hearer hear God through the prophetic speaker. Thus, whatever was holding them hostage is now removed. And that prophetic voice has caused the believer to progress or move closer to God once again.

New Testament Prophetic Message #3 - The Message of Prophetic Encouragement (Comfort)

Who comforteth us in all our tribulation, that we may be able to comfort them which are in any trouble, by the comfort wherewith we ourselves are comforted of God (2 Corinthians 1:4).

The word "comfort" means, "to share in sympathy and empathy." Christian comfort is never done with apathy. Instead, it is done with mercy and love by being relatable. When you comfort someone, you first have to acknowledge that his circumstances have caused him to remain in a certain kind of suffering. For a person may be in a period of mourning, sicknesses, or other issues that have no pending date of release. When this occurs, the prophetic gift of expressing comfort (or encouragement) is not sent to motivate any type of movement. Instead, it is sent to show relation and connectivity through relating with the individuals in distress.

The best way to describe prophetic comfort is to relate it with the exilic ministry of the prophet (we will discuss the exilic matter later). But prophetic comfort is the type of prophetic expression that makes the individual or a people feel that the prophet is right there with them in midst of their circumstances. Again, prophets (like all other five-fold gifts) are direct representatives of God. And comfort may mean crying with others, sharing with them, understanding where they are, and yet also relating to them through human-to-human interaction. But never should you leave the parameters of the word of God. For the prophetic comforter is sent as a helper and not a problem solver:

Rejoice with them that do rejoice, and weep with them that weep (Romans 12:15).

And whether one member suffer, all the members suffer with it; or one member be honored, all the members rejoice with it (1 Corinthians 12:26).

And because comforting is more complex than exhortation and edification, let us dive deeper into the definition. For prophetic comfort also means soothing agony or agitation through the fitting prophetic words of God. And comfort is not always needed for mere moments of sadness. It can also be needed in moments of joy. The goal of comforting or encouraging, then, is to provide emotional connection to the individual who is targeted for this specific reach.

The words "comfort" and "encourage" also mean to help provide relief to a conflicted, tormented, or discouraged individual or people. Prophetic words provide a greater measure of peace when the prophetic expression of encouragement is provided. There is also a measure of strengthening the individual or a people when providing prophetic comfort, which is the means of showing ambassadorial skills in Christ.

When we comfort others, we show compassion and care. People need to know that God always cares (1 Peter 5:7). And God will forever continue to do so. As prophetic vessels and prophetic people under God's watch and care, it is important that the message of prophetic comfort is applicable and active within today's church. There are many afflicted people, wounded and confused, and they need the simplicity of God's word to just reach them and say, "God cares."

Conclusion of the Three Prophetically Graced Messages

When the prophet speaks under any of these three mandates, he will achieve a better outcome. Also, the person or people receiving such messages will be uplifted (edified) or motivated to move (exhorted) or provided with compassion (encouragement/comfort). These three mandates are simple steps for leading people to God.

It is easy to discern when a person needs each type. The easiest way is through prayer first and prophetic speech second. In cases of unction and delayed unction, we are told that the simplest approach to such prophetic properties brings the intended recipient to greater worship:

But if all prophesy, and there come in one that believeth not, or one unlearned, he is convinced of all, he is judged of all: and thus are the secrets of his heart made manifest; and so falling down on his face he will worship God, and report that God is in you of a truth (1 Corinthians 14:24-25).

Herein resides our goal: love others, lift them up, and live among them! If the prophet can do this as he prophesies, then the Lord will be pleased. And the people will grow to love the Lord more, while appreciating the ministry of the prophet as well. But we must first trust his grace before we can exhort, edify, and encourage others to experience the same grace even more!

Thus Saith the Lord versus Thus Saith the Spirit:

"...The prophet...shall presume to speak a word in my name...or...speak in the name of other gods" (Deuteronomy 18:20a/c).

The prophet who prophesies will speak only on behalf of another. Prophets are assigned to speak in the name of God. Or they will assume their own name, or other types of gods. But the true prophet proclaims God's name within his message, under his mantle, through his ministry, and through a specific medium. We who are of God through Jesus Christ must learn that there are two major prophetic formulas of endorsements. We can call these formulas the methodology of prophetic endorsements. Simply put, this is stamping the approval of a word by using the currently manifested name of God.

If we were part of the Jewish nation of Israel, the first church created in the wilderness, we would use the name Jehovah. This is where we get the methodology for our first prophetic endorsement: "thus saith the Lord." But those of us who are called to speak in the name of Jesus Christ, under the ministry of the Holy Ghost, can be more led to say: "thus saith the Spirit." Honestly, whether we use "thus saith the Lord," or "thus saith the Spirit," both Christian and Jewish believers accept these statements as valid endorsements.

Prophetic Endorsement #1 - Thus Saith the Lord

This title is not uncommon for believers both past and present. "Thus saith the Lord" was first referenced when Moses was instructed to speak before Pharaoh. God gave Moses this formula to ensure Pharaoh that Moses was not speaking in his own name or agenda. But rather that it was God himself whom Pharaoh was standing against:

And thou shalt say unto Pharaoh, Thus saith the Lord, Israel is my son, even my firstborn (Exodus 4:22).

When seeing or hearing this prophetic phraseology of authorization, we must understand, of course, that the King James Version has translated this statement. And this version of the prophetic authorization phraseology is most frequently quoted in today's church and kingdom. But as we break the phrase down, we can discover that there is more behind its meaning.

The words "thus" and "saith" come from the same Hebrew word *amar* [Ah-mar]. This means to bear forth, or to bring to light by saying or expressing. And the Hebrew name for Lord is the word "Jehovah," which means "the existing one." Hence the prophetic phraseology of authorization in the Old Testament was designed to bring to light, unto what was not revealed, by saying that, through the true and existed God, Jehovah, it is now revealed. Without the prophet's endorsement, the words uttered could be rejected, refuted, or resisted.

But saying that it is God speaking and revealing through the messenger adds more weight to the words within the mouth of the prophet. And throughout Old Testament scripture "thus saith the Lord" becomes the format and methodology of proper prophetic utterances. Moses' successor, Joshua, prophesies within this same format:

And Joshua said unto all the people, Thus saith the Lord God of Israel, your fathers dwelt on the other side of the flood in old time, even Terah, the father of Abraham, and the father of Nachor; and they served other gods (Joshua 24:2).

The prophets during the ministry of the Judges also prophesy with this same formula:

That the Lord sent a prophet unto the children of Israel, which said unto them, Thus saith the Lord God of Israel, I brought you up from Egypt, and brought you forth out of the house of bondage; and I delivered you out of the hand of the Egyptians, and out of the hand of all that oppressed you, and drove them out from before you, and gave you their land (Judges 6:8-9).

The master-prophet Samuel used this same phrasing as well, which implies that the band of prophets of Gibeah used it too:

And Samuel called the people together unto the Lord to Mizpeh; and said unto the children of Israel, Thus saith the Lord God of Israel, I brought up Israel out of Egypt, and delivered you out of the hand of the Egyptians, and out of the hand of all kingdoms, and of them that oppressed you: and ye have this day rejected your God, who himself saved you out of all your adversities and your tribulations; and ye have said unto Him, Nay, but set a king over us. Now therefore present yourselves before the Lord by your tribes, and by your thousands (1 Samuel 10:17-19).

The master prophet Elijah (and by implication Elisha) used this as well, which implies that the sons of prophets used the same phrasing:

Now therefore thus saith the Lord, thou shalt not come down from that bed on which thou art gone up, but shalt surely die. And Elijah departed. (2 Kings 1:4).

And this prophetic phraseology was used throughout the prophetic ministry of all the Old Testament prophets. But for the sake of finalization, we see that the phrase is consistent up until the ministry of Malachi:

Whereas Edom saith, we are impoverished, but we will return and build the desolate places; thus saith the Lord of hosts. They shall build, but I will throw down; and they shall call them, the border of the wickedness, and, the people against whom the Lord hath indignation forever (Malachi 1:4).

Prophetic Endorsement #2 - Thus Saith the Spirit

The new flow of authorization for the prophetic voice is clearly under the authority of the Holy Ghost in this church era and dispensation of grace. Therefore, the former phraseology "thus saith the Lord" can be replaced with "thus saith the Holy Spirit." The only warning in this area is to assure that God is the one speaking, whether through the voice of the Lord, Spirit, or an angel, for there is grave danger when someone is lying in the name of God, regardless of the dispensation and name designation they decide to use (Jeremiah 29:31).

The methodology of prophetic endorsement only serves as clarification of action and practice, not as a means of disrupting or destroying the authenticity of the prophet's ministry. The basic principle is this: every prophet must have the name of God endorsed within his messages. If there is no methodology for prophetic endorsement, then there is no necessity for acceptance of the utterance. And for speaking in a comedic tone, there was a time when every prophetic word was uttered in the style of the King James Version. But now we are learning that it is certainly the proper interpretation of God's move more than what dialect, slang, or language is used to convey the right word. We still have to question whether God speaks with "doest," "speakest," or "lovest" anymore, or whether his speech has progressed. I think it is at the discretion of the prophet's creativity, as well as the understanding pulled from the mind to convey prophetic voice. Based on the triune manifestations of God, the word teaches there are three within heaven who are one:

For there are three that bear record in heaven, the Father, the word, and the Holy Ghost: and these three are one (1 John 5:7).

Jesus taught the disciples about the new administration of the Holy Ghost, also saying that it is soon to come. He reveals on several occasions the true intent of the Holy Ghost's presence within the world:

But the Comforter, which is the Holy Ghost, whom the Father will send in my name, He shall teach you all things, and bring all things to your remembrance, whatsoever I have said unto you (John 14:26).

Nevertheless I tell you the truth: it is expedient for you that I go away: for if I go not away, the Comforter will not come unto you; but if I depart, I will send Him unto you (John 16:7).

Howbeit when He, the Spirit of truth, is come, He will guide you into all truth: for He shall not speak of Himself; but whatsoever he shall hear, that shall He speak, and He will show you things to come. He shall glorify me: for he shall receive of mine, and shall show it unto you. All things that the Father are mine: therefore said I, that He shall take of mine, and shall show it unto you (John 16:13-15).

It is now the Holy Spirit's job to establish the mindset of God within the earth. The Holy Spirit's presence is the main source of the gift and spirit of prophecy. And since the Holy Spirit is the authorized manifestation of God's holy presence, it seems fitting that the prophetic allocates its assignment under and through this truth. Below are other examples in the New Testament of the prophetic moving with the endorsement of the Holy Ghost –

The Prophets of the Church in Antioch shifted to this paradigm:

Now there were in the church that was at Antioch certain prophets and teachers…As they ministered to the Lord, and fasted, The Holy Ghost said, Separate me Barnabas and Saul for the work whereunto I have called them (Acts 13:1a, 2).

The Judean prophet Agabus employed the same paradigm:

And when he was come unto us, he took Paul's girdle, and bound his own hands and feet, and said, Thus saith the Holy Ghost, so shall the Jews at Jerusalem bind the man that owneth this girdle, and shall deliver him into the hands of the Gentiles (Acts 21:11).

The Apostle Paul speaks under the inspiration of the Holy Spirit:

Now the Spirit speaketh expressly, that in the latter times some shall depart from the faith, giving heed to seducing spirits, and doctrines of devils; speaking lies in hypocrisy; having their conscience seared with a hot iron (1 Timothy 4:1-2)

Forth-telling versus Foretelling

When you think of defining the gift of prophecy, you can define it as a divine ability working in and around natural time. And in respect to time, the prophetic is either a forth-telling moment (meaning in present time) or a foretelling moment (meaning in future time). Regardless of the time's dimension, the prophetic word will always correspond with some realm of time (past, present, and future). Even more deeply, prophetic time, eternal time, and natural time do not always correspond. In fact, the majority of the time they do not have to converge, as long as God so desires. Thus, a prophet must pray for the discernment of the times like the sons of Issachar (1 Chronicles 12:32).

Now that we have established that a prophetic work is created to function within certain realms of time, we must learn the moments of such prophetic operation. But before we begin, there is one more issue we must handle: There is a tendency that accompanies people's working definition of what is truly prophetic. This tendency is epitomized and stereotyped that prophesying is only the ability to foretell the future. But the truth is that prophecy is about so much more than futuristic time. Prophecy is also about voicing the Lord at an appointed time. But never is the Lord restricted to any form of time.

So the prophetic is able to work in the realms of "now" as well as the realm of "later." And prophecy has no purpose without the past! When we understand it in this vein, we see that prophecy is so much more than what we have limited it to be!

Foretelling versus Forth-telling Prophetic Abilities

Forth-telling: The prophetic usage in the forth-telling dimension of the prophetic ability is when a believer decrees the word of God in modern times. A simple way of expressing this type of word is through the use of a commonly used word of confirmation or revelation.

Yes, we all know that the gift of prophecy is said to be one of the most controversial subjects of scripture. This stereotype and misrepresentation of prophesying cause some to feel that they are incapable of prophesying. But it is beneficial for all. Even when we are simply declaring the Gospel or a given scripture, this is when we take on the same prophetic dimension as John the Baptist. For never does he give a foretelling (or futuristic message) or utterance. However, he is called the greatest prophet to have ever lived, simply because he was the forerunner to the emerging ministry of Jesus Christ (Matthew 11:7-14, 17:10-13).

So, when we do this under the Spirit's leading, we are, in essence, becoming a prophetic agent of forth-telling. A more modern example of this ability is when the psalmist or the praise and worship leader uses scripture during ecstatic worship. In his exhortation may rest a *rhema* word. This is also part of the forth-telling realm of prophecy, and it can be distinguished when a prayer warrior or intercessor uses the word of God during public or private prayer. It is also when the preacher or teacher proclaims the word in such a way that it seems as if God is speaking directly to the individual. It is in the minister's unique display and dissertation of his sermon that this can suddenly become forth-telling.

So prophesying in the forth-telling dimension simply is when God talks directly to you through hearing the written word of God. This means that a written or spoken word, used timely and applicably to a given situation, can be prophetic. For the word of God is always prophetic. And when we read the Bible, and we hear the voice of the Holy Spirit within us speak *rhema* and revelation – again that's prophetic – this is because the word is always prophetic. And we are a prophetic people because Jesus Christ is the source of all prophecy! This is the true definition of a prophetic flow!

Foretelling: The prophetic process of using the foretelling dimension is the prophetic ability to proclaim a futuristic timeframe to certain manifestations of God's will. The word is clearly a futuristic word of confirmation or revelation. Thus, it has a time and date stamped on it for such validation.

This aspect of prophesying seems to be the most controversial in modern times. There are many theologians and scholars that assert that there is nothing more to predict. They further asset that with the fullness of the manifestation of Christ and his complete redemptive work on the cross and empty grave – they say that the spirit of prophecy has ceased. But I strongly beg to differ. Even predictive properties within the prophetic still exist. But the issues are in the spirit of error. Not the ability to prophetically predict!

The spirit of error attacks this beautiful dynamic. Prophesying with a predictive quality has been demoralized to soothsaying and divination, which also has been on the borderline of witchcraft. But when we are truly predictive we must be prophetically, scripturally, and spiritually sound. For any prophetic word is best protected when it is done in association with God's holy word. Therefore, the closer we stay in the context of the word of God, the safer our prophetic words will be.

Simply put, prophesying is about the scheduling of God's will within the earth's realm. God has mankind on a unique timetable. The ultimate timetable is Israel's prophetic calendar and clock with God. And anything predictively uttered will always be in congruence with God's original plans that he made with Abraham, Isaac, and Jacob. Even though we are an extension of such plans, by way of the church, the church receives the next prophetic assignment because of the Jewish Messiah, whose name is Jesus Christ.

And on a more personal level, there are events and unrevealed mysterious that coincide with a person's life that God's will must be released strategically and rightfully during an established time. But ultimately predictive prophesy is for the kingdom and not for personal usages. Take for example the story of Queen Esther. When Mordecai (Esther's uncle) exhorts her to interrupt the king, he released a phrase that supported prophecy. He said, "for such a time as this!" Thus Esther used this phrase to justify her abrupt entrance into the king's court, as she selflessly went on the behalf of her people. But like this distinct time, prophecy, too, is about a specified time that God has allocated in the world!

So it is with the foretelling capability of the prophetic. We foretell because it is not yet time for certain aspects of God's plan to be released. This level of prophesying is about scheduling. Never is it isolated to merely validating the prophetic power of the prophet. Yes, this is an Old Testament criterion that we still use to vet our current prophets. But it has expanded to this New Testament concept. As long as all prophecy glorifies Jesus and edifies his church, there will be no harm when expressing this perspective on prophetic anointing:

But if all prophesy, and there come in one that believeth not, or one unlearned, he is convinced of all, he is judged of all; And thus are the secrets of his heart made manifest: and so falling down on his face he will worship God, and report that God is in you of a truth (1 Corinthians 14:24-25).

Thus, the predictive quality of foretelling speaks to God's sovereignty more than man's presence. Mankind has his known and unknown secrets within him by way of a marriage between him and God's spirit. Such a marriage was determined on the date of our salvation. When we become saved, our spiritman is made alive again. And God enters permanently to dwell with man, inside the spirit of man (1 Corinthians 6:17). It is from there that everything spiritual happens.

So the prophetic comes to use prediction (foretelling) and proclamation (forth-telling) to initiate both dynamics within every man who is willing to be used by God. The prophetic voice, then, is the means of determining what God wants revealed and confirmed at each moment. And the major purpose of prediction is not only about God's scheduling. All things of God are slated to happen during a specific season and time, as Ecclesiastes explains (Eccl 3:1). So the purpose of prediction is for the proper discernment of the season that coincides with a specified time.

Finally, even though the fulfillment of Jesus has come – and we know that the prophets of old desired to see within – we still have prophecy as a means of directing and informing the saints of current and future events. This becomes applicable when world events may affect the welfare and works of the church. A great example is the prophet Agabus. It was Agabus who came to prophesy to Paul about the next step in his ministry (Acts 21:11,16). But it was this same prophet that revealed to the church that a famine was soon to come (Acts 11:27-28).

So prophesying can be used as a means of bringing clarity and sobriety based on the applicable time and dimension. We must find a way to balance forth-telling with fore-telling prophetic demonstrations. Now, this raises questions: Is the prophetic word for modern times? Or is the prophetic word just for the future? The answer is this: if God has not changed, neither will the prophetic windows of time. We must now speak for God (by forth-telling). And we must also speak for God concerning the future (by foretelling). But everything is done in part by the hand of God!

Revelation versus Confirmation in Prophecy

The spiritual gift of the word of knowledge (1 Corinthians 12:8) is the ability to know things without prior training, teaching, or apprehension. It is when God instantaneously provides divinely imparted information to a person for the sake of knowing. Usually, the prophetic manifests with the word of knowledge, either as confirmation or as revelation. Words of confirmation and revelation actually help facilitate the movement of the prophetic anointing. When the word of knowledge, under the prophetic ministry brings confirmation, it is a sign that God has already shared with the prophetic recipient.

But if all prophesy and there come in one that believeth not, or one unlearned, he is convinced of all, he is judged of all. And thus are the secrets of his heart made manifest, and so falling down on his face he will worship God, and report that God is in you of a truth (1 Corinthians 14:24-25).

However, aside from confirmation, there is another aspect of the word of knowledge that combines with the prophetic anointing. This secondary diversity is called revelation. Revelation is the ability to reveal things that have not yet been told to a prophetic recipient. Revelation is always harder than confirmation. For confirmation confirms the prophet's integrity immediately. Revelation, however, is based on an honor system that is often later confirmed.

The equivalence of confirmation is very much like forth-telling, whereas the equivalence of revelation is like foretelling, so it is rather convenient to reveal a confirming word. But it is rather challenging to reveal a revelatory word. However, we do have examples of prophetic works attached to revelatory messages that are classified as words of knowledge (with foretelling properties):

This charge I commit unto thee, son Timothy, according to the prophecies which went before on thee, that thou by them mightiest war a good warfare (1 Timothy 1:18).

Neglect not the gift that is in thee, which was given thee by prophecy, with the laying on of the hands of the presbytery (1 Timothy 4:14).

These two cited references to Paul encouraging Timothy inform others that the prophetic can confirm a calling (which is confirmation) but also reveal a calling (which is revelation). But we must understand this gift, in the context of Paul's motive, when he writes to Timothy. At that time, Paul had pastoral and apostolic authority within Timothy's life. And through proper relationship, he also had a divine right to apostolically and prophetically awaken dormant abilities within him for the sake of exhorting Timothy's spiritual destiny.

Of course, this type of spiritual surgery in the prophetic is one that I advise to be done with caution and sobriety. For the word of God admonishes us to know those we labor among (1 Thessalonians 5:12). And as Timothy's spiritual father and pastor, Paul could exercise his divine right to implement any further development of Timothy's ministry! It is my firm belief that this was a spiritually sound means to explain that prophetic ministry is best received through a strong relationship or connection. This means that the best prophetic moments are between one who knows the individual from which he receives prophecy.

Because the perversion of prophecy occurs when there is no true intercession or pastoral regard within the heart and flesh of those whom we must label renegade prophets. A true prophet is submitted. And, therefore, the true prophet is careful in divulging or digging too deep into a person's spirit and destiny. Timothy, apparently, was immobilized spiritually because of the spirit of fear.

Timothy was apprehensive in discovering and engaging in the fullness of his destiny. These divine aspects of prophesying were not done haphazardly. But it appears that Paul ministered strategically to Timothy over a period of time. And Paul used wisdom and strategy to release such divine information and confirmation. Again, Timothy was Paul's spiritual son. And it is the assignment of a spiritual patriarch or matriarch to assist with the supernatural identity of his or her spiritual children. For confirmation and revelation are the sure means of prophecy.

The Gift of Prophecy versus the Gift of Word of Knowledge

There are many words that can come from God. But not all words are prophetic! Some words are *rhema*, some words are admonishment, some words are discernment, and some words are prophetic! And it is also important to know that the word of knowledge gift and the prophetic gift are not the same gift. Many who operate only in the word of knowledge have been labeled prophets because they can confirm and reveal through this particular gift. However, the differences are clear. The prophet will always speak on behalf of God. But the word of knowledge is just a mere demonstration of revelatory and conformational abilities. What makes a word prophetic as opposed to a word of knowledge is either the phrase "thus saith the Lord" or "thus saith the Spirit."

More exists in the prophetic mantle than just revelation and confirmation, which can be linked to the spiritual gift of the word of knowledge. As we further study, you will see definitive differences between these two gifts. And it is advisable to realize that if the gift of the word of knowledge is more your assignment, than the title of prophet is unadvisable in your pursuit of this positioning.

CONCLUSION OF LESSON 7:

Paul could readily identify with the ways of the prophetic because he, too, was called out and confirmed by the prophetic counsel of Antioch (Acts 13:1-3). Moreover, there is a difference between how these are released. Confirmation released through prophesying was better received, which was solely attributed to the recipient's prior knowledge of what was being prophetically affirmed and confirmed. However, when revealing prophetic revelation that has not yet been confirmed or affirmed, the recipient will receive that prophecy very differently.

Usually, this posture is one of discomfort and uncertainty. Therefore, the prophetic demonstrator must make sure that he has clearly heard from God in his deliberation over the distinct revelations and confirmations provided. Furthermore, there must be proper discernment as to whether the word was for direct impartation, intercession, or general knowledge. Simply put, not everything prophetically revealed is lawful to utter. Sometimes God informs a prophet for a higher purpose. Usually that purpose is for a seasonal period of intercession instead of releasing such information.

And every prophet must learn these lessons very quickly. Is it confirmation or revelation? Or is it time to foretell or forth-tell? Am I being prophetic or is this just a word of knowledge? Discern, discern, discern! And learn how God is using you!

CHAPTER 8

How Does the Prophetic Operate? – Part 3

Now, there are diversities of gifts but the same Spirit. And there are differences of administrations but the same Lord. And there are diversities of operations, but it is the same God "which worketh all in all. But the manifestation of the Spirit is given to every man to profit withal" (1 Corinthians 12:4-7).

Prophetic Regions and Operations

A General Overview of the R.O.A.M Mission

But speak thou the things which become sound doctrine...in all things shewing thyself a pattern of good works: in doctrine shewing uncorruptness, gravity, sincerity, sound speech that cannot be condemned..." (Titus 2:1, 7-8a).

Before venturing further with other advanced teachings, let us review some more basics. The basis of any true revelation is in sound biblical fundamentals. Please remember this important note: the exercise and expression of prophecy certainly has principles. And the purpose of such principles is to protect a product, and the product that needs certain protection is prophecy. Another word for "principles" is "instructions" or "laws."

When instructions are thoroughly understood, you'll reap lasting benefits. You'll also ensure greater safety during operation. The purpose of biblical fundamentals serves as an anchor, even within the ministry of prophetism. Based on this idea, I would like to title this section of information, "The Prophetic Principles and Fundamentals of The Doctrine of Prophecy." Or, the short version, "Prophetic Fundamentals 101!"

The word "doctrine" simply means "teaching." And there are several teachings of necessity for the sound explanation of the current practices of prophecy. When one is acquainted with the fundamental teachings of the prophetic anointing, then one can be fully introduced to the complexities of prospective revelatory knowledge gleaned within the prophetic office. This is the proverbial "crawl before walking."

Here it is again: one's adherence to fundamental teachings produces a greater propensity towards prophetic revelation. And the greater your connection with sound fundamentals, the greater the expansion of the prophet's biblical resources during true moments of prophesying. Just as you cannot skip without learning to walk, you must learn fundamentals before your can venture into advanced revelations.

And every apostolic voice is called to properly disseminate information about the relevance of past biblical references within current situations. For the gift and office of the prophet is not a new gift to the world. In fact, it is the oldest spiritual gift that has been recycled and reformed to uniquely function within this current age and dispensation. This further justifies the importance of proper voicing and finding a correlation among expository information. For the doctrine of prophecy governs by protecting the perimeters of prophesying and ensuring that the gift, and the recipients of such gifts, will receive less damage, and that there will be minimum prophetic dysfunction and liability.

As we thoroughly study these truths, they will surface within the ministry of both the Old and New Testaments. Better prophets are made from harmoniously studying both prophetic groups! For we need the Old Testament because it provides blueprints for suitable prophetic designs. But we equally need the New Testament because it is like a construction team capable enough of erecting the materials so we can build the said gift. So, in balancing the Testaments, we can enhance their beauty and hopefully present a more stable representation of today's practice of prophetic ministry. For true prophecy is seen when it is coupled with sound sobriety.

So learn the apostolic doctrines of prophecy! Open your mind. Allow this teaching (doctrine) to engage your mind. However, do know that I will never impose subjective and dogmatic views. This book is not an opportunity for secret denominational agendas or reformation assassinations. No, it is merely an instrument for reforming the prophet; it is not so much a tool for promoting a denomination or reformation.

I encourage you to keep an open mind. For if you absorb this information without being contrary, great reward will meet you in the end. And upon completion I promise that the outcome of an even greater prophetic maturity will become your harvest. Now that we have clarified the agenda, let us progress forward!

Conclusion of General Overview

Each chapter will provide general scriptures, contextual information, and a subjective apostolic interpretation in order to explain said fundamentals and revelations. Please be advised that you will hear new ideas or information expounded on very differently. It is not the goal of this book, then, to confuse you. If you find yourself confused, it is always good to seek counsel, for in much counsel, there is much safety. In this case, I encourage you to consult your pastor or spiritual mentor or leader. Please engage in dialogue with them about complicated material. My heart's intent is to enhance your ministry. Not to destroy it.

The R.O.A.M-Mission – Part 1

Now there are diversities of gifts but the same Spirit. And there are differences of administrations but the same Lord. And there are diversities of operations, but it is the same God which worketh all in all. But the manifestation of the Spirit is given to every man to profit withal (1 Corinthians 12:4-7).

The Doctrine of Prophecy

When reading this text, in context, we understand the Apostle Paul is soon to reveal nine charismatic gifts of the Holy Spirit. Prior to his listing, Paul establishes several classifications for all spiritual gifts:

#1 – There are different (i.e. diversities of) gifts [meaning different name designations]

#2 – There are different types of ministries (i.e. administrations) for each gift [meaning different specific purposes for each gift]

#3 – There are different types of works (i.e. operations) for each gift [meaning various ways that each gift can become a sub-category of supportive function]

Diversities, ministries, and operations can be used within any pattern of explanation for any or one gift in particular. When referring to the prophetic gifting, certainly there are applicable sub-categorizations. Meaning there are diversities within the prophetic gift, and there are different prophetic ministries and different prophetic works within the same gift and office of prophecy. But to simplify our understanding of such things, we will use the acronym R.O.A.M. This acronym will allow us to memorize certain parts of the prophetic office. It stands for:

R = Regions

O = Operations

A = Administrations

M = Mantles

The actual definition of the word "roam" is to go from place to place without purpose or direction. It means to wander. And, truthfully speaking, there are many who wander around in the portals of the prophetic anointing. These people have no clarity concerning the perimeters that help shape their assignment in ministry.

However, in using the acronym R.O.A.M., we will certainly dissolve the presence of the nomadic prophet. For this acronym explains four important aspects of the prophetic gifting. And within each prophetic ministry, there are three known regions, operations, administrations, and mantles recorded within the Bible.

THE THREE REGIONS OF A PROPHET

The Overview of Prophetic Regions

But contrariwise, when they saw that the gospel of the uncircumcision was committed unto me, as the gospel of the circumcision was unto Peter: (For he that wrought effectually in Peter to the apostleship of the circumcision, the same was mighty in me toward the Gentiles) (Galatians 2:7-8).

There is a simple definition for the purpose of prophetic regions. But before we review this definition, let us resort again with the testimony of Jesus. The spirit of prophecy is the testimony of Jesus Christ. And the office of the five-fold gifts is simply the positioning of ordained elders and preachers of the Gospel within his Holy Church. There are two reasons an elder is ordained. One is for the local work inside a given local ministry. And the other is to travel abroad for the sake of mission work.

It is in the Gospels that we see the reasoning behind Jesus' choice to use the Apostles for Christian work. But it is the Book of Acts that explains the ordination of his apostles for preaching the gospel throughout the world. Before Jesus returned to heaven (in the Ascension), he explained to his Apostles the importance of evangelism. For it is in the explanation of evangelism that the revelation of prophetic regions is born.

A common phraseology, often heard in church when people begin to prophesy, is, "The Lord says that you are a national or international prophet!" This statement, as it is, does not sound harmful when hearing it. But there is much implication attached to it when it is made. And sometimes there are novices who truly lack the concept of what it means to be "national and international" for Jesus!

Furthermore, there is much speculation when one thinks of the phrase "national or international prophet." Automatically, this statement presents more questions: What does a national or international prophet truly mean? And will everyone become national and international within the prophetic ministry? And, of course, there is a logical answer for each question. This is why it is important to start here with the first assignment and sub-category of the prophet.

In the first scriptural reference above (Galatians 2:7-8), Paul and Peter are equal in the office of apostleship. However, such equality does not take them both to the same apostolic region. Peter's apostolic-regional ministry was for the Jewish people. And Paul's apostolic-regional ministry was for the Gentiles. A region is the determination of who God has sent you to minister to. Yes, regions are not so much about "where you are going" and "how far you will go to get there"! Regions are about people and not places!

Paul and Peter's apostolic regions were based on the specific people whom God predetermined for them to reach. Peter could not accomplish Paul's work no more than Paul could fulfill Peter's work. And yet, both works were equally important! Both works had legitimate purposes. But there is clear difference between the regions of Paul's apostleship in comparison to that of Peter's. It was Paul who said Peter's region was in favor of circumcision (or the Jews), while his region was in favor of the uncircumcision (or the Gentiles).

And it is the same with all five-fold gifts (apostles, prophets, evangelists, pastors, and teachers). Even prophets must know their own prophetic region. For God is not sending his servants to minister to random places. But he is always sending them to minister to specific people. Again, the people in those places determine the specific region of ministry. And a prophet's prophetic region is just as uniquely crafted as the assignments of the apostles, evangelists, and pastors. In fact, Jesus reveals a tri-fold paradigm of the regions of his day. And he spoke about the realms of evangelism shortly before his ascension:

But ye shall receive power, after that the Holy Ghost is come upon you: and ye shall be witnesses unto me in Jerusalem, and in all Judea, and in Samaria, and unto the uttermost parts of the earth (Acts 1:8).

It is from this paradigm that we can find the connection to three current regions within any of our five-fold structures. The names of the regions in Jesus' day were Galilee, Samaria, and Judaea. These three regions comprised the entire land of Israel (currently called Palestine). Instead of Jesus mentioning Galilee, he mentioned another place. That location was called "the uttermost parts of the world."

And the main theme here is the association of the three regions of Palestine (formerly known as Israel) with the three designated places of any five-fold gift's ministry. For the name of our regions are local, national, and international. And we will stay in the same vein concerning the prophetic. So each of Jesus' biblical regions is parallel to our regions. So, now that we have biblically confirmed that there are three different types of regions, let us define them:

➢ The region of Judea parallels the local ministry of the prophet.

➢ The region of Samaria parallels the national ministry of the prophet.

> The region of the "uttermost parts" parallels the international ministry of the prophet.

The Local Prophet

Clearly, Judea is the place for local evangelistic witness. It is the representation of local witness because Jesus also mentioned Jerusalem, which was the capital city of the region of Judea. For Judea is another way of saying Judah. And Jerusalem was the major city controlling the entire region of Judea. There is a simple revelation in the designation of this region. For this process implies greater exhortation of crawling before walking.

In essence, not every prophet will be national or international. Somebody has got to take care of home. But the importance of sobriety and sincerity must be met with any regional assignment. And the work is just as great on the local level as it is on the national and international level. For the word of God puts it in this wise: **"Does anyone dare despise the day of small beginnings..." (Zechariah 4:10a, Message Bible).**

What this means is this: if you can witness in your Jerusalem (or local city), then you can witness in all of your Judea (or entire state). The process of any ministry is always placed right before you and never far away. Therefore, national ministry is always predicated on first completing a season of local ministry. If you cannot speak to those within your own region, what can you say to those born in other regions? Yes, a prophet is without honor in his own country! But this does not change the fact that every prophet must never overlook his primary starting point! And every starting point is best described as HOME! Even Jesus actualizes this when visiting his hometown of Nazareth:

And when he was come into his own country, he taught them in their synagogue, insomuch that they were astonished, and said, Whence hath this man this wisdom, and these mighty works? Is not this the carpenter's son? Is not his mother called Mary? And his brethren, James, and Joses, and Simon, and Judas? And his sisters, are they not all with us? Whence then hath this man all these things? And they were offended in him, But Jesus said unto them, A prophet is not without honor, save in his own country, and in his own house. And he did not many mighty works there because of their unbelief (Matthew 13:54-58).

You might say to yourself, "my hometown is not worthy of anything!" For even Nathanael asked the question: "Can any good thing come out of Nazareth?" (John 1:46). But the answer is yes! For Jesus came out of Nazareth! And even though Jesus was born in Bethlehem, making him by national descent a citizen of Judah (i.e. Judea), his ministry was destined to begin in Galilee. For Galilee and Capernaum were actually Jesus' Jerusalem and Judea! This means that

Jesus could not bypass his first place of ministry, because one's first place in ministry is right where you are! Therefore, proper handling of one's local ministry will determine one's overall success in the aspirations of national and international pursuits in ministry.

Thus, a prophet's ministry can often be local. In other cases, it may start local and expand to other regional assignments. But it is not limited to one region and can become an assignment within multiple areas. This is because a certain language is developed for each region. Meaning God requires a tongue of communication on a local level, which differs from that of a national level, and certainly requires an even greater skill of communication for the international level. Again, it must be reiterated that regions are about people and not places.

For when you are a local prophet, your message, language, and target exist only for a people immediately within your vicinity. Your prophetic message ministers directly to the individual. The language of the local prophet speaks directly and primarily, but not exclusively, into immediate society, interpersonal relationships, individual finances, and other factors that concern growth in spirituality or worship.

When beginning prophetic ministry, a person aspiring to become a local prophet is like one who frequently operates with the gift of prophecy instead of the office of the prophet. The only difference between a local prophet and one gifted with prophecy is the authority to pronounce judgment, correction, and rebuke. But one's disposition and demeanors will be similar and sometimes confusing if one is not clear on this particular subject matter.

For it is here on the local level that you work out your soul salvation as well as your true prophetic purpose. As we know, not everyone is called to be a prophet. But everyone is called to be prophetic! Therefore, it is on the local level that you are sharpened incrementally. For this is the phase in which you can discern whether you can become faithful enough to matriculate into ministerial assignment and then the formal ordination of eldership. I strongly advise the practicing prophetic candidate to make sure he has the credentials and the necessary skills before taking on this task and any other realm. Because if you are faithful to these things, then God can make you a ruler of many!

So the local prophet does not have messages for kings and queens. Instead, his messages may reach the local city or government officials, neighborhood churches, and local pastors. Yes, his messages will be tailored to local communities and families. And the local prophet's message again has simple mandates. He may even gain notoriety among the local churches within an entire city. But evolution within the ministry of a local prophet always depends on the original measurement of grace that God has predetermined for him.

A classic example of local prophets is seen in the Old Testament, particularly in the case of prophetic schools. The primary prophetic assignment for the prophetic school was usually within the confines of the city instead of an entire nation. The prophet's city, in other words, defined their locality because it defined the name of his region.

This means that Gibeah's prophets, for example, prophesied primarily in Gibeah (1 Samuel 10:5-7); Ramah's prophets in Ramah (1 Samuel 19:19-24), Bethel's prophets in Bethel (2 Kings 2:1-3), Jericho's prophets in Jericho (2 Kings 2:4-5), and Gilgal's prophets in Gilgal (2 Kings 4:38-44). Though prophetic schools were local prophetic ministries in nature, some of their emerging prophetic leaders had a tri-fold operation within the realms of prophetic ministry (e.g. Samuel, Elijah, and Elisha). I strongly believe that this was based upon experience and the Lord's seasoning.

Now, this does not imply that every prophet within a prophetic school is training for exclusivity within a local prophetic ministry. But it does confirm the idea that the novelty mantles of a prophet should reside for a season within their own local proximity. If you start here, then you can have success over there! And if by chance God does not call you to work outside your immediate city, walk in contentment knowing that God knows what is best for every man's ministry.

The National Prophet

Samaria is a region distinct from Judea and the uttermost parts of the earth. But if you combine Samaria and Judea together, you can compare them to the reach of a national region. During Jesus' ministry, there were three known provinces: Judea, the southern district, Samaria, the central district, and Galilee the northern district. These three regions were like a modern day, accessible tri-state or tri-fold state paradigm. In the Washington, DC, vicinity we have a similar paradigm. Maryland is our Galilee, Washington, DC, is our Samaria, and Virginia is our Judea. You too can make the same paradigm. The state above you will represent your Samaria. The state that's above the state representing Samaria can be your Galilee. And the state that you literally reside can be your Judea.

This teaches us that for a ministry to be national, it has to cover more than one city and state. And certainly, the responsibility of a national prophet is much larger than the local prophet. For a national prophet's calling spans a much larger group of people. They speak to multiple states, and governments of civic and national platforms. They speak to more churches and ministry leaders. An early example of this is the principle national prophet, Moses. Moses' ministry was predominantly for two nations: Egypt and Israel. But his greatest platform chiefly resided among the congregation of Israel:

According to all that thou desirest of the Lord thy God in Horeb in the day of the assembly, saying, let me not hear again the voice of the Lord my God, neither let me see this great fire any more, that I die not. And the Lord said unto me, they have well spoken that which they have spoken (Deuteronomy 18:16-17).

When God came to move Israel out of Egypt, it was not solely for the purpose of deliverance. His goal was to also establish a direct relationship with them. His plan was for them to meet him, as a nation, at Mt. Sinai. There, he became their God, and they his people. Upon arrival, the people felt intense fear, since they were hearing God's voice. They said to Moses that the sight and voice of God was too intimidating for them to handle. Next, they hesitated and were reluctant in approaching the mountain that possessed the power and presence of God. And in fear, they withdrew from Mt. Sinai to another place nearby. At this point, they informed Moses that he should be their representative and remain God's continual spokesmen. Thus, the first national ministry of the prophet was born. On a side note, what also appears from this is the first church in the wilderness, which is the first biblical paradigm for a mega-ministry. Not all national prophets will work with a mega-ministry. But Moses, of course, was a rare exception.

These biblical beginnings demonstrate the national prophet's ministry. In response to the people's request, God agreed and kept Moses as their national liaison (Exodus 20:18-21). But prior to this experience, the prophet's role was more localized. However, the evolution of the local prophet to that of the national prophet certainly did not undermine the differences within the regional assignments. In fact, it complemented them.

In sobriety, I must again caution you to not jump before you have mastered walking. The national ministry comes with a language that is applicable to the entire nation and not just a few locals. Be true to what is coming out of you, even if there is a desire for more. And please wait on God to elevate you into more, and be confident and competently faithful in that which you've already received. For a prodigal prophet is like the prodigal son. If you want the portion that is yours now, because of immaturity, you will squander and lose the placement of assignment and the moments of development necessary for maintaining such a large assignment.

The International Prophet

The largest prophetic region is that of the international prophet's ministry. Jesus described this reach in the evangelistic paradigm of Acts 1:8 as the "uttermost parts." If we stay within that same vein, we can decipher this paradigm to mean Galilee, Judea, and Samaria, but it is also beyond the lands of these three vicinities. An international prophet's ministry is always an assignment for many countries. An example of this type of ministry is seen in the assignment of the prophet Jeremiah. Jeremiah's international assignment, for his prophetic sphere was given at his prophetic inauguration:

"...I ordained thee a prophet unto the nations" (Jeremiah 1:5b).

Jeremiah prophesied to his home nation, Israel, but he also prophesied to the nations of Babylon, Egypt, Edom, Assyria (Philistines), and Moab. (See Jeremiah 9:26; 25:15-27; 47:1-17; and Jeremiah Chapters 50 and 51.) Most of the prophetic discourses were done to these countries. But Jeremiah never actually visited some locations about which he was called to prophesy internationally!

This further shows how one can be an international or national prophet and yet never frequent or visit the realm of his prophetic assignment. The prophet's connection to that realm parallels the prophetic message manifesting from him for that realm. But again, let's be sensible about this assignment. You will reveal the true measure of the prophet inside you by what comes out of you. The heart speaks through the mouth, and thus the heart of the prophet is revealed in the prophet's messages. Under the dispensation of the law and Old Testament, an international prophetic voice had a tougher mandate for foreign nations:

At what instant I shall speak concerning a nation, and concerning a kingdom, to pluck up, and to pull down, and to destroy it. If that nation, against whom I have pronounced, turn from their evil, I will repent of the evil that I thought to do unto them. And at what instant shall I speak concerning a nation, and concerning a kingdom, to build and to plant it; If it do evil in my sight, that it obey not my voice, then I will repent of the good, wherewith I said I would benefit them (Jeremiah 18:7-10, KJV).

For it is quite clear: Jeremiah has a tailor-made word for the people of his homeland. But he equally prophesies for nations abroad. This shows that a prophet's language will match the region within their ministry. A prophet's heart, mouth, and spirit will divinely connect to a specific burden and multitudes of people for which God calls them. They have language and divinely conferred ambassadorial skills for kings, queens, presidents, tribal leaders, government, and local, national, and international civic officials. And they will have a pulse for chief ecclesiastical officers and ministry leaders within every continent of the world. Yes, they are prophetic agents for all communities, both domestic and abroad. Thus, the oil of an international prophet has a broader reach and greater responsibility than the other two realms.

Conclusion of the Three Prophetic Regions

The content of each prophet's prophetic messages certainly gives clues to the regions for which a prophet is assigned. Some prophets are called to all regions. And others may be called to one or two regions. And some are not called to any regions at all (the gift of prophecy). International prophetic voices have international visions, national prophetic voices have national visions, and local prophetic voices have local visions. And those gifted with the gift of prophecy have sporadic prophetic purposes that are not conducive to local, national, and international spheres of prophetic responsibility.

But all are good and perfect works. And again, the process towards the recognition of a local, national, and international prophetic voice is wrapped up in the content of his heart. The prophet's mouth reveals the true direction of his ministry. For whatever leaves his mouth surely comes from his heart. And whatever comes from his heart hopefully comes from his spirit.

There will be certain cultures within each ministry to which the prophet and those particular people will be mutually drawn. Like a magnet, they will find each other. This, then, reveals the prophet's true regional mission. The governing leaders of a region (i.e. congressmen, mayors, presidents, and royals, etc.) will favor each known prophet. And the ministerial leaders (i.e. apostles, bishops, overseers, pastors, etc.) will favor them as well. And based on the jurisdiction of sanctuary ministry (ministry within the church), you will know your true reach. If you are reaching predominantly African American congregations, African congregations, or multi-cultural congregations, then you can map your prophetic ministry based on your prophetic practice within the churches of the Lord, as well as by the world leaders you will strategically meet.

This is not the choice of the prophet! Neither is it the choice of a manipulative people or person. But God is the force behind these choices! And when God distributes talents and gifts, there is always a conditional clause attached to such distributions: "To every man according to his several ability" (Matthew 25:15; Romans 12:6; 1 Corinthians 12:7, 11, 29).

Please take note of all scriptural trends. And do not lie to yourself! Stay within your own means of ministry! In other words, stay within your lane! For the spirit of delusion can infect you! And if it could it would deceive even God's elect. It will make you want to do more and yet not complete that which God has already given. Beloved, this is a dangerous demon. And it is still prevalent in today's church.

Remember, there is nothing new under the sun. For we have many wanting to be more than what they are. But we must remember that with responsibility comes the reality of preparation and endurance for any calling. The scriptures declare that even those who are presently building anything for Christ will someday be tried by fire (1 Corinthians 3:15). Therefore, you can only be as true to your ministry as what God has truthfully placed inside you to do:

"...Every man that is among you, not to think of himself more highly than he ought to think; but to think soberly, according as God hath dealt to every man the measure of faith" (Romans 12:6).

All prophets receive the mandate for their prophetic ministry from the womb. Others may start their mandates by generalizing the operation of the gift during moments of ministry. But, my brothers and sisters, it is imperative that sobriety return to the church. For Paul teaches that men should not think higher of themselves. So let every man, assuming a prophet's mantle and work, work that work within his given measures of grace and faith.

For it is quite clear that one will think about being a prophet before one fully knows that he is one. And these doctrines are written beforehand for any man to acknowledge that the perimeters of prophecy are based solely on the word of God and the predetermined will of God for each prophet:

If any man think himself to be a prophet, or spiritual, let him acknowledge that the things that I write unto you are the commandments of the Lord (1 Corinthians 14:37).

Finally, God will also deposit within the prophet's spirit a specific burden for certain countries, places, and people. When you see such burdens, you must take this as the vision for your ministry. For vision is the assignment of any prophet, as are those whom a prophet is called unto! This means that prophets have three assignments, while others have one or two. And some work seasonally in all three regions, while others may spend their lifetime in just one.

All of this depends on grace, faith, and the uniqueness of one's calling. Again, I cannot stress this enough: prophetic sobriety is fundamental to any ministry. It is very dangerous to overextend oneself beyond the true measure of grace, anointing, and the ministry to which you are specifically called. Therefore, a prophet must properly discern his regional assignment by accessing these attributing factors.

You will immediately discover that a prophet cannot go beyond the means of one's own region. The truth about each prophet's ministry will be loud enough for the prophet to understand and see clearly. If God wants a prophet's ministry in China, for example, he will receive prophetic instructions for China. His connections to the region of China, as well as his insights about the region, will come, even when they are only partially transmitted to him. But if God wants a prophet's focus to be on a local city, or even a state alone, then the prophet's messages will remain exclusively for that jurisdiction. For we dare not glorify one region as greater than the other! Each gifting and expression within their region is equally important, for all regions are reflective of this world. And Jesus came to save the entire world. But we are responsible for the section of the world that he has assigned us to!

The process for finding one's region is simple: listen consistently to the words that prophetically flow from you. Listen to the words of the people who prophesy into your life. Every word is established by two or three witnesses. If you have heard it more than once from more than one prophetic source of credibility, then there is a major possibility that this is the premise of your ministry. But walk in sobriety. And don't let deception fool you. Your messages will not lie. The true context and content of you and your relationship with God certainly determines the outlook of your assignment. Simply put, you know what is coming out of you! And you know whether God is speaking through you by way of a local, national, or international prophetic language. For the language of any true ministry will not lie because God will never lie:

God forbid: yea, let God be true, but every man a liar; as it is written, that thou mightest be justified in thy sayings, and mightest overcome when thou art judged (Romans 3:4).

THE THREE OPERATIONS OF A PROPHET

The Overview of Prophetic Operations

And there are diversities of operations, but it is the same God "which worketh all in all" (1 Corinthians 12:6).

The Greek word for "operations" in this context is the word *energema* (En-er-jay-mah, #1753). It is how a position works. In other words, it is the chief area of its own function. When you are offered a job, there should always be a job description. Similarly, the three diverse operations of the prophetic works provide the overall job descriptions of the specific functions within each prophetic work.

Each prophet has a different type of position or a certain type of work. And everyone who is called a prophet does not work as a prophet in the same vein. And each prophet must find his unique work. The appearance of such prophetic offices or works appears as revelations in the New Testament. These revelations are given to the church through the Apostle Paul's ministry. For Paul repetitively explained the presence and purpose of spiritual gifts in three writings as he wrote to three different churches. And the names of the three different churches are Rome, Corinth, and Ephesus.

It is Paul who revealed that there are actually 18-20 spiritual gifts. And he explained a cluster of gifts in each Epistle. Some gifts become duplicated in the next Epistle. But such duplication is actually an even greater revelation of the prophetic. For each list expands and connects to another. This is because Paul's writings about spiritual gifts were linked and based on the historical timeline of each Epistle's creation. Simply put, Paul wrote first to the church of Corinth, Rome second, and to Ephesus third. In light of this timeframe, we must now count and categorize the gifts in chronological order:

- The Charismatic Spiritual Gifts #1 - 9 are mentioned in 1 Corinthians 12 (verses 8-10). Note: they are Word of Wisdom, Word of Knowledge, Faith, Working of Miracles, Divers Tongues, Interpretation of Tongues, Gifts of Healing and Discernment of Spirits [the final gift in this group is called **prophecy**].

- The Serving Spiritual Gifts #10 - 15 are mentioned in Romans 12 (verses 6-8, 13). Note: they are Giving, Exhortation, Mercy, Hospitality, Ruling, and Serving [**prophesying** and teaching are also mentioned].

- The Governmental Spiritual Gifts #15 – 18 (20) are mentioned in Ephesians 4 (verse 11). Note: They are Apostle, Evangelist, and Pastor [**Prophet** and Teacher are duplicated. See Romans 12].

Notice that only two gifts were mentioned more than once. Those gifts are teaching and prophesying. However, it is the gifts of prophecy and prophesying, as well as the office of prophet, that translate into all three Epistles. This establishes that Paul saw the spiritual gift and work of the prophet and prophecy as the primary gift of those mentioned. And it is this threefold mentioning that the Lord revealed to me, showing me that these are not duplicates. Instead, they are revelations of the different operations of a prophetic work.

- The writings of Ephesians reveal the revelation of the governmental prophet.

- The writings of Romans reveal the revelation of the serving prophet.

- The writings of Corinthians reveal the revelation of the charismatic prophet.

The Revelation of the Governmental Prophet

I therefore, the prisoner of the Lord, beseech you that ye walk worthy of the vocation wherewith ye are called (Ephesians 4:1).

And he gave some, apostles; and some, prophets; and some, evangelists; and some, pastors and teachers (Ephesians 4:11).

These two verses help support the revelation of the governmental prophet. And the reason for titling the first prophetic operation the governmental prophet is because of verse 1 of Ephesians 4. Here, the word "vocation" translates to the Greek word meaning "invitation." A vocation, or calling, is an invitation to some formal place or event.

We are still in the process of being called to such an invitation. And when we arrive to that place, there will be a specific place of seating for each individual. We can understand this when we think of weddings. Not everyone will sit in the seat of the father of the bride or the mother of the groom. Those in charge of the wedding predetermine who sits where. It is the same with leadership invitations (i.e. vocations). And there are five gifts that are the most important seats within the calling of spiritual gifts (apostle, prophet, evangelist, pastor, and teacher). For they are the gifts that lead the Lord's church. And the Apostle Paul also revealed in his first Epistle to the Corinthians that three of the five gifts receive an even greater level of respect and honor:

"And God hath set some in the church, first apostles, secondarily prophets, thirdly teachers..." (1 Corinthians 12:28a).

We must further understand that the vocation of these spiritual gifts is exclusive and preselected by the hand of God. No one can assume such gifts from mere desire. Only can these gifts be appropriated from divine destiny. Simply put, you cannot make yourself a prophet, even though you can be prophetic! God called the prophet before he created the world. And this is why Paul asked these questions:

"Are all apostles? Are all prophets? Are all teachers?" (1 Corinthians 12:29a).

The answer to those questions is no. Thus, even within the diversity of the prophetic office, not everyone will be a leading prophet. Some will be of a supportive voice within the prophetic work, while others will be of a leading voice within the prophetic work. But the presence of the governmental prophet is for the sheer purpose of ruling. This position comes with authority and regard. You cannot make yourself into this position, but you can be born into this position. Just as the five-fold gifts are governmental gifts, with the strongest voice for all spiritual gifts, so are the prophets with the greatest measure of faith, grace, and mercy. For, within the Lord's church, the governmental prophet has the greatest function for prophetic service and work.

The Revelation of the Serving Prophet

I beseech you therefore, brethren, by the mercies of God, that ye present your bodies a living sacrifice, holy, acceptable unto God, which is your reasonable service (Romans 12:1).

Having then gifts differing according to the grace that is given to us, whether prophecy, let us prophecy according to the proportion of faith (Romans 12:6).

The pattern in Romans 12 is much like the patter in Ephesians 4. For the following two verses above help support the revelation of the serving prophet. And the reason for shifting the second prophetic operation in the serving prophet is because of verse 1 of Romans 12. Here, the word "service" translates to the Greek word meaning "ministry."

And the Greek word for "service" is *lateria* (lah-tray-ah, #2999). It means "service rendered for hire." Any service for God that is similar to rendering service and worship of God is like the requirements of the Levitical system. It is dually a priestly and Levitical word. The concept behind this word is performing sacred service. So the service here is that which is rendered in the midst of the sanctuary like a priest and or a Levite of God. This type of prophet is a minister to the sanctuary but not in public. Rather this prophet serves best behind the scenes.

The New Testament explains to us that we all are of the royal priesthood of God through Jesus Christ (1 Peter 2:9). In this new reformation, modern-day priests and Levites have a responsibility of ministerial service within the sanctuary similar to the functions of the Old Testament priests and Levites. Their chief service was that of assisting the people of God in maintaining their worship of God. And this service again was like a "behind-the-scenes" method of prophetic work. They may have been either of a ruling nature, such as the priest, or they may have been of a subordinate nature, such as the Levite. Regardless, their overall service in this capacity was to assist with the tabernacle and temple of God – as a public or private instrument – with a serving heart.

The serving prophet is a prophet of priestly or Levitical function. He is sent to conduct administrative affairs within the household of faith. He is sent to prophesy about the presence of governing prophets and other leading gifts and voices. He is also sent to prophesy privately about the behaviors or issues of a people.

When one serves a prophet, one can either govern like a governmental prophet (but with a priestly anointing) or like a prophet with a serving gift of prophecy. And in his assignment, he must focus on what is "behind the scenes" with both prophetic counsel and wisdom. For when one is gifted with a similar gift of prophecy, as a prophet in office, there is a tendency for him to remain neutral in ministering, and he will never administer harshness of judgment or correction. Rather he will focus on exhortation, edification, and encouragement within his prophetic office of serving. Because the assignment is always greater because it's bigger than himself.

A great example in the Old Testament is the prophetic ministry of Nathan in conjunction with the prophetic ministry of David, for David was a king who happened to also be a prophet (Acts 2:29-30). When Nathan prophetically ministered to David, it was in a capacity of service, for Nathan was sent to help the ruling prophet, King David (2 Samuel Chapter 7). Another example of this is when Nathan spoke to David about his error with Bathsheba (2 Samuel Chapter 12).

Thus, any ruling prophet can take on a supportive and administrative role within prophetic ministry. Though senior prophetic leadership was upon both David and Nathan, the spirit of the prophet is subject to a prophet. David's oil of kingly leadership took a back seat to the prophetic oil of Nathan. But Nathan's goal was not to usurp King David's authority. However, Nathan was sent by God to exhort the king concerning his displacement and the need of his return to proper positioning. So when a prophet comes to assist another prophetic leader it is always done from the vein of edification, never domination. For the position of prophetic servant leader is truly the greatest of all positions within any prophetic functionality. Though the governmental prophet is first, all can stand to submit to another prophet greater, equal or lesser in anointing as Nathan did to David, and as many of us will have to do within our lifetime.

The Revelation of the Charismatic Prophet

Now concerning spiritual gifts, brethren, I would not have you ignorant (1 Corinthians 12:1).

"...To another prophecy..." (1 Corinthians 12:10). The Greek word for "gifts" is the word *charisma* (Kah-riz-mah, #5483). The biblical word and definition of *charisma* is a compound word that means both "grace" (charis [Khah-ris], #5485) and "rejoicing" (chairo [Kh-eye-row], #5463). Thus, it is a public demonstrational gift used to promote worship and praise unto God. These are gifts of spectacle because they are known for always being on display.

Examples of such display are usually combined with some vocal, verbal, or artistic talents, such as singing, speaking, or playing music.

The applicable confirmation of such practices is seen even in the description of the classification of the charismatic gifts listed in 1 Corinthians 12. There are three sub-categories within the functions or operations of such charismatic gifts: the divine ability to know, speak, or act. Each category logically places three of the nine within each sub-division, completing the total of the nine charismatic gifts numerically.

When one prophesies in the dimension of the charismatic operations of a prophetic work, the prophet publically demonstrates with a talent used to draw and to evangelize. It is also given to the church to inspire praise and worship, and it is chiefly seen in the public display of leading worship positions. This operation of this type of prophetic office is not shy, nor is it reserved in temperament. Instead, it is a blatant expression of prophecy seen by all and notice by all. It is upfront and frontline. It is center stage within the prophetic works. It is not a behind-the-scene type of prophetic function. And neither is it contemplative or rigid in its reality. Instead, it is impulsive and has spectacular features.

The Old Testament's Confirmation on the New Testament's Revelation About the Three Prophetic Operations

Again, these three revelations of the prophetic operations are given to us by the revelation of the Apostle Paul. But Paul's revelations confirm an even greater witness of such operations. After extensive research, I have discovered that there is a strong connection between the revelation of the three prophetic operations (serving, charismatic, and governmental prophets) in relation to the Old Testament's manifestation concerning the first company of prophets (Moses, Aaron, and Miriam).

The diversity within the collectivity of the prophetic operations of government, service, and charismatic prophetic gifting was how God actually relieved the children of Israel from Egypt and directed their wilderness journey. In fact, Micah records that it was not Moses alone who led them. But his siblings were also officially recognized as co-prophetic pastors of the first mega-church in scripture:

For I brought thee up out of the land of Egypt, and redeemed thee out of the house of servants: and I sent before thee Moses, Aaron, and Miriam (Micah 6:4).

✓ ✓ ✓

Below is the confirmation of Paul's duplications and revelations concerning the prophetic operations of a New Testament prophet:

The Prophet Moses – The Governmental Prophet

And the Lord came down in the pillar of the cloud, and stood in the door of the tabernacle, and called Aaron and Miriam: and they both came forth. And He said, Hear now my words: If there be a prophet among you, I the Lord will make myself known unto him in a vision, and will speak unto him in a dream. My servant Moses is not so, who is faithful in all mine house. With him will I speak mouth to mouth, even apparently, and not in dark speeches; and the similitude of the Lord shall he behold; whereof then were ye not afraid to speak against my servant Moses? (Numbers 12:5-8)

I will raise them up a Prophet from among their brethren, like unto thee, and will put my words in his mouth, and he shall speak unto them all that I shall command him (Deuteronomy 18:18).

The Prophet Aaron – The Serving Prophet

"...And Aaron thy brother shall be thy prophet" (Exodus 7:1b).

The Prophetess Miriam – The Charismatic Prophet

And Miriam the prophetess, the sister of Aaron, took a timbrel in her hand; and all the women went out after her with timbrels and with dances (Exodus 15:22).

Apostle Sherman D. Farmer

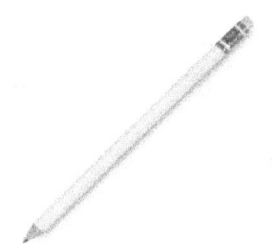

CONCLUSION OF LESSON 8

(THE THREE PROPHETIC REGIONS AND OPERATIONS)

God sent governmental, serving, and charismatic operations of the prophetic office in order to assist Israel. And God is still sending these three types of operations even now unto his church. What Paul did for us, in his three writings to these three different churches, was to provide a revelatory truism. He revealed that the flow of the prophetic gift is graced to operate in one, two, or even every operational capacity.

The truth is, we need prophetic leadership. But we also need prophetic counsel or service, while at the same time we need prophetic inspiration. Each of these expressions of unique operation creates a well-rounded prophetic witness and established word among the later-day New Testament prophet's quorum. Thus, the regions and operations of the prophetic work help pastoring and prophesying to God's people in any and every quarter of the known world. And the manifestation of such revelation dissolves prophetic envy and jealousy whereby some prophets who do not function like other prophets can find their true identity in one of the mentioned positions of prophetic leadership.

Application:

- ➤ Are you a governing prophet (one that is responsible with pastoral leadership over other prophets [i.e., chief-prophet, house-prophet, lead-prophet, under-shepherd-prophet, etc.])?

- ➤ Are you a serving prophet (one that is responsible for administrative and pastoral guidance by way of prophesying behind the scenes [i.e., life coach, counselor, mentorship, prophetic speech writer, prophetic administrator, and or prophetic adjutant, etc.])?

- ➤ Or are you a charismatic prophet (one that is responsible for pastoral leadership that serves in the more public ecstatic presentation of prophesying through prophetic intercession, praise, exhortation, worship, and creative arts [dance, writing, and drawing and public speaking, in areas of public leadership and frontline ministry])?

Yes, everyone fits in somewhere! Now the task is to find out if you operate in one or more of these three leading prophetic offices, or perhaps even all three. For this is based upon God's purpose for your life within his holy church. This is not a matter of personal choosing. Thus, you must find your lane so you can operate properly.

CHAPTER 9

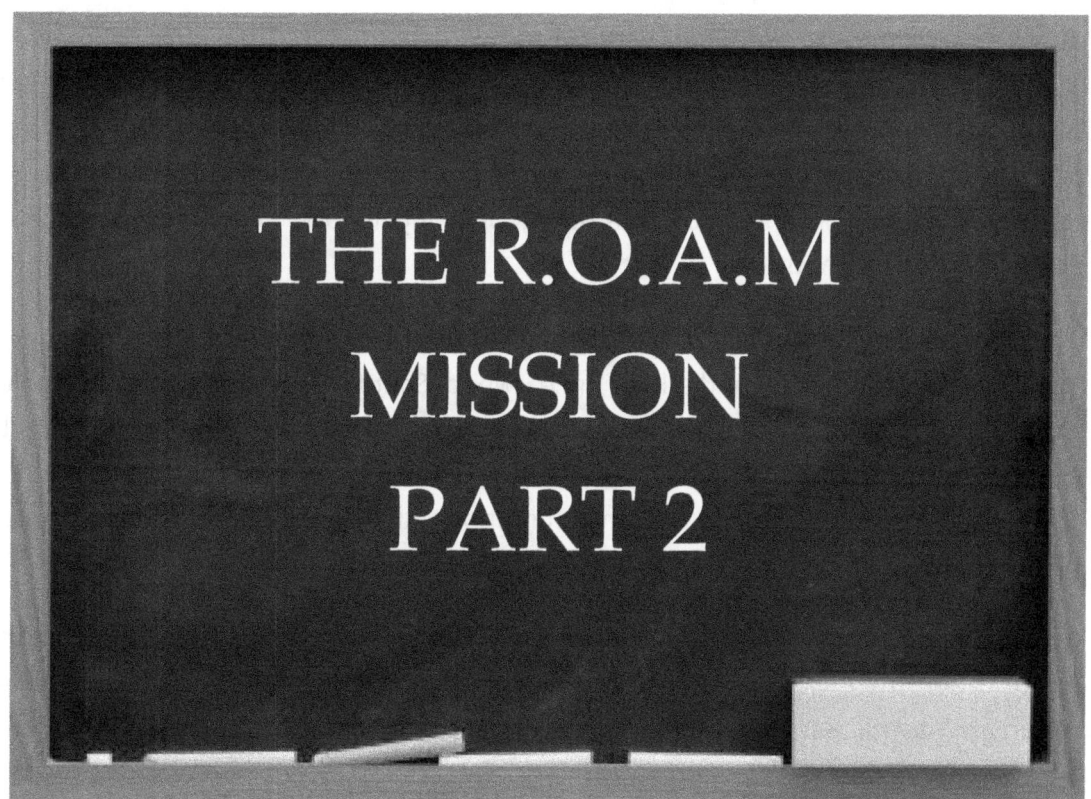

How Does the Prophetic Operate? – Part 4

Now, there are diversities of gifts but the same Spirit. And there are differences of administrations but the same Lord. And there are diversities of operations, but it is the same God "which worketh all in all. But the manifestation of the Spirit is given to every man to profit withal" (1 Corinthians 12:4-7).

Prophetic Administrations and Mantles

THE THREE ADMINISTRATIONS OF A PROPHET

The Overview of Prophetic Administrations

And there are differences of administrations but the same Lord (1 Corinthians 12:5).

The word "administration" has within this word the word "ministry." A ministry is a particular type of service rendered by the one who ministers to a specific people and place. In the Old Testament, a prophet's ministry chiefly dealt with a pending or particular exile a people would or could experience. The definition of "exile" is an enforcement or removal from one's native country. It is also the uncomfortable reality of being forcibly removed from one's initial place of dominion and authority.

Thus, an exile is also a place of bondage because of judgment. It is the process of being taken from one's true dimension and a land once owned. Scripture records two undeniable exilic experiences among the nation of Israel. It is in these exiles, as well as in the experiences before and after such exiles that shape the Old Testament prophet's purposes. We, too, can follow this same paradigm to further understand the conditions that necessitate the presence of a prophetic anointing.

But first we must review the actual storyline of the creation of the two exiles forced upon the nation of Israel. There were actually seven nations that ruled Israel throughout its existence. They were Egypt, Assyria, Babylon, Media, Persia, Greece, and lastly Rome. Apart from Rome, the next main two, out of the seven, were Assyria and Babylon. Assyria's plan was to overtake the northern tribes of Israel. This was the first exile. And the Babylonian siege of the southern tribes created the second exile.

As a result of disobedience, the northern tribes never regained their territory. But the southern nation's remnant eventually returned seventy years later (Jeremiah 29:10, Daniel 9:2). It is also important to note that God was the reason for such exiles. These foreign nations' presence was a form of judgment upon the nation of Israel. Scripture records God's thoughts about nations being used to correct and condition his people so they might return to him:

"Now these are the nations which the Lord left, to prove Israel..." (Judges 3:1a).

And this teaching is strictly from an Old Testament viewpoint. However, its methodology helps to assist the ministry of the current prophet. It in fact reveals how the assignment of a prophet's regional ministry will function. Meaning that there are three known positional aspects of exile. And these three known aspects correspond to what we can now call prophetic administrations:

> **Pre-Exile experiences create a pre-exilic-prophetic administration**

> **Exile experiences create an exilic-prophetic administration**

> **Post-Exile experiences create a post-exilic-prophetic administration**

The position of an exile determines the position of the prophet's administration. Or, more simply, it determines the types of prophetic messages that will be preached. And a modern day exile shapes the overall parameters of any modern day prophetic work. Whereas the region is the location of an assignment, the disposition of a prophet's assignment is based solely on whether a people are in bondage (exiled), coming out of bondage (post-exiled), or about to be in bondage (pre-exile). Another way to look at this teaching is that as long as a people are disobedient, the prophet's ministry will surely be active. For exiles are the very reason prophets are sent to serve within certain administrations. Back then it was for Israel. But now it is for the church and God's kingdom:

> **When a prophet warns a people of a pending bondage, this is the ministry of a pre-exile prophetic administration.**

> **When a prophet is called to minister in a place and time of bondage (alongside those called to a particular judgment of bondage), this is the ministry of an exile prophetic administration.**

> **When a prophet is called to minister in a place designed to bring a people out of bondage, this is a post-exile prophetic administration.**

If we metaphorically extend this concept to the modern purposes of a prophet, a better prophetic clarity will emerge in his assignment. For truth be told: people are always putting themselves in a place of pending spiritual disaster. This is what creates the potential for entering into the unfortunate verdicts of what we now can call a spiritual exile (instead of a literal exile).

Example #1: A Pre-Exile Prophetic Administration Paradigm

The prophet Isaiah was called to speak before and during Israel's bondage at the hand of the Assyrians. Even though Isaiah was a Judean prophet, he could see the pending devastation that God was about to send to the northern tribes of Israel. On a side note, this was because he was an international prophet:

O Assyrian, the rod of mine anger, and the staff in their hand is mine indignation. I will send him against a hypocritical nation, and against the people of my wrath will give him a charge, to take the spoil, and to take the prey, and to tread them down like the mire of the streets. (Isaiah 10:5-6).

When you are called to minister words of warning as a watchman on the wall, you are functioning in the pre-exilic administration of the prophetic anointing. Your job is to warn the people that they are about to place themselves in some type of bondage. It is a warning, though, that now comes with the flow of grace. But it also comes with righteous judgment. The pre-exilic prophetic administration calls for courage to stand up, cry loud, and spare not! This usually is the ministry that is sent to a people before the people are overtaken by their faults. As the Bible says, warning always comes before judgment.

Example #2: An Exiled Prophetic Administration Paradigm

The prophet Jeremiah was called to instruct the people that they could not avoid the seventy years of exile of Babylon. As a result of God's punishment, he instructed them on how to endure exile within Babylon. This was so they might survive and return one day, as a people, back to Jerusalem:

Thus saith the Lord of hosts, the God of Israel, unto all that are carried away captives, whom I have caused to be carried away from Jerusalem unto Babylon: Build ye houses, and dwell in them; and plant gardens, and eat the fruit of them: take ye wives, and beget sons and daughters; and take wives for your sons, and give your daughters to husbands, that they may bear sons and daughters; that ye may be increased there, and not diminished.

And seek the peace of the city whither I have caused you to be carried away captives, and pray unto the Lord for it: for in the peace thereof shall ye have peace...For thus saith the Lord, that after seventy years be accomplished at Babylon I will visit you, and perform my good word toward you, in causing you to return to this place (Jeremiah 29:4-7, 10).

The prophetic exiled ministry is very difficult. It is the hardest of all ministries among the three prophetic administrations. When you are called to an exilic experience of prophetic ministry, you are possibly going to participate in the verdict of the given people to which you are called to this reality. Sometimes this may be the role of a pastor who happens to be prophetic.

And that pastor has to minister to a people who have remained stiff-necked or heart-hardened. The clear example of this is when Moses had to remain with Israel for 40 year in the wilderness. Other examples are Ezekiel and Daniel who are both taken captive from Judah and have to live in Babylon until the judgment is over. It would be Daniel, only, who lived throughout the entire seventy years. But the task of prophesying to a people, in bondage, while also experiencing the same bondage, makes the exilic prophetic ministry very difficult within the prophet's assignment. Of course everyone wants to have a deliverance ministry (or a post exilic prophetic anointing). But we must understand there are some that have to be reached in bondage as well are pre-warned about pending bondage. But the goal of the prophet's discernment in this assignment is to know which position of administration that they are presently therein.

And, we must also understand that administrations of exilic experiences are usually coupled with certain paradigms and patterns, meaning that a prophetic work can start with one administration and then shift to another. In the next section, we will examine some of these biblical clarifications and combinations.

Example #1: The Combination of Exiled and Post-Exiled Prophetic Administration Paradigms

God commissioned from the backside of the desert a formerly adopted Egyptian prince who was a true Israelite. His name was Moses. And Moses became the national prophet. His assignment was to bring Israel out of Egypt (this is an example of a post-exilic experience). And he not only led them out of Egypt, across the Red Sea, but he was assigned to take them to the Promised Land as well. But because of Israel's disobedience in the wilderness, and Moses' lack of patience, both Israel and Moses were disqualified from entering into the land of Canaan. This verdict was decided not only for Moses, Aaron, and Miriam, but also for anyone 20 years old and older (this is another example of an exilic experience):

And the Lord said, I have surely seen the affliction of my people which are in Egypt, and have heard their cry by reason of their taskmasters; for I know their sorrows; and I am come down to deliver them out of the hand of the Egyptians, and to bring them up out of that land unto a good land and a large, unto a land flowing with milk and honey....Now therefore, behold, the cry of the children of Israel is come unto me: and I have also seen the oppression wherewith the Egyptians oppress them: come now therefore, and I will send

thee unto Pharaoh, that thou mayest bring forth my people the children of Israel out of Egypt (Exodus 3:7-8a, 9-10).

I hope you are not missing the meaning of this revelation. God sent Moses to be a post-exilic prophet (calling Israel out of Egypt). But instead the duration of his ministry consisted of being a post-exilic and exilic prophet. This is because the place destined to be the location of their transition (the wilderness) had become the place for a new a level of imprisonment. This, too, can happen in the church. One minute we are helping a people come out of bondage. And the next minute, if a people are not careful, they can place themselves back into bondage because of sin. But regardless of the location, it is that prophet's job to minister to the people based on the present predicament given within each generation.

Example #2: The Trifold Exiled Prophetic Administration Paradigm

In very rare cases, a prophet may be called to the totality of all exilic-prophetic assignments. There is one example of this in scripture. The Prophet Daniel was the only prophet who survived the complete duration of Babylonian captivity. He saw the judgment coming. He lived in the judgment. And he came out of the judgment. Daniel, then, is our greatest example of a prophet called to all three assignments within one prophet's lifetime:

In the first year of Darius the son of Ahasuerus, of the seed of the Medes, which was made king over the realm of the Chaldeans; in the first year of his reign I Daniel understood by books of the number of the years, whereof the word of the Lord came to Jeremiah the prophet, that He would accomplish seventy years in the desolations of Jerusalem. And I set my face unto the Lord God, to see thy prayer and supplications, with fasting, and sackcloth and ashes. (Daniel 9:1-3).

Daniel was taken in the first deportation during captivity. Daniel was possibly a pre-teen or a young teenager when this happened (Daniel 1:3, 4). This shows that the office of the prophet on an international level, such as Daniel's, is not just for men of old. But it is even for those young in age.

When the Babylonian Exile ended, Daniel was in his eighties (and some say possibly his nineties). For Daniel discovered the reoccurring theme of Jeremiah's message during Babylonian exile (Daniel 9:2). The revelation of seventy years of Jeremiah's prophecy stirred Daniel's heart, and Daniel discovered this book around the seventieth year. If he had not discovered it, it is quite possible that Israel would have missed their exodus from Babylon. And thus, the post-exilic ministry of Daniel would have been incomplete! But Daniel successfully completed the period of pre-exilic, exilic, and post-exilic experiences during his lifetime and his prophetic ministry!

The Greatest Spiritual Exile and Diaspora

The Old Testament prophetic-exiled administrations can be seen within a New Testament paradigm. Exiles and expulsions did not begin with Israel. No, the greatest spiritual exiles and diasporas were created by the first parents of scripture. When Adam and Eve sinned, they were also exiled, not only from the Garden of Eden, but also from the Tree of Life that was in the midst of the Garden. This exile and expulsion was both a spiritual and literal one:

And the Lord God said, Behold, the man is become as one of us, to know good and evil: and now, lest he put for his hand, and take also of the tree of life, and eat, and live forever: therefore the Lord sent him forth from the garden of Eden, to till the ground from whence he was taken. So He drove out the man: and He placed at the east of the garden of Eden Cherubims, and a flaming sword which turned every way, to keep the way of the tree of life. (Genesis 3:22-24).

We have clearly been taught that, theologically, man's expulsion from the Garden of Eden was an act of mercy. If man had remained in the Garden of Eden, in his sinful state, and partaken from the Tree of Life, he would have perpetuated himself, and therefore put himself, beyond the pales of redemption. So God's act of mercy was expelling and exiling mankind, since it was the only way to save mankind. As a result, the entirety of mankind lives in a universally understood exilic experience, which is the death of the spirit of man and his displacement from God.

In the creation of exiles, we reach the realm of understanding another word, "diaspora." A diaspora is a migration of people across a particular region. Some diasporas are intentional. Others are forced. The universal spirit of the patriarch and matriarch of mankind is a diaspora directly because of the first man and woman's unfortunate decision. In essence, it is the greatest spiritual exile and diaspora that any human being can experience.

Regarding the prophetic ministry as a primarily spiritual work, the work of the prophet is to prevent and intervene in exiles and diasporas. Thus, the ultimate ministry of the prophet is to minister to mankind under one or more of the prophetic assignments as a means of assisting the candidate in exile with his possible return, which is related to the proper spiritual inheritance and placement of his assignment. That greatest place is in the presence of God, and the spiritual inheritance that is granted to all who become born again will be fully actualized in the ultimate Promised Land, which is heaven:

These all died in faith, not having received the promises, but having seen them afar off, and were persuaded of them, and embraced them, and confessed that they were strangers and pilgrims on the earth. For they that say such things declare plainly that they seek a country. And truly, if they had been mindful of that country from whence they came out, they might have had opportunity to have returned. But now they desire a better country, that is, a heavenly: wherefore God is not ashamed to be called their God: for He hath prepared for them a city (Hebrews 11:13-16).

Conclusion of the Three Prophetic Administrations

Learning from the actual historical accounts of the functions of the exilic-prophetic assignments instructs prophets who are still ministering to a people in pre-exilic, exilic, and post-exilic conditions. And this brings an importance question to pose: What is your prophetic assignment? Is it to exhort people not to go into bondage? Is it to encourage those who are in bondage that they can eventually come out of their bondage? Or is it to comfort those who are called to suffer within bondage until a specified date of deliverance?

We who are prophetic under the dispensation of grace can recognize that we, too, have been called to one or more of these prophetic patterns. It is, then, imperative that the prophet knows the direction of his ministry. He must properly navigate himself and a people to God. This is based on the spiritual condition and location in which he is presently experiencing. The prevailing tendency is for most people to pursue a deliverance prophetic ministry. They want to be like the national and international prophets.

But just as everyone cannot have those larger platforms, all prophets are not called to the same prophetic assignment. Some prophets' callings are with people in bondage, teaching them deliverance and proper development within their bondage. Others are called to warn a people to stay away from bondage or to prepare them for the bondage that is coming because of their disobedience. If all prophets were called to the same assignment, there would be a lopsided prophetic expression of the exilic responsibilities.

Through grace and mercy, and if God's will permits, one can escape a spiritual exile. And this also teaches that the prophetic administration comes to prevent such realities. God sends the pre-exilic-prophetic ministry to exhort the people not to slip into the tendency of spiritual exile. In other cases, God sends prophets into exilic experiences, along with the people he's punishing, to keep them on target for a season and a due date of deliverance. I must add that this type of exilic-prophetic assignment is the hardest of the three. It comes with a need for much tenacity and temperance within the character of the prophets so assigned. For it is easy to warn a people not to go into a bondage, just as much as it is easy to be the hero who brings people out of bondage!

For most prophets want their ministry to be a ministry of deliverance! And every prophet likes to tell the people to come out! But there are times when those people will have to finish a sentence for their crimes. And we must clearly understand that not every prophetic assignment will be one of the pre-exilic or the exilic. There are those like Moses. Their assignment is to go straight to Pharaoh and tell him to let their people go. I again stress the importance of prayer for further clarity about your assignment, as well as for the shifting between assignments. Yes, a prophet is usually moving between several of these prophetic assignments. Like the vacillation of regional prophetic ability, the transition of exilic assignments vacillates too. In other words, the prophetic assignments usually work in some form of combination (i.e. at least two or more), and rarely is one of the assignments done alone.

It is Jesus Christ, who comes now as the second Adam, and the greatest of all prophets. He now comes and provides the world a post-exilic experience, whereby he takes the people of the world out of the world and places them into the church at their moments of salvation. This type of work is the work we all aspire to do. But truth be told, even with the presence of grace, mercy, and the Gospel message, many of men will find themselves drifting back to the exiles of their personal sins. It is then that the prophet's anointing must come forth and help with such conflict of mankind's soul and spirit.

THE THREE MANTLES OF A PROPHET

Overview - What is a Mantle?

We have reviewed and discovered the fact that prophets have at least one of three realms and operations. And prophets also have at least one of three administrations (or assignments in ministry). But there is yet another very important clarity a prophet must have for further prophetic effectiveness. This clarity concerns the unique prophetic expression of each prophet's ministry. For the prophet is a conduit and a beacon of divine information. He speaks of the movements of God. He reveals the very expression of such thoughts through a distinct interpretive means.

This distinct method is biblically called a prophet's mantle. This means that there is biblical distinction for the clothing a prophet wears. A mantle, then, serves as the prophet's uniform. But it also describes the type of style in which the prophet will flow. And throughout scripture, we are given clear examples of various prophetic mantles. Below are a few of those examples. The Prophet Samuel's mantle was accidently ripped when King Saul aggressively attempted to pull Samuel back into a discussion that Samuel had finished:

And as Samuel turned about to go away, he laid hold upon the skirt of his mantle, and it rent. (1 Samuel 15:27).

When the witch of Endor summoned Samuel's spirit back from rest (out of Abraham's bosom), The witch discerned Samuel's age and mantle as a clear distinction that it was truly him:

And he said unto her, What form is he of? And she said, An old man cometh up; and he is covered with a mantle. And Saul perceived that it was Samuel, and he stopped with his face to the ground, and bowed himself (1 Samuel 28:14).

The Prophet Elijah's mantle is the one most famously observed. There are several references to Elijah's unique usage of his mantle:

"And it was so, when Elijah heard it, that he wrapped his face in his mantle..." (1 Kings 19:13a).

When Elijah was to anoint Elisha as his successor, he symbolically took of his mantle and placed it upon Elisha. This was a ceremonial act of bringing Elisha into the prophetic ministry under the uniqueness of Elijah's prophetic style and anointing:

"So he departed thence, and found Elisha...Elijah passed by him, and cast his mantle upon him" (1 Kings 19:19).

Elijah's mantle had his prophetic authority and power within it. On the day of his transition, he took his mantle, wrapped it up, and struck the Jordan waters with it. This act caused the waters to depart, forming a walkway that allowed Elijah and Elisha to pass to the other side of the Jordan River:

And Elijah took his mantle, and wrapped it together, and smote the waters, and they were divided hither and thither, so that they two went over on dry ground (2 Kings 2:8).

But it is the famous mantle of Elijah that demonstrates how a mantle can be passed on to another. This was seen in this case with Elisha. For Elisha asked Elijah for a double portion before he left the earth. Elijah explained the difficulty of this request. He informed Elisha that if God allowed him to see transition, then the request would be granted. And as a sign of God's will for Elisha's life, the request was granted. Elisha released himself from his former garment and prepared to take up Elijah's mantle. When Elisha returned, from seeing Elijah's transition, he used the same method with Elijah's mantle to cross the Jordan once again. When the sons of the prophets at Jericho saw Elijah's mantle on Elisha, they submitted their discipleship to Elisha instead of Elijah (2 Kings 2:9-14). So in the mantle, you will find the spirit of the prophet:

And when the sons of the prophets of Jericho which were to view at Jericho saw him, they said, The Spirit of Elijah doth rest on Elisha. And they came to meet him, and bowed themselves to the ground before him (2 Kings 2:15).

The prophet's unique expression within his region and assignment is heavily connected to the shape of his mantle. The word "mantle," in its literal sense, can simply mean that which covers the physical body of a prophet. Basically, in laymen's terms, it is the style of clothes that the prophet wears! For we know that clothes possess a simple connotation: one's sense of style. Thus, a style articulates a type of expression.

And everyone has a certain style exemplified by the way he dresses. And dressing often reflects the unique personality given to each individual. Thus, the mantle of the prophet is a metaphorical way of expressing the prophet's particular ministry. Not only does it refer to the particulars of prophetic ministry, but it also refers to the actual function of prophetism. For example, the Bible speaks of John the Baptist and how his particular style of garment exemplifies the need to be dissocialized from a people:

"And the same John had his raiment of camel's hair, and a leathern girdle about his loins..." (Matthew 3:4a, KJV).

Thus, each prophet has his own unique style of prophetic delivery based on the presentation of his spiritual mantle. Usually, the metonymy for a mantle is also the oil or anointing that the prophet walks in. Though it is epitomized as fabric, it is much more than a piece of clothing. It is the actual essence of the prophet's ability to prophesy, which is coupled with a unique distinction under his particular prophetic anointing.

Though Elisha was called to be the successor of Elijah's ministry and mantle, he could not be such until it was the time of transition for his leader, Elijah. Ceremonially, this official transition was done privately years ago when Elijah was first instructed to make Elisha his successor. It was in their initial meeting that Elijah took his outer garment (his mantle) and placed it upon Elisha to symbolize his pending transition from normal living to prophetic service:

"...Elijah passed by him, and cast his mantle upon him" (1 Kings 19:19b).

When God finally took Elijah, he honored the initial impartation of his mantle upon Elisha's life. But Elisha had to release his current garment so he could gain Elijah's garment. The power of Elijah's mantle had the same validity and authenticity, even though it was now upon Elisha. When the sons of prophets saw the newly installed Elisha walking with the mantle and operating the mantle properly, they gave full consent to their new leadership.

And Elijah took his mantle, and wrapped it together, and smote the waters, and they were divided hither and thither, so that they went over on dry ground. And it came to pass, when they were gone over, that Elijah said unto Elisha, ask what I shall do for thee, before I be taken away from thee. And Elisha said, I pray thee, let a double portion of thy spirit be upon me (2 Kings 2:8-10).

And it came to pass, as they still went on, and talked, that, behold, there appeared a chariot of fire, and horses of fire, and parted them both asunder; and Elijah went up by a whirlwind into heaven. And Elisha saw it, and he cried, My father, my father, the chariot of Israel, and the horsemen thereof. And he saw him no more: and he took hold of his own clothes, and rent them in two pieces. He took up also the mantle of Elijah that fell from him, and went back, and stood by the bank of Jordan; And he took the mantle of Elijah that fell from him, and smote the waters and said, where is the Lord God of Elijah? And when he also had smitten the waters, they parted hither and thither: and Elisha went over. And when the sons of the prophets which were to view at Jericho saw him, they said, the

spirit of Elijah doth rest on Elisha. And they came to meet him, and bowed themselves to the ground before him (2 Kings 2:12-15).

A prophet must know his region, his assignment, and his mantle (uniformity within prophesying). And there are three types of mantles for the prophetic ministry. And historically speaking, the people of Israel had relationships with a prophet from the days of Moses until the ministry of Malachi. And, based upon the presentation of various prophets, the title designation given to the prophets based on how they related to the people, had changed:

The Biblical Revelation of the Three Mantles

Now the acts of David the king, first and last, behold, they are written in the book of Samuel the seer, and in the book of Nathan the prophet, and in the book of Gad the seer (1 Chronicles 29:29).

The biblical revelation of three mantles is similar to that of revelation of what we call the Holy Trinity. However, instead of referring to it as the trinity, I like to call it three manifestations of the same God. Each part of the triune God is actually distinct within the representation of the same God (1 John 5:7). In the same vein, there are also three parts of man. But each part of man is distinct within his function. Yet each man has the same constitution with God's creation. And so it is with understanding the chief functions of the mantles within prophecy. There are three distinct mantles that shape the same prophetic network. Like a trinity, they work together instead of separately.

We must be very clear about calling it "a prophetic mantle," because the literal mantle of a prophetic person's clothing is not the actual seat of the prophetic anointing. The prophetic mantle also has the ability to interpret the word of God using creative impartations (i.e. writing, vocal, musical, and or dance expressions, etc.). Instead, this mantle is a spiritual mantle of the anointing that becomes part of the prophet's life and style of prophesying. And the prophet's mantle becomes a symbol of the authority given to that prophet.

So there is a distinct anointing upon the prophet's life that moves congruently under the prophetic anointing. This is why we have metonymy, or the parts of a whole concerning the given the association of a prophet's mantle. These three mantles help epitomize the overall association of what we call the prophetic anointing. Finally, historically speaking, Israel saw the prophet in various stages. This is why the name of the prophet changed three times within scripture. And it is from these three changes that our understanding of what God has made becomes three different prophetic expressions:

Before time in Israel, when a man went to enquire of God, thus he spake, come, and let us go to the seer: for he that is now called a Prophet was beforetime called a Seer (1 Samuel 9:9).

Though they are distinct, each functions with a partial distinction to the overall collective. There is one primary example from the Old Testament that captures all three prophetic mantles found in one complete scriptural reference. This reference is 1 Chronicles 29:29. And each time the word "prophet" or "seer" is used, a different Hebraic definition and word are actually attached to it.

Below are the names of the prophetic mantles and their given Hebrew names:

- Samuel, the seer = *raah* [#7200, rah-ah]. (This is where we get the word *roeh* [row-ay], #7203, which means, "one used in divine sight.").

- Nathan, the prophet = nabi [#5030, nah-bee] (This is a derivative of the word *Naba*, [nah-baw], and the Arkaddian word *nabu*, which means, "one used in divine hearing.").

- Gad, the seer = chozeh [#2374, koh-zay] (This is the one used as a visionary, which is the demonstrative prophet.).

The prophet must be clear about the uniqueness of his mantle because his mantle is his distinct prophetic flow. Simply put, when the shape of a prophet's mantle is clear, then the shape of the ability to prophesy and interpret affluently and accurately is also clear. Now that we have disclosed this information, it is time for you to discover which mantle you are wearing. Is it either:

- **The mantle to hear prophetically (The Hearer) – (NATHAN)**

- **The mantle to see prophetically (The Seer) – (SAMUEL)**

- **The mantle to demonstrate prophetically (The Visionary-Seer) – (GAD)**

The Realm of Divine Sight

The *raah* (or *roeh*) anointing (or the mantle of the seer)

Before time in Israel, when a man went to inquire of God, thus he spake, come, let us go to the seer: for he that is now called a Prophet was beforetime called a Seer. (1 Samuel 9:9).

The Hebrew word for seer is derived from the word *raah* [rah-ah (#7200)]. The root of the word is **roeh** [row-ay (#7203)], which simply means, "to see." Additionally, it means, "to see intellectually," or to "inspect, regard, or perceive." Given this derivative, *raah* means, "to see as a prophetic seer." This implies that it does not literally refer to the ability to see from one's natural eye. Instead, it refers to God use of spiritual and supernatural eyesight, so this is the prophet with the anointing to operate in divine sight.

An example of this mantle is within the prophetic ministry of Samuel:

"….These were reckoned by their genealogy in their villages, whom David and Samuel the seer did ordain in their set office" (1 Chronicles 9:22b).

"…Samuel the Seer…" (1 Chronicles 26:28a).

"…The book of Samuel the seer…" (1 Chronicles 29:29b).

So a seer works within an anointing of prophetic discernment. This type of mantle gives one the ability to see into the spirit realm through visions, dreams, and similitudes. Those who consciously function under this mantle experience deciphering of strange trances or are taken into blank or catatonic stares (which causes them to receive such information):

He hath said, which heard the words of God, which saw the vision of the Almighty, falling into a trance, but having his eyes open (Numbers 24:4).

On the morrow, as they went on their journey, and drew nigh unto the city, Peter went up upon the housetop to pray about the sixth hour: and he became very hungry, and would have eaten: but while they made ready, he fell into a trance (Acts 10:9-10).

"And it came to pass, that, when I was come again to Jerusalem, even while I prayed in the temple, I was in a trance; and saw him saying unto me…" (Acts 22:17-18a).

Again, a vision is when there is a conscious manifestation. And a dream is when there is an unconscious manifestation. Both are still ascribed to the mantle of a seer. Thus, the seer is called upon to allow images and symbols to reach their inner being and spirit (similitudes). This ability is done solely through bearing witness with the Spirit of God. It is, then, the job of the seer to articulate these images, and in some cases provide translation and interpretation for such symbols.

And trances result from a release within the prophetic host as a means of inducing the true sight of the seer. This is when God stops the movement of the natural eye to open the movement of the spiritual and supernatural eye. When God speaks through a seer's mantle, he transmits images rather than words:

"...Daniel had understanding in all visions and dreams" (Daniel 1:17b).

Then was Daniel brought in before the king. And the king spake and said unto Daniel, art thou that Daniel, which art of the children of the captivity of Judah, whom the king my father brought out of Jewry? I have even heard of thee that the spirit of the gods is in thee, and that light and understanding and excellent wisdom is found in thee. And now the wise men, the astrologers, have been brought in before me, that they should read this writing, and make known unto me the interpretation thereof: but they could not show the interpretation of the thing: and I have heard of thee, that thou canst make interpretations, and dissolve doubts: now if thou canst read the writing, and make known to me the interpretation thereof, thou shalt be clothed with scarlet, and have a chain of gold about thy neck, and shalt be the third ruler in the kingdom. Then Daniel answered and said before the king, let thy gifts be to thyself, and give thy rewards to another; yet I will read the writing unto the king, and make known to him the interpretation...And this is the writing that was written, MENE, MENE, TEKEL, UPHARSIN. This is the interpretation of the thing: MENE; God hath numbered thy kingdom, and finished it. TEKEL; Thou art weighed in the balances, and art found wanting. PERES; Thy kingdom is divided, and given to the Medes and Persians (Daniel 5:13-17, 25-28).

Joseph also had this same ability when he interpreted Pharaoh's dream. Pharaoh not only made him second in command over all of Egypt, but Pharaoh also gave Joseph a wife and called him by a unique Egyptian name that showed his prophetic ability. This name means "a revealer of secrets" or "the man to whom secrets are revealed."

And Pharaoh called Joseph's name Zaphnath-paaneah; and he gave him to wife Asenath the daughter of Poti-pherah priest of On. And Joseph went out over all the land of Egypt. (Genesis 41:45).

A seer not only can see images, but he can also interpret the images that he sees. With respect to his own subjective function, he is also called upon to be an expert of interpretation for others, informing them of what they see and cannot yet understand. The Bible says that he reveals the secrets to the prophets. Thus, most seers operate in the realm of prophetic interpreters for the Lord Jesus and His holy kingdom.

The Realm of Divine Exploits

The *chozeh* anointing (or the mantle of the demonstrative exploits)

There are two types of prophetic seers. One is the *roeh*-seer, who generally senses through divine sight. But the second prophetic seer has a different directive with his sight. The prophet of this type is called to make visual and demonstrative exploits unto the people as a symbolic means of visually and dramatically prophesying.

The Hebrew name for this type of seer is *chozeh* [chozeh (Koh-zay) (#2374)]. It is the visionary prophet. The visionary prophet is the most creative and has the greatest prophetic assignment. The visionary's assignment is a hard one. The demonstration of the prophetic mantle of a visionary prophet requires a high level of creativity. Not only is a visionary prophet called to creativity, but he is also called to operate in strict confidence of his personal image. For when called upon, this mantle may challenge the very image and identity of the individual summoned to work in such operations. Thus, the visionary prophet performs prophetically divine exploits, by which I mean dramatic and illustrative means.

With respect to studying and discovering such things, there are certain seers considered of the *chozeh* anointing within scripture. The way of discovery, in this case, is only through the knowledge of the translation of the Hebrew Scriptures. But when researching the word "seer," this is usually done in unison. And what you will discover is that there is no distinction made of this type of seer when translating the Bible into English or other languages. However, the revelation of such a prophet comes, and is confirmed, through one's study of the distinction of the two Hebrew words associated with this one English word.

Here are a few direct examples of the *chozeh* anointing:

- *"And the Lord spake unto Gad, David's seer..." (1 Chronicles 21:9a).*

- *All these were the sons of Heman the king's seer in the words of God, to lift up the horn. And God gave to Heman fourteen sons and three daughters. (1 Chronicles 25:5).*

- *"...Hanani the seer..." (2 Chronicles 16:7a).*

- *"...The visions of Iddo, the seer..." (2 Chronicles 9:29b).*

- *"...Asaph the seer..." (2 Chronicles 29:30b).*

> *"...And Jeduthun the king's seer..." (2 Chronicles 33:15b)*

> *"Also Amaziah said unto Amos, O thou seer, go, flee thee away into the land of Judah, and there eat bread, and prophesy there" (Amos 7:12).*

There will be times when the visionary prophet experiences personal embarrassment, major loss, and unusual requests from God. The visionary must demonstrate prophecy rather than just saying or seeing prophecy (the *chozeh* anointing is usually typical of all three mantles in one). And it is when the prophet himself becomes the prophetic word!

Whether it is in the naming his children unique names (Isaiah 8:3; Hosea 1:3-9), or in losing a wife (Ezekiel 24:15-18), forbidden to marry (Jeremiah 16:1-4), commanded to marry a prostitute (Hosea Chapters 1:2, 3:1) and maybe it will be God who requires them to stand outside barefoot and naked (Isaiah 20:3-4), or even shave his head as a prophetic emblem (Ezekiel 5:1). In these cases, demonstrative vision occurs when the prophetic mantle of *chozeh* is manifested as a spectacle unto a people. And speaking in a humanistic manner, no one likes to be used as a test subject, or as the butt of a joke. It will appear at times, when operating in this manner, that God is making a mockery of you. But in all actuality God, is using this mantle to make a mockery of sin, the devil, and any form of rebellion, disobedience, and spiritual inertia.

Another example is a New Testament Prophet, the prophet Agabus, who came and performed prophetic exploits for the Apostle Paul. The Prophet took Paul's belt and tied his own hands as a symbol conveying a set time of affliction that Paul would experience:

And as we tarried there many days, there came down from Judea a certain prophet, named Agabus. And when he was come unto us, he took Paul's girdle, and bound his own hands and feet, and said, Thus saith the Holy Ghost, so shall the Jews at Jerusalem bind the man that owneth this girdle, and shall deliver him into the hands of the Gentiles. (Acts 21:10-11).

It appears that *roeh* and *chozeh* anointings are the sister gifts of prophetic expression. These prophetic gifts are similar, but yet they have distinct assignments. *Roeh* is a subjective prophetic expression, while *chozeh* is an objective prophetic expression. *Roeh* is simply the manifestation of a vision, dream, or similitude. But *chozeh* is an objective assignment in which the prophet conveys the messages of dreams, visions, and similitudes through visualizations.

When the *chozeh* mantle is in effect, one usually senses the presence of awkwardness. This is because the temperament of a *chozeh* mantle defies norms and conventional methods. The *chozeh* anointing is very difficult. Its burden is hard to bear. Usually, people only embrace the conventional means of being prophetic, meaning they can easily verbalize a word from God. And the expression of the *nabi* anointing is not always the expression God wants. This implies that God creates balance within the prophetic mantles. Each mantle, then, is important for building God's kingdom. And present prophets should pray for a higher discernment of their applicable mantle. Every prophet has a unique message that is within his ministry. And every prophet has a unique map that is within his prophetic assignment and his mantle. Know your region. Know your assignment. Wear only your mantle.

The Realm of Divine Hearing

The Nabi Anointing (Or the Mantle of the Hearer)

"...For he that is now called <u>a Prophet</u> was beforetime called a Seer" (1 Samuel 9:9b).

The presence of a prophet was a relatively fresh perspective in the days of Samuel's ministry. The people's testimony of the prophet was literally based on how the prophets ministered. Thus, there was a season of exclusively the seer. However, the season of the seer soon took rest, and then God created the season of another mantle.

The mantle of the prophet who heard was approaching. The title of prophet who worked within the realm of divine hearing was called *nabi* [nah-bee (#5030)]. The definition of the word *nabi* means to "bubble up and over." It denotes an effervescent quality. In studying various derivatives of this Hebrew word, you will discover that other ethnicities ascribe various meanings similar to the Hebrew's expression of this mantle. The derivative word associated with the origin of the Hebrew word is connected to an ancient Akkadian word.

The Akkadian word *nabu* further helps us understand the full meaning of the word n*abi*. The word *nabu* simply means, "to be called." To be called is to summon hearing. This is because in order to be called, one must be available to listen, so the Prophet who allows the spirit to bubble over, which is the meaning of the nabi, is one who allows the inner ear of the spirit of man to hear what the word of the Lord is saying. The prophet Samuel vacillated between these two prophetic expressions:

"Now the Lord had told Samuel in his ear a day before Saul came..." (1 Samuel 9:15a).

Another example of the *nabi* mantle is the ministry of the prophet Elijah. On occasion, God cultivated Elijah's prophetic hearing. One particular cave experience, after fleeing from Jezebel and Ahab, was one in which Elijah's prophetic ear was fine-tuned:

And he came thither unto a cave, and lodged there; and, behold, the word of the Lord came to him, and he said unto him, what doest thou here, Elijah...And He said, go forth, and stand upon the mount before the Lord. And, behold, the Lord passed by, and a great and strong wind rent the mountains, and broke in pieces the rocks before the Lord; but the Lord was not in the wind: and after the wind an earthquake; but the Lord was not in the earthquake: and after the earthquake a fire; but the Lord was not in the fire: and after the fire a still small voice. (1 Kings 9:9, 11-12).

On this occasion Elijah received training in the ability to hear the divine. He was practicing the ability so he could hear the true word and Spirit of the Lord. But Elijah was also seen doing, hearing, and seeing prophetically. Thus, he is an example of prophetic dexterity within his mantle. But in this matter, God revealed to the prophet a voice small in comparison to the boldness of the typical prophetic exploits. The implication here is that God can speak through nature (i.e. earthquakes, winds, and fires). But there are times in which he speaks through audible sound. The fact that Elijah listened teaches that the prophet must be trained with the mantle of hearing. Later in the book, we will discuss prophetic sensitivity. But this is a classic illustration of the nabi mantle.

Apostle Sherman D. Farmer

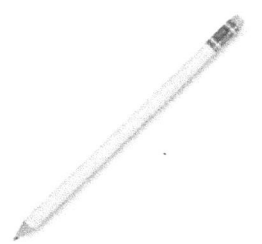

CONCLUSION OF LESSON 9

(The Three Prophetic Administrations and Mantles):

Notice that the text of 1 Kings 9:9 says that the "word of the Lord came to him." The word of the Lord is more the essence and movement of the Spirit and the way in which the prophet interprets and conveys what has come from God. First, the prophet has to make sure that one has clarity of his mantle, which is connected to his region and prophetic assignment. It is very important to remember that God does not move through natural realms when ministering to the natural. Instead, God always moves through supernatural and spiritual realms first and foremost. Then God sends uniquely gifted specialists to transmit that which needs to be uttered in the natural realm:

But as it is written, eye hath not seen, nor ear heard, neither have entered into the heart of man, the things which God hath prepared for them that love Him. But God hath revealed them unto us by His Spirit: for the Spirit searcheth all things, yea, the deep things of God. (1 Corinthians 2:9-10).

These three prophetic mantles, or types of anointing, are clearly mentioned multiple times within the Old Testament to express how God always uses his prophets. 1 Chronicles 29:29 again indicates these types and designations. It was through reading their names that I heard the Spirit of God. These names are actually the mantles that shifted throughout Israelite history based on the type of prophetic expression God wanted and needed to be released at a given time.

I believe that God is still consistent with the current usage of such prophetic expressions. So contemporary prophets seek and find the means, or shall I say mantles, that will best help you to express yourself under the prophetic anointing. This will require prayer and spiritual diligence in so doing. God bless. And enjoy the adventure of the prophetic exploration of your unique prophetic administration and mantle in Jesus Christ.

The Doctrine of Prophecy

Just as we have discussed, there are three manifestations of God in one, three parts of man in one man, and three mantles in the mantles of the prophetic ministry. The manifestation of God as Father is relative to the expression of the *Ro-eh* anointing. He sees and oversees everything. The manifestation of Jesus as Son is relative to the expression of the *Koh-zay* anointing. He sacrifices everything and is the example before the people. And the manifestation of the Spirit is relative to the expression of the *Nah-bah* anointing. He hears, speaks, and relays the Lord's will exactly.

As Jesus said, "he that has ears let him hear what the Spirit of God is saying" (Matthew 11:15, Mark 4:9). So it is certainly time for the prophet of God to know what the Spirit, Jesus, and God (who are one) is saying to the church, through these three divine expressions of one prophetic spirit.

CHAPTER 10

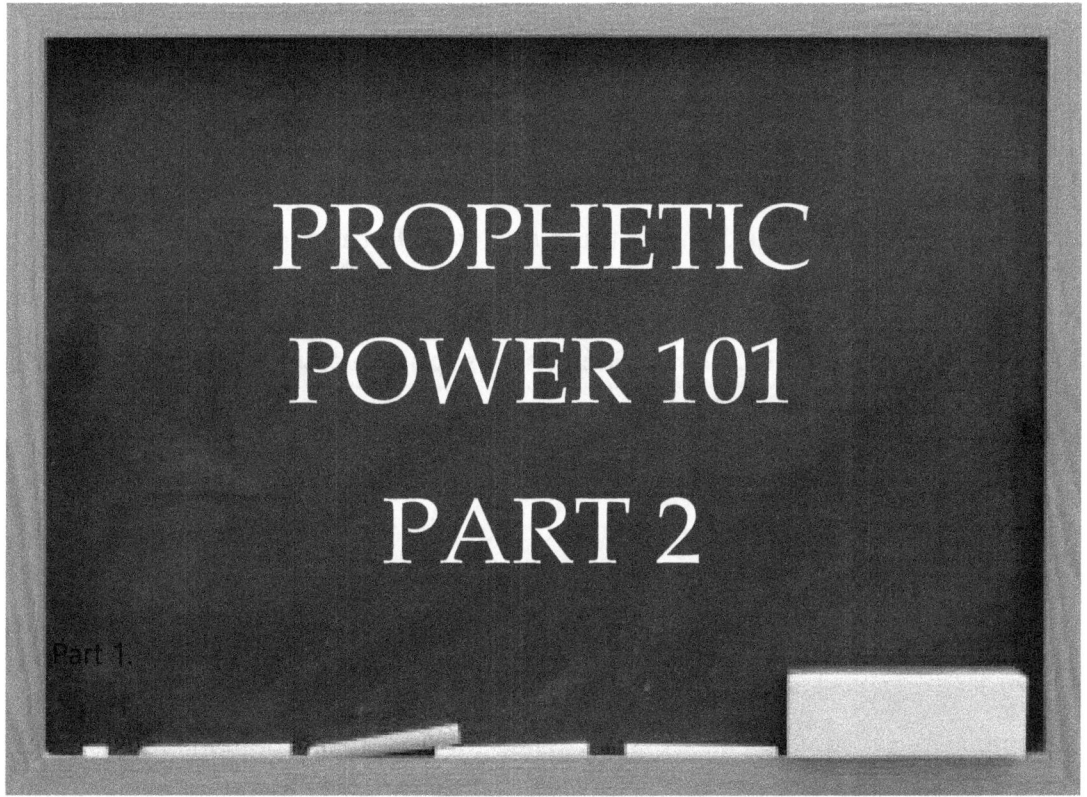

How Does the Prophetic Operate? – Part 5

Do not merely listen to the word, and so deceive yourselves. Do what it says. Anyone who listens to the word but does not do what it says is like a man who looks at his face in a mirror and after looking at himself, goes away and immediately forgets what he looks like (James 1:22-24, NIV).

The Overview & Observations of Prophetic Placement and Sensitivity

Every prophet needs to practice! And there is no better place to practice than the house of God. Just as a person goes to the gym to exercise, it is imperative that the prophet learns the calisthenics of developing prophetic sensitivity, productivity, and vocality within the prophetic ministry. When any of these are neglected, the prophetic ministry will be neglected as well. As wise stewards of any of God's blessings, we are held responsible for the necessary operation of our gifts. Thus, we are to exercise our spiritual gifts properly and soberly.

The healthiness of one's prophetic ministry rests greatly upon one's diligence in finding out everything about the operation of such gifting. But the proper application of such information is to be implemented and not just gathered. But before that, there are two major lessons of distinguishing that we must review before we progress further:

Major Lesson #1: Distinguishing Denominational Prophets versus Christian Prophets

Prophetism does not disdain God's work within denominationalism, especially when it concerns the mission and ministry of Jesus Christ. No, I am not negating the fact that there is a problem between religiosity and true spirituality. But there are major differences in prophetic expressions cloaked with a non-denominational assignment compared to those who operate prophetically with a given denominational affiliation. And within today's prophetism, there is a dramatic difference between these two types of prophets.

I humbly make this appeal: we should not want to make denominational prophetism higher than the assignment of the Universal Church. It is widely known that current practices of the prophetic office have been expressed with abrasive, edgy, unapproachable, and ill-advised temperaments. Moments of self-righteousness and legalism can fuel the thoughts of even the most sincere prophet. But staying within context to Ephesians 4:11, God is not calling us to become denominational prophets. Instead, he is making us into Christian prophets, which is more important than a denominational one.

And the difference between the two is very simple: one who prophecies based on his denominational teaching is what we shall call the denominational prophet. The opposite of this prophet is the one who universally preaches the Bible. This type of prophet is focused on being Christ-like, which is in accordance with a kingdom agenda. And not a church program or denominational agenda! Both prophets may be passionate about their assignments and placements. But only one fits into the Ephesians 4:11-16 paradigm.

What we have learned so far is that there are many different types of prophets according to the Bible. There are Hebrew prophets, Gentile prophets, and false prophets. But the Christian prophet preaches only the kingdom of Jesus Christ! And the Christian prophet preaches Christianity! Therefore, Christian prophets are the most relevant New Testament prophets there are. Sure, the denominational prophet may preach some kingdom and some aspects of the Bible. And if he is not universally dexterous, then his ministry remains in the confines of his organization, reformation, or denominational experience.

But our mandate is bigger than our organizations and denominations. Yes, there will be some work, within the prophetic, that will always be bigger than a denomination. Jesus, in fact, says that our witness is Judea, Samaria, and the uttermost parts of the world (Acts 1:8). Therefore, our witness can be within our denomination, but our denomination must never be greater than our witness.

With this resolve comes an alternative way of thinking about your prophetic assignment. Preach the Gospel, and prophecy to all who profess that they believe. For surely you can do this while also being loyal to your organization. But do it as a kingdom prophet who prophesies more of the biblical mandates of the New Testament church than furthering the advancements of your own denomination.

And this is what we are called to remember: we are under a new covenant and administration! We are under the dispensation of grace and the ministry of Jesus Christ. This is why we must deconstruct this inappropriate practice of the prophetic. And this is the only goal of this section. It is to disarm denominational views and open minds to the universal mandate of all believers.

Here's the bottom line: the prophet's job is to speak in the spirit of Jesus Christ! And Christ has called you to remember his words more than you remember the traditions of men. Therefore, one's traditions may be lawful, but not every aspect of your traditions may be expedient. Even as an apostle of the Lord with a non-denominational view, I am still called to remain true to the universal assignment of apostleship and prophetic ministry. That universal assignment is the gift of Jesus Christ. Herein is the central premise to the doctrine of prophecy!

Major Lesson #2: Distinguishing the Gift of Prophecy versus the Office of the Prophet

The gifts of the office of prophet and gift of prophecy are birthed from the spirit of prophecy, which is the testimony of Jesus Christ (Revelations 19:10). And the best way to understand these differences is to understand that the calling to preach and teach the Gospel (Romans 10:13-15; 1 Corinthians 9:14-17) is in the New Testament prophet's destiny.

When one is called to preach and teach the Gospel, he can do so only through divine conferment in the womb (Jeremiah 1:5; Galatians 1:15-16). This responsibility comes with a vested level of power, privilege, and authority. Remember, the authority of the prophet is different in operation than a believer gifted with the general ability to prophesy. The ordained elder should be recognized with the prophet's authority. But any other believer (who is not ordained by the church) should be given the authority to prophesy under the supervised direction of a pastor and a local congregation.

This is why the prophet can speak within the perimeters of this gift. But his ability extends into pronouncing correction, judgment, and rebuke. However, the believer who seeks to prophesy does not have that same power, authority, or privilege. And the best way to resolve this predicament is to use the doctrine of ecclesiology. Ecclesiology teaches the orders of ministers and the final disposition of one's five-fold calling. A prophet should be an elder of the Lord Jesus Christ first and foremost. And only an ordained elder of the Gospel or an elder who is given laity leadership privileges, can receive true respect within the said office of the prophet. This is the means of properly distinguishing one who is gifted to prophesy, comparing that to the definition of one who is called to be a prophet.

For the prophet is also called to preach and teach God's word. The prophet also walks in the authority allocated to him from the exclusive power of preaching and teaching God's word (Hebrews 4:12; 1 Thessalonians 1:5) with revelatory ability. This is why double honor is given to the elder who labors in the word (1 Timothy 5:17). And it is the position of eldership that differentiates the other spiritual gifts outside of the five-fold capacity. Even during biblical times, Apostles were ordained as elders for authority purposes (1 Peter 5:1). Therefore, it is the anointing and formal appointment of an elder that can differentiate between one having the gift or the office (Acts 13:1).

Simply speaking, when you are a prophet, your office is your gift. But when you are operating with the gift of prophecy, the Holy Spirit officially moves through you to operate the generalities of this gifting. One is a gift, entirely. The other is a gift for someone who is gifted by the Holy Spirit. Both cannot function authentically and legally without the presence of Jesus Christ. Even though one stands greater than the other, the source of such ability is still the same! This is why God requires everyone to prophesy (1 Corinthians 14:1). But never does God call all to be a prophet! Finally, a way to distinguish the power of the prophet from the power of a prophetic believer is by the authority of each given prophetic word. For as we listen to the authority and demonstration of the prophecy, discernment will always reveal the difference between the gift and the office:

"...Upholding all things by the word of His power..." (Hebrews 1:3b).

Proper Discernment of Prophetic Sensitivity:

A Lesson That Takes Time

Moreover the word of the Lord came unto me, saying, Jeremiah, what seest thou? (Jeremiah 1:11a).

The major lesson for any prophet then, is to learn prophetic sensitivity. This is the ability to listen and respond to the voice of God. This active listening and responding is done by way of a specific prophetic mantle (i.e. a seer, a hearer, or a visionary). And prophetic sensitivity has two channels. The first is when the prophet properly hears the voice of God. The second is when the prophet obeys the voice of God by conveying exactly what God has said. Again, this is done through the uniqueness of each prophet's ministry.

All prophetic instructions received should be clearly deciphered before disseminated. And each prophetic utterance should be properly made. When we prophesy, people want specifics and not vagueness. When God called Jeremiah, for example, a part of his training involved reciting what God had spoken and shown. God asks Jeremiah what he sees. Jeremiah's sight was pretty impressive in the spirit, being a new prophet. And for clear sight, God openly rewarded him by saying, "Jeremiah you are seeing very well!"

But prophetic sensitivity even for Jeremiah was a life-long lesson that took time to develop. Thus, it is the lesson of prophetic sensitivity that intimidates the novice prophet. The weaker your prophetic antennas, the less inclined you will be, or even inspired you will be, to prophesy. Just like it is the goal to put training wheels on a bike to ensure that the rider enjoys riding his bike, so is prophetic sensitivity designed to put "training wheels" on the beginnings of your prophetic gift and office. This method is to motivate the prophet to listen and properly respond.

The Primary Fundamental of Prophetic Sensitivity: Anthropomorphizing God

When God gives a prophet a moment of prophetic sensitivity training, this process can often become very challenging. The novice and advanced prophet are equal sometimes regarding this matter. Meaning, it does not matter how long you've been in the prophetic; there are things we all learn every day! And though one is new, while the other is a life-long student; both are always learning how to interpret the voice of God.

And the development of prophetic sensitivity is repeatedly seen throughout scripture. When the Spirit of God moves upon the spirit of man, the prophet receives a supernatural impression. It is then the prophet's job to accurately interpret the essence of this move. The prophet provides common phraseologies, anecdotes, metaphors, etc. And the accurate articulation of the prophetic word assists a worshipper or inquirer in their pursuit or reconnection with God. In theology, there is word that has a strong connection to prophetic sensitivity. That word is "anthropomorphisms." Using anthropomorphisms ascribes human attributes given to God. These different metaphors assist prophets in their expression of the actions, thoughts, and intentions of God.

There are several categories for anthropomorphism:

- Human actions (change of mind, relents, remembers, rests)
- Human emotions (sorrow, jealousy, pity, regret)
- Human physique (hands, face, mouth, eyes, arm)

Here is an additional common list of mostly used anthropomorphisms in the bible:

- God's voice walks (Genesis 3:8a)
- God changes his mind (Genesis 6:6a; Exodus 32:14)/Regrets (1 Samuel 15:35)
- God stretches out his hand (Exodus 3:20; 7:5)
- God talks in plural form (Genesis 1:26; Isaiah 6:8)
- God sings (Zephaniah 3:17)
- God rests (Genesis 2:2)
- God's feet (Isaiah 66:1)
- God's face (Numbers 6:24)
- God's mouth (Psalm 33:6)
- God's eyes (Psalm 34:15)

> God's arm (Psalm 80:10)

It is very important that we not forget these facts when using anthropomorphisms:

> ***God is not a man, that He should lie; neither the son of man, that He should repent: hath He said, and shall He not do it? Or hath He spoken, and shall He not make it good? (Numbers 23:19).***

> ***God is a spirit: and they that worship him must worship him in Spirit and in truth (John 4:24).***

> ***"...The heaven and heavens of heavens cannot contain thee..." (1 Kings 8:27b).***

Scripture declares that God is not a man. But God is a Spirit. As much as we hate to admit it, God is vast and beyond human comprehension. However, God has given prophets a creative ability to interpret his actions. I call God's actions extraterrestrial movements within our terrestrial plain. Thus, this is when the prophet uses the image of man to explain the image of God.

Of course, with the exception of the manifestation of Jesus Christ, God is predominantly understood to be pure and eternal divine Spirit! This means that he does not possess hands, feet, eyes, ears, nose, or human mouth. God also does not cry, sing, laugh, or even speak an exclusive earthly language. Again, God is supreme spirit. He is also universal and eternal spirit. Not only that, but God is the only uncreated spirit. He is the supreme spirit always existing. And man has to learn how to engage God. The strategy of such engagement is through prophetic sensitivity and a wise prophet who can properly anthropomorphize God.

The prophet makes the intangibility of God become more tangible. This creative bridge allows man to cross over to a world beyond him and past his comprehension. And God still uses the prophet to bridge such affects. This is why it is the prophet's job is to properly convey the essence of God as well as what he is actually articulating to a people. But for the prophet, this ability requires a lifetime of learning. Scripture shows that for new and seasoned prophets alike learning prophetic sensitivity through anthropomorphisms can sometimes be improperly conveyed. But if that prophet learns how to patiently become turned in, they will gather the correct voice and image necessary to bring a people closer to the true and living God!

Prophetic Sensitivity Lessons

Prophetic Sensitivity Lesson #1: Carrying a Heavy Word in Uncertain Times!

The prophet Abraham is our first lesson of prophetic sensitivity. His lesson is a very important one. One that all prophets will experience. Abraham's major lesson in prophetic sensitivity happens when God tells Abraham that he must sacrifice his son, Isaac. Abraham's instructions are incremental. And the instructions were for Abraham to take his son to an unknown location in a mountain and sacrifice him there upon that mountain:

And He said, take now thy son, thine only son Isaac, whom thou lovest, and get thee into the land of Moriah; and offer him there for a burnt offering upon one of the mountains which I will tell thee of. (Genesis 22:2).

This reference shows there is no clear distinction between the mountains of Moriah. Of course, there was a specific mountain Abraham had to reach for personal hardship and sacrifice. And it apparently was not made clear until God was ready to make it clearer. Until then, Abraham was to walk around until he found the specific mountain that God wanted him to do this very act upon. So here is an example of carrying a very hard word in an uncertain time.

But even in this short hard word, it was still specific, very general and incremental. And the Bible is clear: prophesying is done in parts, and knowledge is incrementally given (1 Corinthians 13:9). So Abraham moves this very hard and incremental word towards a mountain in a vast land. As he travels towards the mountain regions of Moriah, I can imagine that he is equally thinking "How can I take my son's life? And which mountain is it?" But out of obedience to God, he forges ahead.

What is amazing is Abraham's unwavering receptivity to the voice of God. His obedience was impeccable. The trust Abraham exhibits, even though he doesn't understand God's reasons, teaches an important lesson in prophetic training and sensitivity. You'll need to use your imagination. Visualize Abraham walking and talking. He had his son, a few servants, and supplies for the sacrifice. As he forged from mountain to mountain with a heavy word, imagine how the journey was gut wrenching for him.

What do you do when you're prophetically groping in the dark and you're carrying a heavy word? You know it's a word that you personally do not want to complete. But because you are submitting and being compliant to the voice of God, you obey! This lesson is strictly about obedience with spiritual receptivity. And to become obedient and receptive, you must go through proper training. The story ends with Abraham fulfilling the Lord's commands. Isaac was nearly sacrificed. But the ram in the bush replaces Isaac, and he is ultimately saved.

From this lesson, we must learn that no matter how conflicting and contradicting God's move may be, a prophet must never question the voice and word of the Lord. Prophetic sensitivity relies heavily on a prophet's obedience. Even when he is void of understanding and he cannot see clearly what the Lord wants, a prophet must always be ready for active duty. And he must readily be compliant with the directives of the Lord. Prophetic sensitivity, then, is about full submission with utmost obedience.

Abraham relinquishes all ideals, thoughts, and pursuits to follow exactly what God wants. This type of prophetic training is like walking in the dark. It is like a form of combat training. The task is to overcome the need for natural resources and rely solely on the divine, even at the expense of personal comfort and one's happiness. In Abraham's case, the temporary loss of his happiness soon returned. When God made the initial request for Abraham to take Isaac's life, I can imagine Abraham's response was filled with much pain and mental suffering. But this further confirms that you cannot fail or lose if you ultimately follow God. Prophetic sensitivity is about following God at all costs.

Prophetic Sensitivity Lesson #2: Deciphering Self-Consciousness from God-Consciousness!

And it came to pass at that time, when Eli was laid down in his place, and his eyes began to wax dim, that he could not see; and ere the lamp of God went out in the temple of the Lord, where the ark of God was, and Samuel was laid down to sleep; that the Lord called Samuel; and he answered, here am I. And he ran unto Eli, and said, here am I; for thou calledst me. And he said, I called not; lie down again. And he went and lay down. And the Lord called yet again Samuel. And Samuel arose and went to Eli, and said, Here am I; for thou didst call me. And he answered, I called not, my son; lie down again. Now Samuel did not yet know the Lord, neither was the word of the Lord yet revealed unto him. And the Lord called Samuel again the third time. And he arose and went to Eli, and said, Here am I; for thou didst call me. And Eli perceived that the Lord had called the child. Therefore Eli said unto Samuel, Go, lie down: and it shall be, if He call thee, that thou shalt say, speak Lord; for thy servant heareth. So Samuel went and lay down in his place. And the Lord came, and stood, and called as at other times, Samuel, Samuel. Then Samuel answered, Speak; for thy servant heareth (1 Samuel 3:2-10).

The Prophet Samuel's humble beginnings in the prophetic serve as a classic example of one fine-tuning his ability to discern the audible pitch of the voice of God. When Samuel grew up, he no longer had to deal with his issues with prophetic utterances and receptivity. But his initial encounter was one of learning the difference between the voice of the Lord and a voice of another. Because he was familiar with the voice of Eli, his priestly mentor and spiritual father, it was Eli's voice that he thought he heard.

This also teaches us the importance of being clear about the voice we are listening to during any prophetic moment. In Samuel's case, he truly heard the voice of God. And apparently there was something both familiar and unfamiliar about Eli's voice. That familiarity caused Samuel to question Eli. An important note is made with this fact: the voice of your spiritual leader should never outweigh the voice of God. Regardless of how significant the voice of your leader is to you personally, hopefully God's voice is still the most important.

Scripture shares the idea that Samuel did not have a direct relationship with God prior to his initial introduction into the prophetic. It is of utmost importance and urgency that the prophet develops a strong and close relationship with God. The scripture also suggests the importance of having a prophetic mentor and or prophetic father. This subject matter is discussed further in my first book, *The New Prophetic Generation*.

But the lesson continues. A prophet should be an example of consistency in his fellowship and relationship with the Lord. Misrepresentation or miscalculation of God's voice is a serious offense in the prophetic world. The consequences of inaccurate prophecy can be grave. Nevertheless, three times God called Samuel. Patiently, God waited for him to hone what he had heard. This became the beginning of Samuel's prophetic sensitivity. God speaking to Samuel was not about his lack of awareness alone. In fact, it can be suggested that God was speaking into each dimension of Samuel's image (i.e. his body, soul, and spirit) – See 1 Samuel 3:4, 6, 8.

➢ The first time God called Samuel's name was to tap on his physical body (1 Samuel 3:4).

➢ The second time was to reach deeper into the soul to grasp Samuel's mind, intellect, personality, and emotions (1 Samuel 3:6).

➢ The third time God began to penetrate the deepest place within his candidate: Samuel's spirit (1 Samuel 3:8).

➢ But the fourth time God awakened his prophetic service (1 Samuel 3:-9-10).

Eli's wisdom led Samuel to understand that God was calling him (1 Samuel 3:9). And Eli provided a greater strategy for learning prophetic sensitivities on an elementary level. Eli released a simple process.

Eli's school of prophecy reveals that a candidate of the prophetic gift or office must avail one's inner ear. This inner ear is only found within the spiritman. It took four times before Samuel got it right. Eventually he did with the help of someone who was aware of how to properly communicate with God prophetically! The following guidelines given to Samuel by Eli also can be used in initial stages of an emerging prophetic candidate's prayer life. In fact, it does not hurt to say this words even now. For the clause is easy to remember and recite: "Speak Lord, for thy servant hears."

Prophetic Sensitivity Lesson #3: Detoxing from Prophetic Ruts of Complacency

There are many times when true prophets become jaded and prophetically impaired. Usually, this is due to stress or emotional imbalance from ministering a prophetic word in a particular season. Regardless of prophetic displacement, the mandate and requirements still hold a specified charge. And that charge is to always be adaptable to the move of God more than you are to a prophetic season in God. But when the prophet becomes a victim of prophetic inertia, the only remedy is to detox from prophetic complacency.

Prophetic complacency, in short, is when the prophet can only see and hear what he thinks God is saying. The prophet under this struggle usually does not know how to move from the last prophetic assignment into his new one. Like a soldier who becomes excessively connected to a station that's not his home, a jaded prophet can become too connected to a word that is for the church or the kingdom in a specific season. This is when God has to send a dramatic experience to jumpstart the necessary process of prophetic detox.

In another biblical account, we learn this great lesson when Elijah experienced a personal meltdown during one of his darker moments in ministry. The prophet Elijah had just finished ministering a strong and sharp word to Israel's current wicked king and queen, Ahab and Jezebel. After delivering the word, he fled to a nearby cave for protection. During his experiences in the cave, God teaches Elijah a very importance lesson. For God teaches Elijah that the prophet must never become complacent or comfortable within any modality of his prophetic abilities:

And he came thither to unto a cave, and lodged there; and, behold, the word of the Lord came to him, and he said unto him, What doest thou here, Elijah? And he said, I have been very jealous for the Lord God of hosts: for the children of Israel have forsaken thy covenant, thrown down thine altars, and slain thy prophets with the sword; and I, even I only, am left; and they seek my life, to take it away. And he said, go forth, and stand upon the mount before the Lord. And, behold, the Lord passed by, and a great and strong wind rent the mountains, and broke in pieces the rocks before the Lord; but the Lord was not in

the wind: and after the wind an earthquake; but the lord was not in the earthquake: and after the earthquake a fire; but the Lord was not in the fire: and after the fire a still small voice (1 Kings 19:9-12).

Elijah thought God was in the wind, which broke rocks into several pieces. But the Lord was not in the wind. Elijah then thought the Lord was in the earthquake, which occurred after the wind. But God was not in the earthquake either. Then God manifested a fire. And Elijah again assumed that God was in the manifestation of fire. Logically, it appears that God was not in the wind, fire or earthquake. But the scripture says that the voice and presence of God was absent in each of these episodes involving nature.

But nature does not always speak for God. This means that catastrophe and calamity are not always part of God's mind. Sometimes they have their own voice, apart from God. And nature's disasters come as a result of cause and effect. But the truth remains: God is in control. He should never be disregarded during any conventional occurrence of nature, even with the random violent acts nature can sometimes demonstrate.

In the same manner, a prophet must remain sensitive to God, who is not here to comfort or conform. The answer finally came to Elijah. God presented himself as a still small voice. But the good news was seen in the process. It may have taken time for Elijah to get to it, but eventually he did come to hear what God was saying. And yet, notice that the pericope begins with the prophet's displacement (1 Kings 19:9). God asks a question: "What are you doing here Elijah?" When I read this question it reminded me of God asking Adam "where are you?" (Genesis 3:9). This is the moment of a prophetic detox. Sometimes, the detox can be sin, self, or the insensibility of our emotions.

And it appears that Elijah had the wrong answers because he was hearing the wrong things. The inaccuracy of his response reveals that he was spiritually inert. This teaches a very important lesson. It is imperative that we do not become too comfortable with the normalcy of God's manifestations. We must always remain open and available, and we must be available to any move of God's presence, because God can switch it up at any time. This again speaks to how prophetic sensitivity can be a hard lesson to learn. Prophetic sensitivity takes time and great practice to gain strength for clear prophetic interpretation. Even when you think you've mastered the prophetic realm in God, you will and can experience moments like Elijah did in the cave. Thus, a prophet must continue his spiritual training, even if he is considering an advanced placement within prophetic works.

For it takes time to learn the flow of the prophetic. If the prophet becomes available and obedient, and he walks in faith, then there is a greater opportunity for receiving the voice of God within that prophet's ministry. Abraham's, Samuel's, and Elijah's examples are vivid examples of so many lessons to learn about prophetic sensitivity. The prophet will experience moments of dark places filled with series of uncertainties. The prophet will be challenged by many thoughts, emotions, and personal agendas. The prophet will be challenged to fight complacency. The prophet will always need to tweak his sight, hearing, and flesh for the sole purpose of ensuring a pure prophetic ministry. Trust God! He will help you to detox and will deliver you from all things, because the agenda God has for the prophet is bigger than the misunderstandings a prophet might feel and face from time to time.

Prophetic Sensitivity Lesson #4: Decoding Prophetic Messages from Angelic Visitations

Within the prophet's ministry, there will be angelic visitations and communication. The Bible reveals that prophets are heavily inundated with the presence of angels, which are known and released by God to speak to prophets in their dreams, visions, and similitudes:

And he dreamed, and behold a ladder set up on the earth, and the top of it reached to heaven: behold the angels of God ascending and descending (Genesis 28:12).

"And the angel of God spake unto me in a dream..." (Genesis 31:11a).

Jacob, though not literally considered a prophet, is like the prophets because of his encounters with God. In both references above he was spoken to by the voice of angels. And similar to Jacob are other prophets of the Bible. Isaiah, for example, experiences the ministry of the seraphim during his prophetic commission (Isaiah 6:1). Ezekiel experiences the ministry of the cherubim during his prophetic commission (Ezekiel 1:5-12). And Daniel experiences the ministry of archangels during his prophetic ministry (Daniel 8:26; 9:21).

It is the same ministry of the archangel Gabriel that visited John the Baptist's father, Zechariah, when the enunciation of the prophet John's birth was soon to come (Luke 1:13, 18-19). It was this same Gabriel who visited Mary, the mother of Jesus, and also explained the birth of Christ (Luke 1:26). Even Jesus spent times with the ministry of angels (Luke 22:53). And, as we know, Jesus is like Moses. When Moses encountered the burning bush, it was the actual angelic representative of God and not of God himself (Galatians 3:19b). Jesus says that he, too, was represented in his work and ministry by an angel: Revelation 1:1b.

So it is the prophet's job to assess when angels are speaking to them from the mind of God. For God spoke to Moses face-to-face, making him the greatest of all prophets ever to live

(Exodus 33:11a; Deuteronomy 34:10). But even Moses had received the laws of God, not through just God's presence alone, but also at the hands of the ministry of angels:

And when forty years were expired, there appeared to him in the wilderness of mount Sina an angel of the Lord in a flame of fire in a bush. When Moses saw it, he wondered at the sight: and as he drew near to behold it, the voice of the Lord came unto him (Acts 7:30-31).

"...The same did God send to be a ruler and a deliverer by the hand of the angel which appeared to him in the bush" (Acts 7:35b).

This is he, that was in the church in the wilderness with the angel which spake to him in the mount Sina, and with our fathers: who received the lively oracles to give unto us (Acts 7:38).

The Greatest confirmation of a prophet's ministry is communication and contact with the angels of God. Whether cherubim, seraphim, angels, or archangels, the ears, eyes, and spirit of a prophet have the power to discern an angel's presence and purpose. This takes time to develop and to learn to pray for such awareness.

The prophet Elisha had to pray for his servant to see angelic activity when a great army surrounded the city of Dothan. Once Elisha prayed for his prophetic adjutant, he experienced clarity, and the servant was able to see just as Elisha saw the angels. The implications of this text remind us of why we need a prophetic father or mentor, for they can see what we cannot. And they can also help to oversee and develop the discernment of such activity:

And when the servant of the man of God was risen early, and gone forth, behold, an host compassed the city both with horses and chariots. And his servant said unto him, Alas, my master! How shall we do? And he answered, Fear not: for they that be with us are more than they that be with them. And Elisha prayed and said, Lord, I pray thee, open his eyes, that he may see. And the Lord opened the eyes of the young man; and he saw: and, behold, the mountain was full of horses and chariots of fire round about Elisha (2 Kings 6:15-17).

The prophet's spiritual sensitivity is not limited to just the voice of the Holy Ghost speaking to his spirit. The prophet is also gifted to hear the voice of the Lord through the ministry of angels. And this special privilege distinguishes prophets (and apostles) from other ministerial gifts:

Then said I, O my lord, what are these? And the angel that talked with me said unto me, I will shew thee what these be...And the Lord answered the angel that talked with me good

words and comfortable words. So the angel that communed with me said unto me, cry thou, saying, thus saith the Lord of hosts; I am jealous for Jerusalem and for Zion with a great jealousy...And I said unto the angel that talked with me, what be these? And he answered me, these are the horns which have scattered Judah, Israel, and Jerusalem (Zechariah 1:9, 13-14, 19).

CONCLUSION OF LESSON 10:

The task of spiritual sensitivity, then, is a matter of time and of adjusting to things of the spirit realm. For the natural is in competition with the spiritual (Galatians 5:17; Romans 7:14-23; Matthew 26:41; 1 Corinthians 2:14). But principle interpretation of the word of God is part of the prophet's sensitivity training. And it cannot be avoided.

Prophetic sensitivity comes with much responsibility, as well as a necessary submission to proper accountability. For a strong discerning ear must be able to distinguish the tongues of angels (1 Corinthians 13:1) from the tongues of men, for there is a difference between language and dialect. It would appear that God could have made it easier for us and only speak to us through his son. Chiefly, he does this even now, as the word declares. But we must not limit the move of God or the prophet's ability within a prophetic work. For God is the same today as he was yesterday, and he will remain the same forever. And with that being the case, we can understand that there is nothing new under the sun. The modern prophet, then, is called upon to operate within these same realms of prophetic sensitivity training.

CHAPTER 11

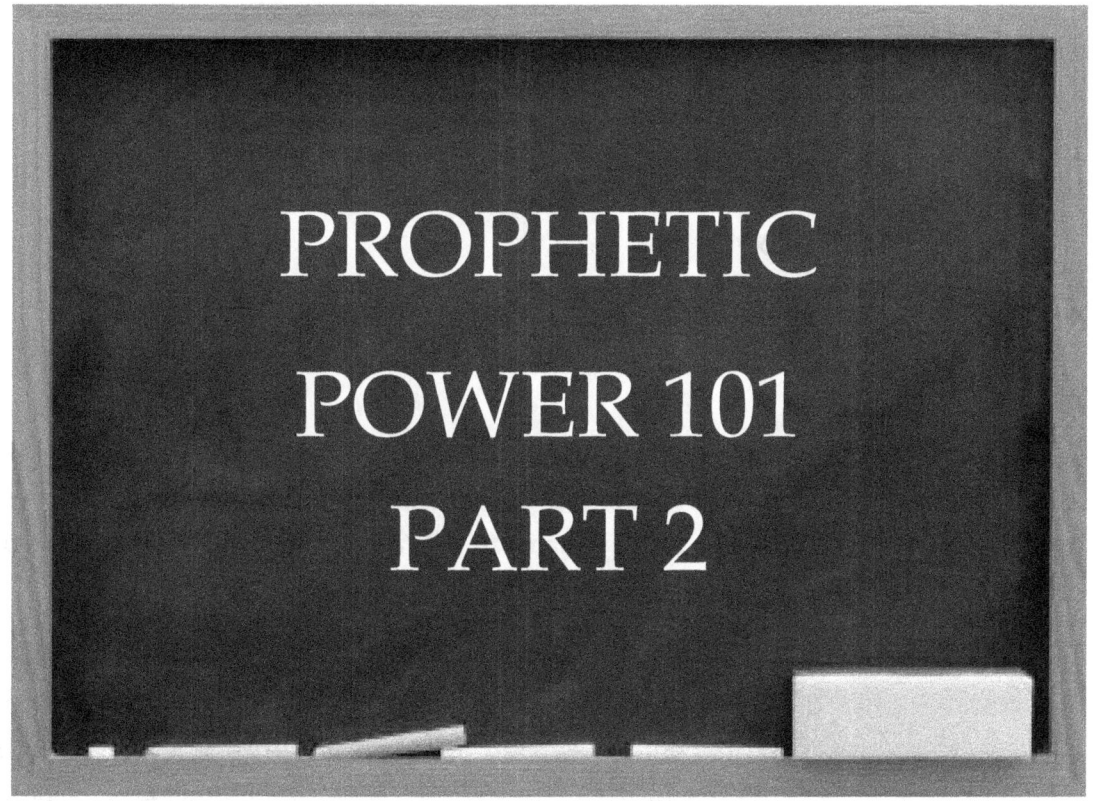

How Does the Prophetic Operate? – Part 6

Do not merely listen to the word, and so deceive yourselves. Do what it says. Anyone who listens to the word but does not do what it says is like a man who looks at his face in a mirror and after looking at himself, goes away and immediately forgets what he looks like (James 1:22-24, NIV).

Proper Development of Your Prophetic Productivity

The Three True Sources of Prophetic Power:

The prophet's sensitivity helps with his spiritual discernment. But the prophet's productivity helps with his power. There are several sources of fueling prophetic power. For the prophet is only as great as his authority and power. And when the sources of prophetic power are consistent, they allow the prophet to operate powerfully. Here are the major known tools needed to fuel prophetic productivity:

- **The Spirit of God**
- **The Consistency of Prayer**
- **The Application of Incremental Fasting**

The Spirit of God

But as it is written, Eye hath not seen, nor ear heard, neither have entered into the heart of man, the things which God hath prepared for them that love him. But God hath revealed them unto us by His Spirit: for the Spirit searcheth all things, yea, the deep things of God (1 Corinthians 2:8-10, KJV).

We have countless examples of how prophets like Ezekiel or Jeremiah would get caught up in their feelings while the Spirit of God moved upon them during prophecy (Ezekiel 8:3; Jeremiah 20:9). In some Old Testament cases, God subdued his prophetic vessels and their freewill. This was due to the urgency of the matter as well as the different dispensations they were in. But regardless of dispensation, the prophet of every age grows in intimacy with the Spirit of God. The Spirit of God is the first power of prophecy whether the prophet personally wants to deal with God or not!

For a major prophetic release was more important than the prophet's feelings and personal desires. The Old Testament teaches that a prophetic word emerges based on the time of crisis. And if the prophet would not relinquish control of self, God would either force him to operate or punish him severely (in the case of Jonah, for example). The prophet would then have to quickly shift from their personal placement. And finally he would not have a choice regarding God's desire to move prophetically through him. But the Spirit of God is the supreme source of the prophetic anointing. After all, the anointing to prophesy is a spiritual gift (1 Corinthians 12:1, 10; Romans 12:6) and a spiritual office (Ephesians 4:11).

This is why power within a prophetic mantle needs to be diligently sought, and not haphazardly or inconsistently, but fervently and seriously. Because due diligence is critical in the development of the productivity of every prophet's gift. What helps enhance such a search is the Spirit of the living God must become apart of the life of the designated prophet. That is why the power of the prophet chiefly centers on the move of the spirit first! Then, grace follows! And finalizing its power is the gift of faith! And even faith and grace are virtues, but they are also specific dimensions, like prophecy is within the spirit (Zechariah 12:10; 2 Corinthians 4:18).

This means that all prophetic anointing may be unique, but the process of prophetic release and its results are generally the same. The prophetic release comes from God. God then sends his Spirit unto ours. Our spirit then sends it to our heart. And from our heart, the prophetic moves towards our mouth or body. And this is always the manner in which God speaks, through a man to a people.

This means that no prophetic presence has exclusive rights to prophetic revelations or scriptural interpretations. For it is the same Spirit of yesterday that moves on the prophets of today. Furthermore, there are no copyrights within any prophetic mantle. Regardless of diversity, administration, or operation, it is the same Spirit, Lord, and God that work in all (1 Corinthians 12:4-7).

This simply shows how no single prophet holds absolute authority. All prophetic authority originates from the same place. And the Spirit of God is that place! If the Holy Spirit is absent of the prophetic ministry, one is operating in grace, but not in the fullness of prophetic power. The dangerous zone outside of that is what we call the spirit of divination. This can be very destructive. For the Spirit of God protects all true mantles of any prophet. And furthering his ethics comes as a protective measure, because God wants to ensure that all prophesying is congruent, and from the same origin.

Even within these voluntary or involuntary acts, the prophetic mantle is still at the discretion, release, and leading of the Holy Ghost. But it is also true that prophesying wasn't something men did secretly to promote their ministry or their society. Whether a person is given direct prophecy, or whether he receives prophecy after worship, prayer, or listening to music, prophecy does not go from the spirit of man into the heart of man until the Holy Spirit is willing to impart such experiences:

The main thing to keep in mind here is that no prophecy of Scripture is a matter of private opinion. And why? Because it's not something concocted in the human heart. Prophecy

resulted when the Holy Spirit prompted men and women to speak God's word (2 Peter 1:20-21, Message Bible).

Without the Spirit of God, a prophet has no right to speak. God's spirit is the source of all prophetic productivity! Meaning that the prophet must properly receive God's spirit so he can connect to the network for all prophets! Thus, the prophet's centralization is of the Holy Ghost. Or we can say it like this: the Holy Ghost is the headquarters of all prophetic voices. If there is no Holy Ghost, then there is no prophetic anointing!

This is why one must make sure that his life and connection to the Spirit are valid and active. And in order to receive the gift of the Holy Spirit within this dispensation, one must receive the gift of salvation through Jesus Christ (John 3:16). It is then that the candidate of the office of prophet will have more validity with this gift. Certainly, a former operation of the temporal anointing from the womb, as well as the gift of prophesying performed without salvation, are still possible (Matthew 7:21-23). And God's gifts and callings are without repentance (Romans 11:29). But when we accept these gifts, we must experience the permanency of the gift of the Holy Ghost, which is the foundation of all prophetic power.

- Every prophet must pray for prophetic power.
- Every prophet must pray for prophetic authority.

For both are essential in the Holy Ghost's operation, along with the prophetic anointing.

Prayer, as well as the prophet's lifestyle, must be free from the controlling and destructive strongholds of sin. Many prophets prophesy within their own level of understanding, instead of from a place of spiritual maturity. The only way to build up the most holy faith is by praying in the Spirit (Jude 20). For not practicing is walking dangerously. And in doing so, you walk a fine line between the spirits of divination and the true spirit of prophecy.

The Consistency of Prayer

The Old Testament prophets are classic demonstrators and foundational examples of how one should avail himself to a lifestyle of service in God. Their major service, which kept their prophetic productivity accurate, was through prayer. Consistency in one's prayer life is the means to the next phase of producing great prophetic power. And a major example of a prayer warrior was that of the prophet Daniel:

Now when Daniel knew that the writing was signed, he went into his house; and his windows being open in his chamber toward Jerusalem, he kneeled upon his knees three

times a day, and prayed, and gave thanks before his God, as he did aforetime. Then these men assembled, and found Daniel praying and making supplication before his God (Daniel 6:10-11).

When a prophet enters the zone of diligent prayer, God can entrust greater moves upon him. He is then propelled into greater moments of prophetic power, and prophecy will manifest evenly and accurately as a result. The prophetic expression will also be matured because the prophet has created a lifestyle of ascertaining prayer within his spirit and heart. If Jesus, who was both God and man, prayed, then the prophet, too, must give himself more to a greater prayer life as well.

Jeremiah and Ezekiel were both priests before becoming prophets. Moses was educated as a prince and Egyptian before becoming a prophet. David learned shepherding on the backside of the dessert while tending to his father's sheep before becoming a prophet. Amos' skills as a farmer, and Daniel's and Isaiah's connection to royalty were apparent before their prophetic ministries. But all these dynamics play vital and pivotal roles in their prophetic productivity. Yet the greatest activity that all these prophets have in common was their constant communication with God.

We may not become too scholarly like priests or theologians like Paul. And we may never have royal ancestry like Daniel and Isaiah. But we always will have the power of prayer. For a prophet that does not pray is a dangerous prophet. Prayer is a prophet's major means of connecting to his prophetic power. The definition of prayer simply means "one who talks with God." Thus, the question comes to mind: How can one prophesy if he does not pray?

Thus, prayer and prophesying work hand in hand. They are wholly connected. We pray in the Holy Ghost to build up our most holy faith (Jude 20). We pray in the Holy Ghost for better spiritual understanding (1 Corinthians 14:15). We also pray in the Holy Ghost to speak expressively and expressly what the Spirit of God is saying to the church in these last and evil days (1 Timothy 4:1a). If we do not pray in the Spirit, we do not have true prophetic connection. And if you are not talking to God, how can you speak for God?

This takes us back to the Gospel when Jesus requested that his closest disciples pray with him for one hour (Matthew 26:40). I truly believe that within even a mere 60 minutes, if we prevail in consistent prayer, we will reap an even greater allotment of power by the time the hour is over. Here is another revelation: there is so much power in one hour of prayer! And every prophet should practice spiritual prayer in the Holy Ghost for a minimum of one hour. As the love of prayer grows within the life of the prophet, so, too, does the purpose of one's prophetic ministry.

And a prophet's consistency in prayer will build greater clarity, accuracy, and sobriety of one's office and voice. For prayer also helps to condition the prophet's temperament. And prayer ensures that the prophetic work is never stifled by one's personality. When men come and seek your prophetic expertise, they should hopefully find you coming or going from prayer. For the lifestyle of prayer will perfect the prophetic anointing inside of you!

The Application of Incremental Fasting

Fasting is another activity that can help ensure purity within the life of the believer. It is the means of progressing in one's sanctification in Christ. And it is the means of breaking free from earthly control in order to grow in discipleship. When one fasts, it is not about form or fashion. In fact, we never fast to prove our spirituality or to be self-righteous. Fasting should always be conducted in secret:

Moreover when ye fast, be not, as the hypocrites, of a sad countenance: for they disfigure their faces, that they may appear unto men to fast. Verily I say unto you, they have their reward. But thou, when thou fastest, anoint thine head, and wash thy face. That thou appear not unto men to fast, but unto thy father which is in secret: and thy father, which seeth in secret, shall reward thee openly (Matthew 6:16-18).

Oftentimes, life, as well as life's issues, can disconnect a person from his true spiritual power. But fasting helps reconnect the two. And fasting can draw authority and power from the heavens, for we are baptized with the Holy Ghost to gain access into heaven. And we are also taught that we are seated with Christ in heaven. These revelations are in fact two different aspects of our spiritual baptism. But just because we are baptized in the Spirit does not mean we are yielded enough in the Spirit. A prime example of this is when the disciples could not cast out the demon that was afflicting a young boy at the bottom of Mt. Transfiguration. The issue at hand was because their spiritual power to handle such things was weakened by a lack of faith. Not only faith, but also the process of incremental fasting:

Howbeit this kind goeth not out but by prayer and fasting (Matthew 17:21).

Another example is when Jesus conducts his fast before his ministry. The moment Jesus came out of the fast, the scripture explains that a powerful release of more anointing and connection with the Spirit of God occurred. So, a fast is for this very purpose. It helps decrease the appetites of our sinful natures so that we may progress in our spiritual identities and natures instead. Herein determines if we are ready to be promoted in our ministries:

And Jesus returned in the power of the Spirit into Galilee: and there went out a fame of him through all the region round about (Luke 4:14).

We must never fast to achieve earthly perfection. For fasting will never make any of us perfect. It will, however, improve the heavenly gift of prophecy, allowing it to properly operate in or through us. This, too, is a legitimate source of prophetic productivity. The more we fast, the more success we will have within our prophetic anointing and gifting. For fasting is never about God. Instead, it is about you and your growth in God. When we fast, we crucify our flesh and allow the Holy Ghost more activity and unction within us. We also fast to ensure better prophetic purity! And in the practice of this, I guarantee you there will be greater prophetic power.

Conclusion of Prophetic Productivity

When the prophet establishes a consistent regimen of prayer and fasting in order to be filled by the Holy Ghost, a greater prophetic surge will happen. Every prophet needs to assess the scriptures and pray strategically about the prophet's actions in scripture. This increases the content of one's prayer life. And it also increases the prophet's power to be more prophetically productive. In a job, it is important to remain productive. Stagnation can be grounds for suspension, docked pay, and, in worse case scenarios, termination. If the contemporary prophet is not careful, he will be in danger of any one of those. And in the same manner, it is important to pray, fast, seek the spirit, and read God's word.

Acts 16:16 speaks of the spirit of divination. And the Greek word for "divination," is also the word "python." A python is a non-poisonous member of boa constrictor family. Boa constrictors seize their prey by entangling them and then suffocating them. To fight the false spirit that brings entanglement and spiritual suffocation it will take the prayers of the righteous and the student of the word, who is seeking to be continuously filled with the Lord Jesus' spirit. If you are that candidate, then you will receive the power of prophetic productivity!

Proper Distinguishment of the Conduits of Prophetic Vocality

I know that we have covered much. But there is one final lesson that we must review in this semester before this book must come to its close. After one has learned prophetic sensitivity and productivity, the prophet must then learn the greater levels of prophetic vocality. This, simply, is the process of learning how to use natural talents along with one's prophetic mantles.

And from a biblical point of view, when researching the scripture, there are three major natural talents that are commonly used along with the prophetic mantles mentioned earlier:

The Three Conventional Conduits for Prophetic Vocality

- The conduit of spoken words (the talent of speaking)
- The conduit of music (the talent of vocal and instrumental music)
- The conduit of written words (the talent of writing)

Overview: The Most Common Conduit is the Speaking Voice

Out of all prophetic manners, mediums, or modalities that are biblically expressed, the most popular talents associated with the prophetic are those of a vocal expression. Using one's voice is the most common. For the vocal expression of the prophetic is the most sound and is recorded biblically as the most conventional of all natural talents used as conduits to perform prophetic vocality:

As He spake by the mouth of His holy prophets, which have been since the world began (Luke 1:70).

Dark Speeches

But sometimes the vocal expression of the prophetic does not come in the language of its intended audience. When God spoke to Moses, for example, he spoke directly, and Moses would then speak directly to the people. And when God spoke with Moses, it was through a direct encounter unlike any other – but it was still vocal in nature:

And the Lord spake unto Moses face to face, as a man speaketh unto his friend..." (Exodus 33:11a).

"With him will I speak mouth to mouth, even apparently, and not in dark speeches; and the similitude of the Lord shall he behold..." (Numbers 12:8a).

I have also spoken by the prophets, and I have multiplied visions, and used similtudes, by the ministry of the prophets (Hosea 12:10).

But there are times when God creatively uses the vocal arts, along with poetry or parables, to speak to a people. The best examples of these would be verse or prose. And depending on the design of God's spirit, the prophetic can also use those forms. One of the greatest examples of the prophetic in parabolic form comes from the days of Jesus' ministry. The Bible says that Jesus spoke mainly in parables, which is frequently seen, too, among the ministry of the Old Testament prophets.

Prophetic Parables

The Parable of the Ewe Lamb

> *And the Lord sent Nathan unto David. And he came unto him, and said unto him, there were two en in one city; the one rich, and the other poor. The rich man had exceeding many flocks and herds: but the poor man had nothing, save one little ewe lamb, which he had brought and nourished up: and it grew up together with him, and with his children; it did eat of his own meat, and drank of his own cup, and lay in his bosom, and was unto him as a daughter. And there came a traveler unto the rich man, and he spared to take of his own flock and of his own herd, to dress for the wayfaring man that was come unto him; but took the poor man's lamb, and dressed it for the man that was come to him. And David's anger was greatly kindled against the man; and he said to Nathan, as the Lord liveth, the man that hath done this thing shall surely die: and he shall restore the lamb fourfold, because he did this thing, and because he had not pity. And Nathan said to David, thou art the man, thus saith the Lord God of Israel, I anointed thee king over Israel, and delivered thee out of the hand of Saul (2 Samuel 12:1-7).*

The Parable of the Wild Grapes

> *Now will I sing to my well beloved a song of my beloved touching his vineyard. My well beloved hath a vineyard in a very fruitful hill: and he fenced it, and gathered out the stones thereof, and planted it with the choicest vine, and built a tower in the midst of it, and also made a winepress therein: and he looked that it should bring forth grapes, and it brought forth wild grapes. And now, O inhabitants of Jerusalem, and men of Judah, judge, I pray you, between me and my vineyard. What could have been done more to my vineyard, that I have not done in it? Wherefore, when I looked that it should bring forth grapes, brought it forth wild grapes? And now go to; I will tell you what I will do to my vineyard: I will take away the hedge thereof, and it shall be eaten up; and break down the wall thereof, and it shall be trodden down: And I will lay it waste: it shall not be pruned, nor digged; but there shall come up briers and thorns: I will also command the clouds that they rain no rain upon it. For the vineyard of the Lord of hosts is the house of*

> *Israel, and the men of Judah his pleasant plant: and he looked for judgment, but behold oppression; for righteousness, but behold a cry (Isaiah 5:1-7).*

The Parable of the Eagles and the Vines

> *Son of man, put forth a riddle, and speak a parable unto the house of Israel; And say, Thus saith the Lord God; a great eagle with great wings, longwinged, full of feathers, which had divers colors, came unto Lebanon, and took the highest branch of the cedar: He cropped off the top of his young twigs, and carried it unto a land of traffic; he set it in a city of merchants. He took also of the seed of the land, and planted it in a fruitful field: he placed it by great waters, and set it as a willow tree. And it grew, and became a spreading vine of low stature, whose branches turned toward him, and the roots thereof were under him: so it became a vine, and brought forth branches, and shot forth sprigs. There was also another great eagle with great wings and many feathers: and, behold, this vine did bend her roots towards him, and shot forth her branches toward him, that he might water it by the furrows of her plantation. It was planted in a good soil by great waters, that it might bring forth branches, and that it might bear fruit, that it might be a goodly vine. Say thou, Thus saith the Lord God; shall it prosper? Shall he not pull up the roots thereof, and cut off the fruit thereof, that it wither? It shall wither in all the leaves of her spring, even without great power of many people to pluck it up by the roots thereof. Yea, behold, being planted, shall it prosper? Shall it not utterly wither, when the east wind toucheth it? It shall wither in the furrows where it grew (Ezekiel 17:2-10).*

Using a parable as an extension of the vocal form of the prophetic is biblically revealed as both common and proper. The overall purpose of the parable was to help the hearer become an intense listener, whereby, if they allowed the parable to grasp their mind's eye, they could properly transfer the metaphor's meaning. And whether the prophetic word is done in prose or verse, the vocalized prophetic word of God is the superlative of all prophetic expressions. It is the superlative of all conventional tools, and of all prophetic mediums, especially when the prophet speaks of a vision, dream, or similitude. However, the vocal expression and derivatives are not the only expressions.

The Conduit of Music

Then sang Moses and the children of Israel this song unto the Lord, and spake, saying, I will sing unto the Lord, for he hath triumphed gloriously: the horse and his rider hath He thrown into the sea. (Exodus 15:1).

Prior to the massive exodus of the Israelites from Egypt, there is no biblical reference for music, except for the awareness of the father of music, Jubal (Genesis 4:21). Interestingly enough, when Jubal's song was created, the position of the prophetic anointing for using music as a prophetic medium was also confirmed through Moses' sister, since she responded to the song of praise and victory:

And Miriam the prophetess, the sister of Aaron, took a timbrel in her hand; and all the women went out after her with timbrels and with dances. And Miriam answered them, Sing ye to the Lord, for He hath triumphed gloriously; the horse and his rider hath He thrown into the sea (Exodus 15:20-21).

Here, the musical activity of Israel emerged. Not only did the musical emerge, but the first prophetic musical expression also appeared biblically. When researching the Hebrew word for "sang," translated in verse one of Exodus 15, we discover that the word means to "generally sing."

But further research of this word leads us to discover another root word for this same word. And that definition led us to the phrase, "strolling minstrelsy." In the Hebraic understanding the word "minstrelsy" comes from the Hebrew word that is called the "minstrel." Moreover, the Hebrew definition for the word "minstrel" means "a singing and traveling musical poet." In other words, to sing poetically is to be the type of minstrel, which is mentioned in the scriptures. But as we go even deeper with study a minstrel is, symbolically, another form of a prophetic musician:

"And Elisha said, as the Lord of hosts liveth, before whom I stand, surely, were it not that I regard the presence of Jehoshaphat the king of Judah, I would not look toward thee, nor see thee. But now bring me a minstrel. And it came to pass, when the minstrel played, the hand of the ord came upon him (2 Kings 3:14-15).

This reference explains how a minstrel can become prophetic and not just musical. Just as Moses and Miriam were not merely singing; they were also prophetically singing through music. Though audible words and melody were provided on that day, the content of their message was so much deeper. God had taken music and turned that talent into a conduit in order to assist prophecy. For not only does prophecy flow through singing, but it also flows through instrumental music as well.

So, after the great deliverance from Egypt, God brought singing back to the people. And Moses flowed poetically and musically like a minstrel when he created his song at the other side of the Red Sea, while he watched Pharaoh's entire army drown. But notice that the definition also mentioned the word strolling, meaning that the actions of the minstrel are to sing, walk and create a new song spontaneously. This is the art form of singing poetically and extemporaneously. Thus, when Moses sang this song extemporaneously, he was walking and singing simultaneously. This was the first feature of the prophetic flow of music and the creativity that coincided with it.

From the beginning of music to more advanced music as a prophetic gift, we must mention the fact that when Samuel became the prophet of the people, during the last administration of the judges, God allowed him and King David to establish a system of prophetic guilds for the regiments and services of worship rendered within the tabernacle:

"…These were reckoned by their genealogy in their villages, whom David and Samuel the seer did ordain in their set office" (1 Chronicles 9:22b).

And it is very clear why God required King David to assist with the organization of the prophetic musical guides within the temple, along with Samuel. For the Bible teaches that David was indeed a prophet who flowed prophetically while writing his music:

Men and brethren, let me freely speak unto you of the patriarch David, that he is both dead and buried, and his sepulcher is with us unto this day. Therefore being a prophet, and knowing that God had sworn with an oath to him, that of the fruit of his loins, according to the flesh, he would raise up Christ to sit on his throne; he seeing this before spake of the resurrection of Christ, that his soul was not left in hell, neither his flesh did see corruption (Acts 2:29-31).

When Peter gave his apostolic dissertation and revelation concerning David's additional identity, he cited one of David's prophetic psalms:

Therefore my heart is glad, and my glory rejoiceth: my flesh also shall rest in hope. For thou wilt not leave my soul in hell; neither wilt thou suffer thine Holy one to see corruption. Thou wilt show me the path of life: in thy presence is fullness of joy; at thy right hand there are pleasure forevermore (Psalm 16:9-11).

And since David was familiar with music and the prophetic, he could work with Samuel to create such a paradigm for prophetic and musical families so they could worship daily and consistently within the temple:

Moreover David and the captains of the host separated to the service of the sons of Asaph, and of Heman, and of Jeduthun, who should prophesy with harps, with psalteries, and with cymbals...The sons of Asaph under the hands of Asaph, which prophesied according to the order of the king...six, under the hands of their father Jeduthun, who prophesied with a harp, to give thanks and to praise the Lord..Heman the king's seer in the words of God, to lift up the horn...All these were under the hands of their father for song in the house of the Lord, with cymbals, psalteries, and harps, for the service of the house of God, according to the king's order to Asaph, Jeduthun, and Heman. So the number of them, with their brethren that were instructed in the songs of the Lord, even all that were cunning, was two hundred fourscore and eight. And they cast lots, ward against ward, as well the small as the great, the teacher as the scholar. (1 Chronicles 25:1a, 2b, 5a, 6-8).

Thus, the prophetic flows within the musical ministry of ancient Israelite culture. And the musical ministry is the second most common of the conventional talents that often connect with prophetic ability.

The Conduit of Written Word

And the Lord answered me, and said, write the vision, and make it plain upon tables, that he may run that readeth it. For the vision is yet for an appointed time, but at the end it shall speak, and not lie: though it tarry, wait for it; because it will surely come, it will not tarry (Habakkuk 2:2-3).

"...It is written in the book of the prophets..." (Acts 7:42).

It is the will of God that prophets write down their prophetic words, visions, and dreams. And the prophet Habakkuk is the prototype for this understanding. As we venture into the word of God more, we see that other prophets had the same mandate in their lives. John the Apostle, for example, although he was not officially a prophet, was sanctioned to write prophesies for the Book of Revelation for other believers to read (Revelation 22:7, 10, 18-19, KJV).

> ➤ The goal of the prophetic words written was to provide additional blessings to the hearers and observers of a given prophecy: *Blessed is he that readeth, and they that hear the words of this prophecy, and keep those things which are written therein: for the time is at hand (Revelation 1:3).*

- Even the musical prophets that were in the tabernacle and temple wrote their music fresh and taught it quickly for worship: ***And Moses came and spake all the words of this song in the ears of the people, he, and Hoshea the son of Nun (Deuteronomy 32:44).***

- And King David would also follow this same paradigm: ***And he appointed certain of the Levites to minister before the ark of the Lord, and to record, and to thank and praise the Lord God of Israel....Then on that day David delivered first this psalm to thank the Lord into the hand of Asaph and his brethren (1 Chronicles 16:4, 7).***

This is why the prophet was called on to write down the words of the Lord for future generations. It appears that the prophet was not only a recorder of the prophetic words, but also a recorder of the history of the people:

"And Moses wrote all the words of the Lord..." (Exodus 24:4a).

Now the rest of the acts of Solomon, first and last, are they not written in the book of Nathan the prophet, and in the prophecy of Ahijah the Shilonite, and in the visions of Iddo the seer against Jeroboam the son of Nebat? (2 Chronicles 9:29).

Now the acts of Rehoboam, first and last, are they not written in the book of Shemaiah the prophet, and of Iddo the seer concerning the genealogies?" (2 Chronicles 12:15a).

And even in prophetic correspondence, the word of God was written as a letter, which confirms it as another additional means of prophetic transport. Mere letters of prophecy were sent out as a means of reaching an intended audience when the prophet was unable to reach his audience directly. It was also God's will to have the prophet keep a journal of the prophetic words that consisted of major shifts in the history of the Israelites.

Regardless of the purpose, letters and journals are biblically sound conduits for prophetic ministry:

"And there came a writing to him from Elijah the prophet..." (2 Chronicles 21:12a).

Moreover the Lord said unto me, take thee a great roll, and write in it with a man's pen concerning Maher-shalal-hash-baz (Isaiah 8:1).

Take thee a roll of a book, and write therein all the words that I have spoken unto thee against Israel, and against Judah, and against all the nations from the day I spake unto thee, from the days of Josiah, even unto this day (Jeremiah 36:2).

And it came to pass, that when Jehudi had read three of four leaves, he cut it with the penknife, and cast it into the fire that was on the hearth, until all the roll was consumed in the fire that was on the hearth (Jeremiah 32:23).

Even in the story of Jeremiah, writing the prophetic word via letter or an entire book that contained over twenty years of prophetic utterances, the King Jehoaikim attempted to destroy it because the prophetic word was so penetrating and convicting. God gave Jeremiah creative insight to employ a prophetic scribe (who wrote both manuscripts), and Jeremiah vocalized the Lord's thoughts on the wicked king:

Then Jeremiah called Baruch the son of Neriah: and Baruch wrote from the mouth of Jeremiah all the words of the Lord, which he had spoken unto him, upon a roll of a book (Jeremiah 36:4).

Then the word of the Lord came to Jeremiah, after that the king had burned the roll, and the words which Baruch wrote at the mouth of Jeremiah, saying, take thee again another roll, and write in it all the former words that were in the first roll, which Jehoiakim the king of Judah hath burned....Then took Jeremiah another roll and gave it to Baruch the scribe, the son of Neriah; who wrote therein from the mouth of Jeremiah all the words of the book which Jehoiakim king of Judah had burned in the fire: and there were added besides unto them many like words (Jeremiah 36:27-28, 32).

CONCLUSION OF LESSON 11:

When God wanted to get a prophetic word to a people, it did not matter what means he used. These three highly quoted and referenced means are not the only ones. But again, they are the main ones. In today's expression, other art forms have been added, including prayer, dance, visual arts, and other forms. But the trueness of the definition of the prophetic centers around one prevailing theme: the prophetic must clearly speak the revelation and will of God through whatever means they operate. Thus, the voice of the prophet is not limited to mere conventional expressions, as long as the true essence of the Spirit of God is properly conveyed during the set time of its release. And this is properly done within the ordained manner of God's divine choice.

For I have discovered that most prophets are artists by profession or hobby. They are writers, poets, singers, dancers, musicians, graphic artists and public speakers. Thus, God has demonstrated, through the various methods of prophesying, that the vocal arts of the prophetic are foundational. But many other talents, as conduits with specific prophetic mantles, are presently emerging.

Now it is common to express the prophetic in liberated and unconventional means. For there are now prophetic praise dancers, prophetic exhorters, prophetic psalmists, prophetic preachers, prophetic teachers, prophetic writers, and the list goes on. We must, then, use the unique shapes of our lives and talents to allow God to be God. And to allow God to move through these talents as he pleases while we are called to use our spiritual gift of prophecy. For this is why the unknown writer of Hebrews states that God spoke through the prophets in different manners (Hebrews 1:1). Now the assignment is yours to seek. Seek it thoroughly and honestly because you can only be true to the true you. And the unique way that God has made you!

PART 3

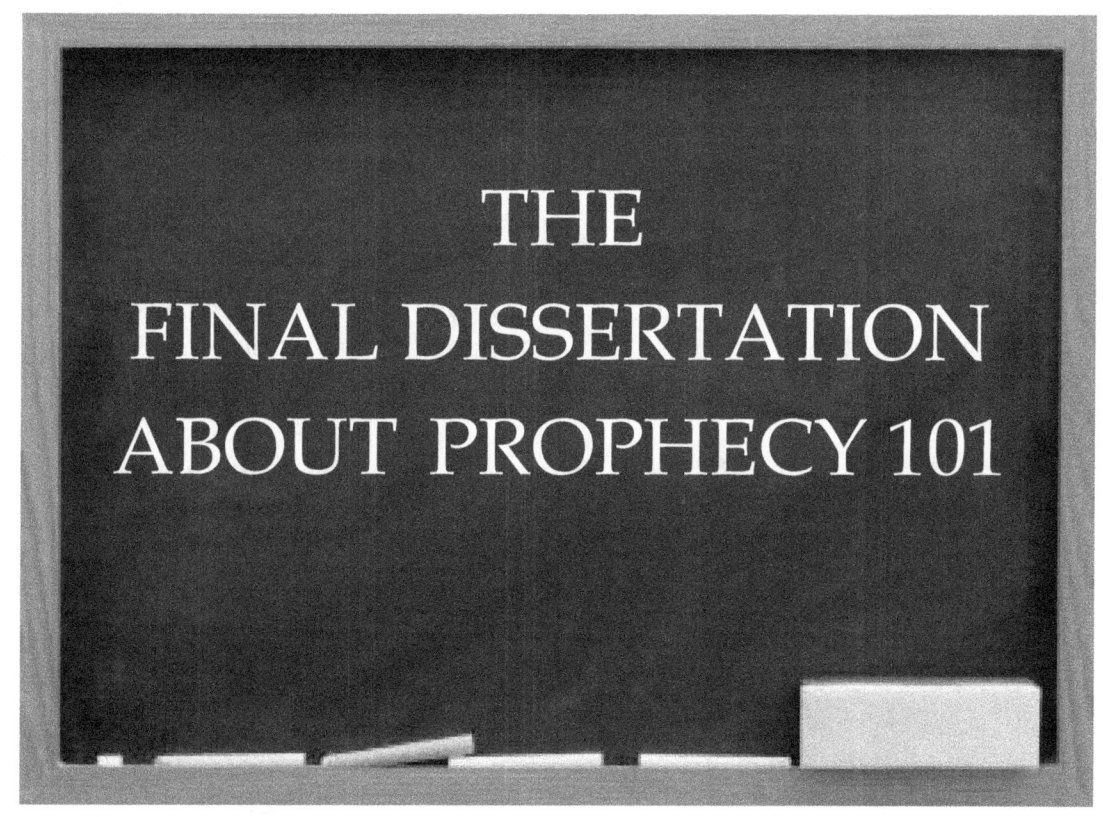

THE THIRD INTRODUCTION

Part 3: The Final Dissertation About Prophecy 101

The gift of prophecy and the office of the prophet are vast. But this book of various teachings on the doctrine of prophecy was meant to inspire awareness of some of the basic who, what, when, where, why and how of prophecy. Hopefully, you have received that inspiration. And hopefully you have taken many notes on the concepts and revelations mentioned. Regarding the current practice of New Testament prophecy, I must share these final perspectives with you!

The word of God declares that prophecy is the best of all spiritual gifts used in his church:

"Follow after charity, and desire spiritual gifts, but rather that ye may prophesy... Wherefore, brethren, covet to prophesy..." (1 Corinthians 14:1, 39a).

The Apostle Paul also confirmed prophecy as the superlative spiritual gift of all spiritual gifts. Simply put, the purpose of the prophetic is highly important. Paul literally called the prophetic one of the best gifts God has given the church by way of his Holy Spirit. And every believer is called on to covet the best gifts for the purpose of the maximizing Jesus' ministry:

But covet earnestly the best gifts: and yet show I unto you a more excellent way (1 Corinthians 12:31).

If Jesus Christ is the superlative of all true prophets, then prophecy is the superlative of all spiritual gifts. And herein is the major premise behind the doctrine of prophecy. For this reveals that prophecy and Jesus are the same, just as love and God are the same. This is why the Apostle Paul taught that the pursuit of prophesying should be as strong as pursuit of *agape*-love. For *agape*-love is God, and God is *agape*-love:

"...God is love..." (1 John 4:16b).

Following love means that you seek to apprehend it. The Greek explanation for the phrase "following love" means to run quickly and swiftly towards loves as an attempt to chase it down so that one might catch it (with the intention of never letting it go). This also means that there is a tempo to the prophetic and the love of God. Prophecy is, therefore, a movement and not just a destination. Meaning prophecy moves within time just as much as love moves in and out of time. Therefore, he who pursues these two divine virtues must always realize that there is an urgency of exhortation. And that exhortation is that if you are in love with God, you surely do not want to miss God's moves.

And in 1 Corinthians 12:31 and 14:1, Paul uses the word "covet." The Greek definition for the word "covet" is "to burn with zeal," which further shows that we must be eager to prophesy. This means the following: God wants us to pursue quickly the prophetic (i.e. follow after it or have passion for it). This also means that God wants us to desire the prophetic (i.e. to be moved or envious of it), which means taking a negative intention and making it positive. Therefore, he wants us to stalk prophesying as much as we should stalk God's love.

Let's think about this for a moment. When you envy something, you desire to have something that's not directly yours. This is the desire to have something that belongs to another. And positive envying of prophecy is when you want to experience the influence, power, and presence of the anointing that operates within the truly prophetic, even if the prophetic is not your main spiritual gift assigned.

CHAPTER 12

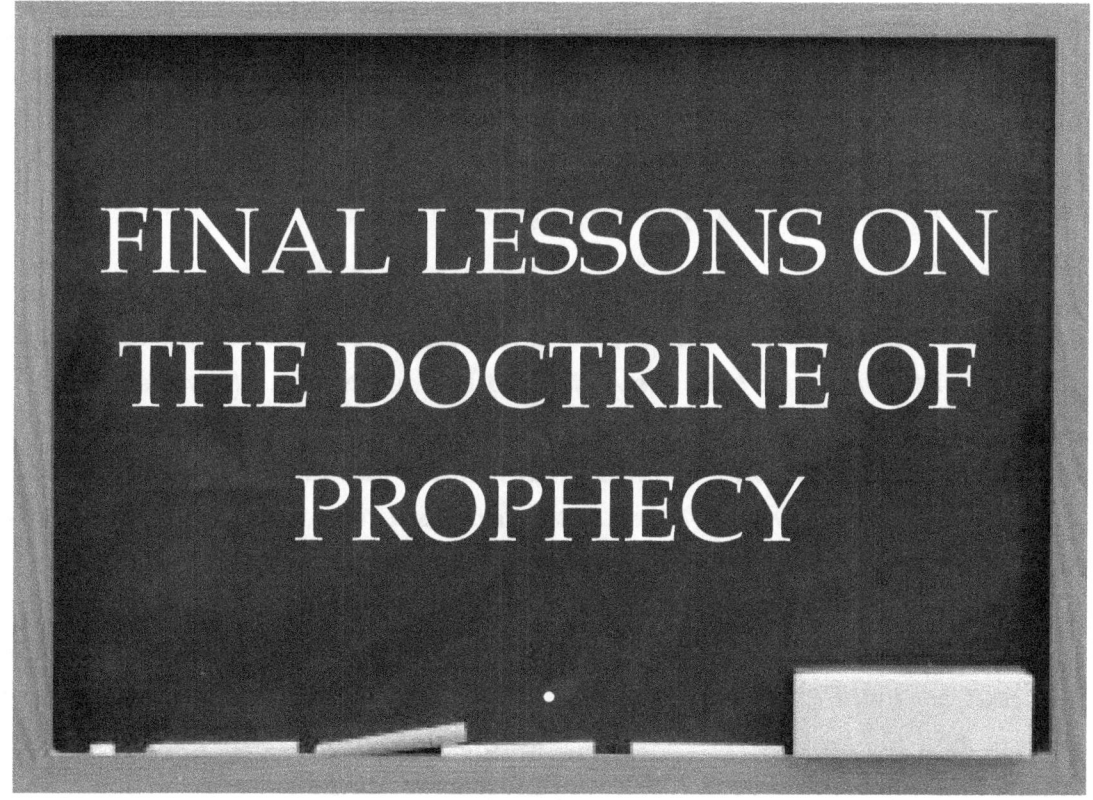

Final Scriptural Thought:

"...Prophecy...is for believers, not for unbelievers..."
(1 Corinthians 14:22b, NIV).

The Doctrine of Prophecy

An Old Testament Prayer Fulfilled

"And the Lord came down in a cloud, and spake unto him, and took of the spirit that was upon him, and gave it unto the seventy elders: and it came to pass, that, when the spirit rested upon them, they prophesied, and did not cease...And Moses said unto him, enviest thou for my sake? Would God that all the Lord's people were prophets, and that the Lord would put his spirit upon them!" (Numbers 11:25, 29).

It was the prayer life of the Prophet Moses that confirmed Joel and Peter's revelation regarding the prophetic anointing that was destined to be generational rather than individual. Moses experienced this struggle when handling the matters of local and national proportions of ministry among the entire nation of Israel. In simpler terms, Moses was exhausted. Yet he still attempted to answer all matters of the congregation of Israel alone:

Then Moses heard the people weep throughout their families, every man in the door of his tent: and the anger of the Lord was kindled greatly; Moses also was displeased. And Moses said unto the Lord, wherefore hast thou afflicted thy servant? And wherefore have I not found favor in thy sight, that thou layest the burden of all this people upon me? Have I conceived all this people? Have I begotten them, that thou shouldest say unto me, carry them in thy bosom, as a nursing father beareth the suckling child, unto the land which thou swearest unto their fathers? Whence should I have flesh to give unto all this people? For they weep unto me, saying, give us flesh, that we may eat. I am not able to bear all this people alone, because it is too heavy for me. And if thou deal thus with me, kill me, I pray thee, out of hand, if I have found favor in thy sight: and let me not see my wretchedness. And the Lord said unto Moses, gather unto me seventy men of the elders of Israel, whom thou knowest to be the elders of the people, and officers over them; and bring them unto the tabernacle of the congregation, that they may stand there with thee. And I will come down and talk with thee there: and I will take of the spirit which is upon thee, and will put it upon them; and they shall bear the burden of the people with thee, that thou beat it not thyself alone (Numbers 11:10-17).

In this reference, several things occurred. The first was a situation concerning the vast number of complaints that Moses had constantly heard and become highly irritated by. As a result of this irritation, God manifested a fire that burned and began to destroy the camp of the Israelites (Numbers 11:1). The scripture says that Moses became God's intercessor and dissolved the fires (Numbers 11:2-3).

But then a second situation arose concerning the daily distribution of manna. There was a mixed multitude growing within the congregation, and their lust caused competition in the consumption of the manna. Again, the complaints of the Israelites began to manifest (Numbers 11:4-6). In Moses' frustration and desperation, he went to God and vented. During his venting, we see the clarity of Moses' complaints to God (Numbers 11:10-15).

God then sent Moses a divine solution. God instructed Moses to pick elders of each tribe, who were already leaders, to receive the prophetic anointing that was upon Moses' life (Numbers 11:16). This again confirms another teaching on how the mantle of the senior prophet is in the anointing of the supportive prophet. And that distinct anointing can permeate a people if God so desires (Numbers 11:17). God takes the prophetic anointing on Moses and places it on 70 leaders. 68 of them were present when this transfer happened. But two of them were in another location within the camp. And yet, because the specified 70 were chosen, it did not matter what location there were in. What was important was the matter in which Moses chose whom he picked to receive his mantle.

This reveals that it does not matter who you are, or if you are destined to be a prophet or be prophetic – you will surely be what God wants you to be. For the people in Moses' time were destined to receive the spirit of his anointing, regardless of their locations. But the enigma of the two out of the seventy, who were already prophesying in the camp and were absent from the initial impartation, is the basis for our reception of prophetic prayer, for a corporate body of prophets is revealed. Moses' desire was expressed when he wished that God anoint all of his people with the prophetic so he did not have to be so exhausted. The accounts share that an eyewitness came to Moses and informed him. Joshua, Moses' successor, demanded Moses stop this ordeal:

"However, two men, whose names were Eldad and Medad, had remained in the camp. They were listed among the elders, but did not go out to the Tent. Yet the Spirit also rested on them, and they prophesied in the camp. A young man ran and told Moses, "Eldad and Medad are prophesying in the camp." Joshua son of Nun, who had been Moses' aide since youth, spoke up and said, "Moses, my Lord, stop them! But Moses replied, "Are you jealous for my sake? I wish that all the Lord's people were prophets and that the Lord would put His spirit on them!" (Numbers 11:26-29, NIV).

It appears that Moses' prophetic prayer request had come to pass. The fulfillment of this confirmation occurred not just for Israel, but also through the Apostle Paul's dissertation and apostolic command for all New Testament believers to pursue after prophesying and being prophetic.

Even I never knew personally how my zeal for being prophetic was actually biblical until I started studying these references. It is clear that God wants the body to be a prophetic institution of baptized, spirit-filled believers who can tap into the prophetic and not be at the mercy of itinerant prophets. This revelation does not negate, or make invalid, the position of the office of the prophet. But it does share in the revelation that all can be prophetic, and that all can pursue the prophetic for corporate, personal, and spiritual matters.

But this lesson gives us the greatest lesson about prophecy, which, as stated earlier, is that the superlative of all prophets is Jesus Christ, and that all prophets, past and present, operate under the spirit of prophecy, which is the testimony of Christ (Revelation 19:10b). This revelation ultimately means that each prophet does not deliver a distinction of his own spirit and personality, but rather that all leading or governmental prophets can only pass on a true mantle and anointing that is from the Spirit of Christ.

An Apostolic Charge

As I traveled between the Testaments, watching the patterns of the Apostle Paul's training and the specific accounts of the Old Testament prophetic training, I felt the urgency to pick up the mantle and burden of this apostolic assignment to help New Testament ministries that are intimately with a prophetic mantle. But the first assignment for restoring this gift is to receive the governing principles of the commandments that God refreshes us through the Apostle Paul's and Jesus Christ's ministries. Unfortunately, there are so many rogue prophets that will probably refuse the potential for prophetic growth, just as they did during Jesus' and Paul's times and ministries. And if there are any rogue prophets present within your ministry, then this next verse certainly applies to them:

But if any man be ignorant, let him be ignorant (1 Corinthians 14:38).

The goal of this book is to provide you with the basics of prophetism. There are, of course, some levels of advanced thought and subjective apostolic revelation. However, the final means is to charge you to remain sober, because of the damages seen day to day with the prophetic gift of God. A strange fire is being raised among the people of God. And that fire is among those who inordinately ascribe to the apostolic and prophetic offices. This book, then, serves to combat the falsities that these agents perpetrate:

For God is not the author of confusion, but of peace, as in all churches of the saints....Let all things be done decently and in order (1 Corinthians 14:33, 40).

For prophetism is a beautiful instrument as well as responsibility. And prophetism has come with many setbacks because darkness always competes with the light. But darkness does not stop the presence of the true appropriation of the prophets. A prime example of such prophetic preserving power is seen in the story of Obadiah, when Jezebel attempted to destroy all of God's prophets. Obadiah hid 100 prophets in a cave to preserve the prophetic vision of God:

And Ahab called Obadiah, which was the governor of his house. (Now Obadiah feared the Lord greatly: For it was so, when Jezebel cut off the prophets of the Lord, that Obadiah took an hundred prophets, and hid them by fifty in a cave, and fed them with bread and water.) (1 Kings 18:3-4).

What we need now is the power of prophetic preservation! And we need more modern day prophetic preservers and crusaders with the spirit of Obadiah. Obadiah was a mere man who wanted the prophetic life to remain within the earth's realm! He was a man after God's own heart. But he also was a man who knew the importance of prophecy and the serious need for continuing a prophetic anointing. If the spirit of Jezebel can resurrect (Revelation 2:20), surely the spirit of Obadiah can too! Never do we imply this in the sense of reincarnation. But always by the sense of function and purpose can we become a modern day Obadiah.

The chapters and information in this book will help you navigate prophetic infection and contamination. It will keep you sane and sober as you matriculate through the many disconcerted attempts of those, who may be earnest, but yet ill equipped to explain and foster such principles and communities. The design of this book is to give you foundational understanding of how: we who are prophetic must strengthen our resolve to formalize a proper prophetic doctrine! Not just for this generation alone! But also for other generations to come.

Now that I have raised your consciousness, I exhort you to intercede on behalf of the prophetic office and gifting throughout the world. For your intercession of our community thus showcases that you have submitted to the major assignment of being prophetic. Furthermore, it will demonstrate that you are not interested in the trifles of badly learned behavior. For there is a massive amount of badly learned behavior being done among current prophetic practitioners! For they have continuously and demonically let such practices infiltrate the spiritual body of Christ:

"And we have the word of the prophets made more certain, and you will do well to pay attention to it..." (2 Peter 1:19a, NIV).

THE FINAL CONCLUSIONS OF THE DOCTRINE OF PROPHECY

Prophesying is Greater Than Speaking in Tongues

I would that ye all spake with tongues, but rather that ye prophesied: for greater is he that prophesieth that he that speaketh with tongues, except he interpret, that the church may receive edifying (1 Corinthians 14:5).

The ultimate goal of this superlative spiritual gift and office, then, is to build up people. It is not meant to downcast other gifts, nor is to say that the gift of prophecy is the exclusive gift. It is, however, the premiere gift that all can ascertain if they will and yield to its true presence within the church. It is also important to share that the same Holy Spirit present during the lives of the Apostles, the day of Pentecost, and the prophets of the epistles, is the same Holy Spirit who endows us with the gift of prophecy.

This is why prophesying is even greater than speaking in tongues. For we know that speaking in tongues is the newest of all spiritual gifts. And something new would seem to have more influence than the old. However, prophecy is greater, not just because it is older, but because it is about Jesus. When you truly prophesy, you are actually speaking for Jesus. And speaking in tongues is about prayer and witness. Thus, prophesying is about gathering a greater witness for the kingdom of God, by representing Jesus to his Holy church!

The Prophetic is Interpretation of the Will and Purposes of God

The gift of prophecy and the office of the prophet certainly are about the unique ability to receive secrets that only God and men can know. This gift is also the ability to discern, through prophetic interpretation, the purpose of such secrets, whether they are transported via dreams, visions, or similitudes and spontaneous utterances. When the creator of the Amplified Bible, a woman by the name of Frances Siewert, articulated the prophetic understandings of the Apostle Paul, she presented it to us in this way:

- "...Prophetic insight (the gift of interpreting the divine will and purpose)..." (1 Corinthians 12:10, Amp).

- "...Second prophets (inspired preachers and expounders)..." (1 Corinthians 12:28, Amp).

- "...Are all prophets (inspired interpreters of the will and purposes of God)..." (1 Corinthians 12:29a, Amp).

- "...Prophetic powers (the gift of interpreting the divine will and purpose)..." (1 Corinthians 13:2a, Amp).

- "...Prophesy (interpret the divine will and purpose in inspired preaching and teaching)" (1 Corinthians 14:1b, Amp).

- "...The one who prophesies [who interprets the divine will and purpose in inspired preaching and teaching] speaks to men for their upbuilding and constructive spiritual progress and encouragement and consolation" (1 Corinthians 14:3b, Amp).

- "...He who prophesies [interpreting the divine will and purpose and teaching with inspiration] edifies and improves the church and promotes growth [in Christian wisdom, piety, holiness and happiness]" (1 Corinthians 14:4b, Amp).

- "...But more especially [I want you] to prophesy (to be inspired to preach and interpret the divine will and purpose. He who prophesies [who is inspired to preach and teach] is greater (more useful and more important)..." (1 Corinthians 14:5b, Amp).

- "...Prophecy (inspired preaching and teaching, interpreting the divine will and purpose) is not for unbelievers [on the point of believing] but for believers" (1 Corinthians 14:22b, Amp).

- But if all prophesy [giving inspired testimony and interpreting the divine will and purpose] the unbeliever or untaught outsider comes in, he is told of his sin and reproved and convicted and convinced of all, and his defects and needs are examined (estimated, determined) and he is called to account by all (1 Corinthians 14:24, Amp).

- "...Set your hearts on prophesying (on being inspired to preach and teach and to interpret God's will and purpose)..." (1 Corinthians 14:39b, Amp).

I share her translations in excess to show you how important it is to become a better student of prophecy. Because to be a prophet, you must have the ability to interpret the move of God accurately, soberly, and with clarity! For the prophet has been gifted with the ability to properly interpret such spiritual and biblical facts. But this only comes from a life of study.

For the word "interpret" simply means, "to explain, or tell the meaning of something." It means to present things in understandable terms. The function of interpreting, then, is to serve as a representative of two speakers from two different languages. Thus, the gift of the prophet is to be the conveyer of the language of God while doing so through one or more of the languages of men.

Yes, the tongue of God is different than the tongue of men. And God has chosen the prophet to be able to listen, hear, and properly decipher the things of the spirit realm! When you find a great interpreter of the will and purposes of God, you are standing in the presence of a great prophetic student.

Thus, the gift of prophecy is most successful when the prophet has cultivated the ability to interpret the divine will and purposes of God. Like Daniel, this ability is a gift that is developed through prayer. And like Joseph, he was genetically predisposed with the assignment to interpret his own dreams and even the dreams of Pharaoh. But it was Daniel and his three friend's prayer lives that helped find the truth behind Nebuchadnezzar's rant from a previous nightmare. Daniel had no clue what was said in Nebuchadnezzar's dream. But God did! God knows all and will reveal all – if he so chooses. The choice is always God's. But the process of gathering such ability is relatively the same. And that agenda is proactive prayer with a clear agenda for studying the word of God in order to become a better prophetic conduit!

We must become better interpreters of the will and purposes of God. No! We are never called to translate. For we could never speak totally for God – only God can do that! But we can surmise and gather, through our own discipline, the ability to properly articulate God's will and purposes in such a way that man will know that it is God speaking to them, through us! And each generation has a newer responsibility to creatively hear what the Spirit of God is speaking to his Holy Church.

This is why you must become very detail oriented and investigative during your pursuits of the prophetic assignment. It is also equally important that just as we asked the basic questions of who, what, when, where, why, and how within this book, you must now also continue to ask these questions within your very own private studies. In fact, I am insisting that you do this every time we are not in class together! For the extra credit in God is up to you:

Keep on asking and it will be given you; keep on seeking and you will find, keep on knocking [reverently] and [the door] will be opened to you (Matthew 7:7, Amplified Version).

Well, this ends the classroom session for our semester. The bell has rung. And school is out for the moment. However, practice the principles and the perspectives we have discussed. For the doctrine of prophecy class will soon continue.

ABOUT APOSTLE SHERMAN D. FARMER

Apostle Sherman D. Farmer is a visionary and prophet entrusted with the vision of God to shepherd millions of souls into the kingdom. Over 20 years, his soul-saving messages have reached the hearts of men and women throughout the world. Apostle Farmer's distinct and unparalleled ability to impart training of integrity through the compassion, empowerment and inspiration of the Holy Spirit has caused his ministry to flourish.

Founder of The New Apostolic Prophetic Reformation of the United and Covenanted Churches, a subsidiary of the New Gibeah Ministries for Christ, Inc. and Straightway Apostolic Ministries located in Capitol Heights, Maryland, he also serves as the Chief Apostle to Redeeming Touch of Love. Helping prophets establish and fully develop proper functioning of their gifts through biblical and doctrinal aptitude courses, he is the founding visionary of the New Kohath Prophetic Institute.

He is also the visionary behind several entities of ministry, including The NGMC Worship Center, a prophetic house of fellowship, worship, ministry, discipleship, and evangelism; The House of Benjamin Annex, bridging the gap between educational, vocational and secular systems; The Delores O. Farmer School for Christians in the Performing Arts, serving those gifted in theater, visual arts, music, dance and vocational arts; Straightway Ministries, imparting wisdom, knowledge and understanding in an instructional environment through an international outreach; and The NGMC School of Ministry, training ministers, pastors and other religious leaders in various areas.

Apostle Farmer is a renowned teacher and a highly sought after leader with life changing Bible study sessions including: The Prison Epistles, teaching believers how to work heavily in ministry under the stress of spiritual warfare; Project MAPP (Ministry Assignment Placement Program), providing believers with the tools to understand and identify their spiritual gifts; and The Life of Christ, equipping believers with the required full armor on the parables, historical timelines, genealogy and spirituality of Jesus Christ in order to become effective witnesses.

As an advocate for finding creative venues to reach millions of souls, Apostle Farmer has directed benefit concerts for guest artists from Yolanda Adams to B.J. Crosby. He has conducted seminars in the areas of praise and worship and art, praise and worship reformation training, and served as one of the campaign coordinators for the *40 Days of Purpose Program*. In 2000, he created the Band of Prophets Online Ministry, teaching spiritual leaders how to become a Five-Fold Kingdom Builder.

Apostle Farmer's primary apostolic assignment is to legitimize the prophetic and apostolic voice in today's spiritually deprived world. He is forming a revolution of spiritual revivals within the Body of Christ by encouraging leaders to become more transparent and accessible. As Apostle Farmer continues to lead the people of God to their destiny, he stands firmly on the words of Isaiah: *"Also, I heard the voice of the Lord, saying, Whom shall I send, and who will go for us? Then said I, Here I am; send me."* (Isaiah 6:8 KJV)

Connect with Apostle Farmer or Share Your Feedback on:

amazon.com

goodreads.com

barnesandnoble.com

WWW.ABOUT.ME/SHERMANDFARMER

Personal note from the author:
Throughout this book, you will see certain names, words, and terms which are widely used in the theological society. These instances are not to be perceived as poor grammar.